THRI

What Every Engineer Should Learn from Star Wars

Adam Shostack

The Empire doesn't consider a small, one-man fighter to be any threat or they'd have a tighter defense.
—General Dodonna

About the Author

Adam Shostack is a leading expert on threat modeling. He's also a consultant, expert witness, and game designer. He has decades of experience delivering secure products and systems. His experience ranges across the business world from founding startups to nearly a decade at Microsoft.

His accomplishments include:

- Helped create the CVE; now an emeritus member of the Advisory Board
- Fixed Autorun for Windows XP and Vista
- Led the design and delivery of the Microsoft SDL Threat Modeling Tool (v3)
- Created the *Elevation of Privilege* threat modeling game and helped create *Control-Alt-Hack*
- Wrote *Threat Modeling: Designing for Security*, and coauthored *The New School of Information Security*

Beyond consulting and training, Shostack serves as an advisor to many companies and academic institutions. He is an Affiliate Professor at the Paul G. Allen School of Computer Science and Engineering at the University of Washington.

You can learn more at shostack.org.

Acknowledgments

This book would be different from cover to cover if not for the stunning and deep worldbuilding by George Lucas, and the crew and cast of Star Wars who first brought it to life. That first crew not sweating the details could have robbed us all of so much.

This book has been a five-year mission to clearly explain security to engineers. In 2017, a gentleman in Cupertino asked me the simple question, "Where do I go to learn more about these threats?" I didn't write down his name, but if you see this, thank you for the question, and sorry it took so long to answer.

In my explorations, I've spoken with hundreds of people about the frame of "what every engineer needs to know." I want to gratefully acknowledge all their contributions, and whatever errors remain are mine.

My amazing team of teachers at Shostack + Associates (Valery Berestetsky, Jamie Dicken, and Caroline Emmott) also read the entire draft (sometimes more than once) and helped ensure the many lessons from our students are included and the many questions they ask are answered.

While I worked on this book, I also worked on a set of courses with LinkedIn Learning. My team there, including Alyssa Pratt, Rae Hoyt, and Andrew Probert, were warm, supportive, and coaching throughout. Working with them on a set of STRIDE courses while I worked on this book improved the separate content in each.

Loren Kohnfelder did more than create the STRIDE mnemonic (with Praerit Garg) that forms the foundation of this book. He also read most of this book in early draft form, and I treasured our long conversations about the specifics and also the structure.

Dean Tribble and Jonathan Shapiro reminded me of Mark Miller's work on Authority as a way out of the messy thinking around privileges and permissions. That challenge could have ended the mission. Similarly, the chapter on parsing became much clearer and richer when I read the work of the LangSec community. Jeff Williams provided thoughtful perspective on early drafts. Izar Tarandach gave the text a close read, even though he has a somewhat competing book. Jim Bell explained how spacecraft on Mars track time.

Some of these improvements to early drafts were to text that's evolved so much that the improvement is no longer visible. I am extra grateful to those people because they helped the book in a way that's less visible but no less vital: Michael Roytman suggested date formats for canonicalization pendulums, and those are way easier to parse than my URL examples. Kim Wuyts helped with the definition of predictability and its privacy impacts.

Thanks also to Jon Callas, Chris Eng, Mark French, Tom Galhager, Shawn Hernan, Jeff Jarmoc, Arron Johnson, Christoph Klaaßen, Lucky Munro, Daniel Ostermeier, Ian Poynter, John Poulin, Morgan Roman, Anant Shrivasta, Peleus Uhley, Tarah Wheeler, and Charles Wilson.

Cypherpunk and lawyer Doug Barnes was the friend who wrote "'and then the cops show up' is a rotten step to include in your protocols," quoted in the repudiation chapter. The sentence and paragraph were complex and so I acknowledge him here.

Others have used Star Wars to illustrate: *The Ultimate Star Wars and Philosophy* (Wiley, 2015), *Star Wars Psychology* (Sterling, 2015), and *The World According to Star Wars* (Sunstein, 2016). I learned from each, and my use of Star Wars is more focused and nuanced for having them to guide the way. Kellman Meghu pointed out that until

Darth Vader shows up, the Empire is running a pretty solid breach response executive meeting, and I haven't found a way to work that into the text. And while mentioning Star Wars content, I especially want to thank those readers who are less familiar with it for pointing out where I went too deep. While they have not failed me, they remain safely anonymous.

Last, but not least, I want to thank my team at Wiley: Jim Minatel for asking provocative questions again and again as I figured out why this is more than a chapter of another book and then advising me how to write a book that draws on a beloved universe. Kelly Talbot has been a fantastic project editor, embracing the humor and challenges. Kim Wimpsett edited carefully where it was needed and fixed that which shall not be named. And speaking of not named: there were many people involved who I never got to meet. Much like the anonymous Rebels so frequently in the background, you helped make this great.

—Adam Shostack

Contents

Preface

How does R2-D2 know who Ben Kenobi is? How does he decide to play the recording of Princess Leia for Ben, but not Luke? How does Princess Leia tell R2 her intentions? These three questions touch on fundamental issues of security: authentication, authorization, and usability. (Star Wars geeks have an answer to the first from the prequels, but Leia does not know that answer.) What's more, the way the world of Star Wars engages with technology and computers gives us a familiar base from which to learn about how technology works in our world.

I was a Star Wars fan before I ever wrote a line of code and long before I broke my first system. As I became an expert in computer security, it became clear to me that we in the field are much better at code than with stories, and while it's tempting to say "That is why you fail," telling better stories is not our only hope. As I reflected on Star Wars, I realized that as the crawl fades, the camera descends onto Princess Leia's ship being pursued over…a stolen data tape! I realized Star Wars is not only the story of Luke's hero's journey and growth into adulthood but also a story of information disclosure and its consequences. Over the last decade, I've used Star Wars to tell the story of computer security because the epic stories give us reference points and illustrations of important issues.

In this book, almost every reference is to the original trilogy. There is material I could use in *Rogue One*, in the prequels and sequels, and in the TV shows, the books, and more. But I'll assume that most readers have only watched and rewatched the core three: *Star Wars*, *Empire*, and *Jedi*.

Like the Force is a property of all living things, security is a property of all technological systems. And like the Force has a light side and a dark side, security has defenses and attacks. This book is focused primarily on the attacks, the threats, the problems. You need to understand the threats to select appropriate defenses. It's dramatic to watch the Emperor unleash purple force lightning on Luke Skywalker, but better training could have alerted Luke to the threat and how to defend against it. Neither a firewall nor a checklist will block force lightning.

If you want to make a home secure, you need to think through the many things that might go wrong. Some are natural (floods), some can be natural or manmade (fire), and some (theft) are the acts of intelligent beings.

We have implicit models of what a home is, the types of homes, and the common types of problems. Those problems vary somewhat: the central plain of the United States has tornados, southeast Asia has monsoons, and the Middle East has sandstorms. But you can go to your insurer and get a list. (It's split across "optional coverage" and "exclusions.")

Our implicit models of how technical systems are set up are weaker. Technology has more variety and more rapid change than our homes or office buildings. Three-tier architectures are unlike microservices. Microservice cloud deployments differ from the virtual machines deployed a mere decade ago.

Technological builders and defenders have a disadvantage: it's hard to get away from thinking about making the system work. We all know it's hard to make a system work. That there are trade-offs and compromises made to get the code to work, to get it to customers, and even to deploy it.

Security's traditional response to this has been an exhortation to "Think like an attacker!" That's hard. In response I encourage people to think like a professional chef, planning for hundreds of diners to sit down tonight. Most of us wouldn't know where to start. But we don't have to "think like an attacker" to get different perspectives on the systems we're working on.

Security also differs from other potential problems because we have intelligent attackers who can learn and adapt. If we think about a person wanting to steal your stereo, then they can come through the front door in many ways: they can kick it in, jimmy the latch, pick the lock, or steal a key. Some attacks exploit vulnerabilities: the lock has a weak front plate that's easily drilled because of a defect in the casting. Some exploit design flaws: the lock has only a few pins, making it easy to pick. They can bypass our defense, walking over to a window. And in technological systems, the range of attacks seems endless and perhaps unknowable—a problem this book solves.

One of the reasons that we fail at making secure systems is attackers have a great many advantages. They can study their target, plan their attacks, and launch them only when they feel confident. They can do what they will to take control of a system, make it misbehave, or embarrass its creator. And some of what attackers do is really very clever, and all of it is unexpected. That's tremendously important. In a great little video *The Death Star Architect Speaks Out*, the architect says, "The shot was literally not possible unless you had magic powers. Maybe if someone would have told me to account for space wizards when designing the exhaust ports, we would still have a Death Star!"

He has a good point. Too often, security researchers get publicity for taking a completed system and pointing out flaws…like engineers not knowing a torpedo could fly through miles of piping without turbulence deflecting it. It can feel like security experts are judging you and answering every question by rolling their eyes and saying "Search your feelings." This book focuses on the important threats.

Security expert and author Bruce Schneier once wrote, "When I visited the National Security Agency, I asked to see the 'big book of attacks.' They told me there's no single place where it's all written down." This book aims to fix that. It's important because understanding "the attacks" is easier if there is a defined set of "the attacks." This is not an attempt to categorize every attack or to be comprehensive. That last is probably surprising and may even worry you. But the reality is that security issues are violations of security requirements.

The requirements for different systems are different. Should I include violations of the requirements for nuclear bombs or currency printing? ("Fewer than two people can activate the system" or "Another customer can obtain the same paper stock.") Completeness would obscure the more common attacks and make it hard to quickly reference threats that may inspire and enable you to reason by analogy and discover attacks on your own systems. Understanding the threats is the crux, and until now they've been hard to understand.

Someone else wrote "All interesting systems surprise their creator." That's the property that takes them from useful to interesting. And security issues are often issues of surprise. They rely not only on mistakes in what's there, but in the failure of architects to develop defenses.

Human attention is a harsh master. It is hard to perceive what is missing. My intent in cataloging common issues is to say: these matter. These must be considered and, by collecting, organizing, and presenting them, provide some clarity about what is in the set of things "you must consider." If what's in this book is ignored, maybe it's reasonable to claim that is a failure of the engineer. That's not to say "You can ignore anything else." Just as a pilot must land the plane beyond the checklist or a surgeon must treat the patient, what must be addressed is not limited to what's in the pages of this book.

Human attention is really a harsh master. Daniel Kahneman is a Nobel Prize–winning founder of behavioral economics. In his lovely book, *Thinking Fast and Slow*, he uses only a single acronym: WYSIATI. What You See Is All There Is. The importance of what's in front of you is so great, it crowds out our efforts to "remain aware" and to "keep in mind." Yet as an engineer you must do exactly that—keep in mind reliability, performance, usability, maintainability, and a great many other properties. We have many tools for managing such things, including automation, checklists, and the judgment of diverse teams.

For this book, I am making a design trade-off and assuming that defenses are known and understood, or at least understandable once you understand the threats. So I focus on the threats and touch briefly on the defenses. That's a conscious trade-off to make the book shorter and more approachable.

Introduction

My students teach me so much. As I hear the questions they ask and read the assignments they submit, I learn where they face challenges in securing their systems. I learned about threats over a decades-long career, from a few wise teachers and from many mistakes. As I mention in the acknowledgments, this book really was catalyzed by a simple question: "Where do I go to learn about the threats?"

A bit like "There's good in him, I've felt it," I've felt that question in so many conversations. The word *security* subsumes a great deal of complexity and nuance. I was going to say we tend to learn about threats by osmosis, but that's not true. We tend to learn about threats when something blows up. Even when that something is smaller than a Death Star, the lessons are often traumatic, sometimes career-changing. Tragedy is a bad teacher.

If we want to be systematic in our search for threats to our products, we must be structured in how we learn and teach about those threats.

Who This Book Is For

This book is for every engineer.

It will be most useful to those who build or operate complex software-rich systems. There are hard trade-offs in engineering, which are made harder when security goals are obscure or vague. The book is focused on systems that incorporate code, but these days, what doesn't? Engineers who work in more traditional parts of the field (aerospace, chemical, civil, mechanical) are finding that these more elegant systems from a more mechanical time are being supplanted. Your systems must now interface with code, and you must address its security properties.

Over the last few decades, the job of software development and systems operation has changed. We've learned that our hopes of retrofitting properties from accessibility to reliability to usability have cost us dearly and that we need to incorporate each from the start. We are learning that security is much the same way. Choices made during system development have consequences. We see the need to address security earlier and more holistically.

This book is also for security professionals and enthusiasts. There are many pathways into many fields focused on security and hacking. Few of them provide a broad framework that will serve to organize the flood of information about threats, vulnerabilities, and exploits that you'll encounter. My hope is that this book serves all of them.

This book is for every engineer, even if they're not a science-fiction fan, and if you are, whatever world you love. As I spoke about this book, Star Trek fans came out of the nebulas to ask "Why?" And I love Trek. I love the optimistic view of the future, how the series reveres competence and science, and the writing and character development. I turned in the manuscript with the dedication: "to boldly secure what no one has secured before," as an attempt at a loving homage. My team told me that it was too jarring for the opening, and they were right.

What You'll Gain from This Book

Security.

More specifically, you'll gain the understanding of security in ways that enables you to build and operate systems that perform despite the efforts of adversaries. Much like understanding force (the mass times acceleration kind) allows us to think about many different parts of the world and bring it to bear on our projects, this book provides you with an enduring framework to anticipate threats.

It's traditional to include a breathless list of security flaws here, in the hopes of motivating readers. It hasn't seemed to work, so I'm not going to bother. In 2023, the issue with security is no longer why. It's what and how.

A Few Words for the Nonengineer

This book is written for engineers: people who build or operate complex technical systems, especially the algorithms, chips, sensors, and actuator parts of those systems. It's written to be as clear as reasonably possible, and if you're a nontechnologist looking for advice, I want to include the three things you should do.

First, turn on automatic update on everything, most especially devices, operating systems, and web browsers. The updates that engineers ship often address security problems that can be exploited automatically. If your vendor mixes functionality changes with security fixes, complain loudly. But this step is a crucial defense against those exploitable problems.

Second, use a password manager, and have it create long, random passwords for you. One of the ways security fails is when websites leak your email address and password. Attackers gather and trade those lists, and they test the combinations on every website they can. They also test variants. They know that my Amazon password might be "adamamazon" or "amazonas1?" and computers are very good at testing those sorts of combinations, along with amazon-feb and the others you've thought of. Use a long, random password. If I expect I'll need to type it in regularly, I'll use the feature that gives me three or four random words as a password. By the way, I use 1Password from Agilebits as my password manager and recommend it. (We have no business relationship.)

Third, trust your feelings. If you feel a website isn't safe, leave. Find the company by searching or with a bookmark. If you think an email is suspicious, call the person or entity that claimed to have sent it. Use the number on the back of your card to call your bank. In each of these cases, you're taking control, and you're using resources that an attacker can't influence.

Maybe an attacker can replace the card in your wallet, and if you have attackers like that, seek professional help. I'm not saying that sarcastically. If you're up against a spy agency who will spend the time and energy to create a card and put it in your wallet, this advice isn't going to save you.

Two more optional steps if you want extra safety. First, craft special email addresses for special relationships. Set up something like hiufd-suapre8wafdsjkf@gmail.com and use it for either one bank or all your banks. This protects you if an attacker takes over your main email account, and it helps you sort out phishing emails. If you only use that for your bank, then any mail from "your bank" in your main account is automatically suspicious. See above about trusting your feelings.

Lastly, I use a different browser and browser profile for online banking. Browser software is pretty solid these days, but with all the attacks, I feel more comfortable having a low-use browser for that. (These days, one is Firefox, the other is Chrome. At other times, it was two different Firefox profiles, with two dramatically different visual themes.)

That's it. That's my advice. Thank you for buying this book. You're welcome to read it or pass it on to a technologist or budding technologist who you know. Either way, I'm going to assume a technical reader, so we start speaking the binary languages that underpin both a galaxy far, far away and our own world.

Let me draw your attention to a principle that underlies the advice: isolation. A password manager isolates sites from each other, as does using two email accounts or two browsers. Leaving a site or calling your bank leaves the locus of an attack. That isolation, separating parts of a system from each other, is also the reason we have different computer accounts, firewalls, and a host of other defensive techniques.

Of course, each layer of isolation comes at a cost of convenience. Not allowing software to seamlessly work together means you have to do the things that make them work together, because that way attackers have to trick you into doing those things.

This advice is sadly not the advice you'll get from everyone. We lack information on the root causes and history of incidents that would help us prioritize, which is a problem I write about elsewhere and don't dwell on much in this book.[1]

Security Terminology

This book is about *threats*. We all know a threat when we hear one— "Give me your money, or else!" "I have altered the terms of the deal. Pray I do not alter them…any further." I use threat to mean a future problem and one that can often be averted if we take preventative action.

Security folks use the word *threat* in a variety of ways. We call an attacker a threat, or sometimes a threat agent. The anti-malware part of the industry calls each virus or bit of malware a threat.

Carrying out a threat is an attack. Each of the threat, its manifestation, and its impact can be a concern. The law considers a credible threat as assault; the act of hitting someone is the battery in "assault and battery." These can result in injury. In cybersecurity, we often worry about both the threat and its result. If someone breaks in by spoofing a legitimate user, they can quickly chain other threats, such as tampering or information disclosure. Especially as you are learning, being specific about the relationship between mechanism and impact can be helpful. A *risk* is the quantified refinement of a threat, and those quantifications often involve probability of success and the magnitude of the impact in dollars or lives.

---

[1]You can find more on that at shostack.org/resources/lessons.

An attacker uses an *exploit* to take advantage of a vulnerability. An exploit (as a noun) is a bit of software that allows its user to do something that the system owner would like to prevent. To exploit (as a verb) is to use that software against a target. A *vulnerability* is either a specific code issue (a bug), a flaw where design requirements have been overlooked, or the result of a trade-off made by designers or operators. Sometimes specificity helps with clarity; other times it descends into pedantry.

The word *trust* is used a lot in computer security and can be trusted to trip up the unwary. In normal English, trust means "a firm belief in someone's reliability, honesty, or ability." Trustworthy means someone who lives up to that trust. In computer security, trusted means something with the ability to break your security. Cambridge University professor Ross Anderson provides an example: "The spy caught selling secrets was trusted but not trustworthy." Others have pointed out that the word is often used in a passive or Orwellian voice. A "trusted system" fails to specify who trusts it. The Galactic Empire often labeled systems as "trusted" to bypass any discussion of their impact on the people it touches.

Aphorisms

There are a few bits of pithy wisdom I'd like to share because they can broadly inform your work as it touches on security.

"Attacks only get better; they never get worse." Bruce Schneier attributes this as a saying at the American National Security Agency (NSA). While defenses do get deployed, the lesson of an attack is never lost. The tools developed to execute it don't go away. They're honed and refined.

"Theories of security come from theories of insecurity," said Rick Proto of the NSA. Those attacks get better, and the collection of attacks inform how we think about what security is.

"All models are wrong; some models are useful." British statistician George Box said this.

"Computer security is perverse. When you want something to be difficult, it's easy, and when you want it to be easy, it's hard." (Me.) Consider file deletion. When you want to make a file really disappear, it's difficult, and when you want to recover it, it is surprisingly hard. It's hard to really make a file disappear because deletion usually just removes the pointers within the file system. If you try to overwrite the bits on a magnetic disk, it turns out that the physical records on the disk vary in size and so can be read after overwriting. And flash drives make it tough to ever write to the same locations. Similarly, randomness is easy to find when you want predictability. Computers seem unpredictable and heisenbugs are common, but just try writing a safe random number generator.

"Attackers will spend their budget how they want, not how you hope." (Me again.) You may hope that attackers will behave in very specific ways, but then they wouldn't be attackers.

"Security is a systems property." It's unclear who first said this. This is a true claim, and what it means is that system security is often limited by weak links. This book helps you remove the obviously weak links.

"Shipping is a feature." This is a common saying at Microsoft. All the new features that have been built do no good until they're being used by your customers, so delaying to add a few more is often unwise. Similarly, delaying delivery in the hopes of achieving perfect security means no one can use your new features. I'm making that same call in shipping this book now: I hope its virtues outweigh its flaws.

"The devil is in the details." Whoever said this wasn't thinking of security, but they could well have been. A great many things turn out to be less secure as one delves in, and security experts have great respect for talented reverse engineers who pry systems apart to understand their inner workings and in doing so discover unexpected properties of the system.

How This Book Is Organized

This book starts with STRIDE, a classic way of thinking about threats. STRIDE stands for Spoofing, Tampering, Repudiation, Information Disclosure, Denial of Service, Expansion of Authority. STRIDE is a mnemonic that helps us remember six major groups of threats, covered in the first six chapters. Those are followed by chapters on predictability, parsing, and kill chains.

Most chapters in this book follow the same general plan: start with an explanation of the threat, then how it manifests in specific technologies, the mechanisms that attackers use, and finally a short section on defenses.

There are many organizational choices to make writing a book like this. I grappled with the different ways computing now works and the way various threats impact them. Those ways include the Internet of Things, mobile, the cloud, and AI/ML. The specifics in these sections are in addition to the broader points made in the chapter, not a replacement for them—the fact that a computer has the shape of an internet of things teddy bear doesn't mean the rest of the chapter doesn't apply. A few of these sections in other chapters have additional sections because the nature of the threat has interesting properties in a specific scenario that's worth discussing.

The sole emergent technology not treated in this way is quantum computing. Most of the STRIDE threats will work on the systems that surround a quantum core, and probably work on that core. For example, the power draw of the mirrors in quantum cryptography leads to important information disclosure attacks. (Quantum crypto uses spin information to distribute cryptographic key information in ways that are hard to eavesdrop on, often relying on fiber between sites. It is very different from the use of quantum mechanics for computing.) The primary early impact of quantum computing seems to be breaking most classical asymmetric cryptography by discovering the keys, an information disclosure threat. If you're curious about quantum, *Law and Policy for the Quantum Age* (Hoofnagle and Garfinkel, 2021) is an excellent primer.

Another crucial organizational choice is to revisit threats. I've learned from teaching the first time someone encounters some information, it may not sink in. Coming back to it from a different angle often helps.

Style and Conventions

Many organizations and products are named. Product names are used to make examples concrete, and no malice is meant toward the creator or trademark owner. The passe convention of including a "for example" with each one wastes the time of most readers for the possible benefit of a few particularly literal-minded ones, who might be confused however many clarifiers are included.

A Few Words from a Jedi Master

Yoda:…a Jedi's strength flows from the Force. But beware of the Dark Side. Anger, fear, aggression; the Dark Side of the Force are they. Easily they flow, quick to join you in a fight. If once you start down the dark path, forever will it dominate your destiny, consume you it will, as it did Obi-Wan's apprentice.

Luke: Vader…Is the Dark Side stronger?

Yoda: No, no, no. Quicker, easier, more seductive.

Luke: But how am I to know the good side from the bad?

Yoda: You will know…when you are calm, at peace, passive. A Jedi uses the Force for knowledge and defense, *never* for attack.

The dark path is the path of ignoring security. Easily, the code flows. But once you start down that path, forever will it dominate your destiny. The easy choice is to ignore security and focus entirely on features that are more visible to customers. Modern languages make complete static analysis feasible by constraining some of the seductive power of pointers. There's a cost: the dark side of C is faster code, but forever will it dominate your security advisories. And 20 years ago, when security mattered less, that was a choice many companies made, often thoughtlessly. It was the choice that Microsoft made in its heyday.

But Yoda was right: "Consume you it will." I worked at Microsoft for most of a decade, and I have tremendous respect for my colleagues who have been bolting security onto Office and Windows and replacing parts of their guts. They have achieved far more than I would have thought possible. But the very different innards of IoS and ChromeOS allow those competitors to move faster today.

Lastly, there is a security career path open to you, a path of attack. It's flashy. It's powerful: "Let me show you how I can pwn your system." And if you want to follow that path, my only request is that you do so ethically, using your skills and knowledge to conduct authorized attacks to build stronger defenses. My own path started with vulnerability discovery but lately has been focused on delivering stronger systems. It's a harder path, but the impact long term can be much greater.

1 Spoofing and Authenticity

Shortly after we first meet Luke Skywalker, he is cleaning his newly acquired droids, and R2-D2 teases him with part of a message that is only supposed to play for Obi-Wan Kenobi. How does R2-D2 know who Obi-Wan Kenobi is? How does he decide to play the recording of Princess Leia for Obi-Wan, but not Luke? As I mention in the book's introduction, these questions are multifaceted. Let's go deeper into questions of names and authenticity.

As we look at this interaction, I'll treat droids as computers. And so we can ask questions like "How does a computer identify a human?" This is one of several crucial types of authentication. We can also ask how a human identifies a computer, or one computer identifies another. Star Wars is full of problems that stem from challenges with how humans identify other humans. In the prequels, why don't the members of the Jedi Council realize that the Chancellor is also the Sith Lord Darth Sidious?

Authentic means something is "the genuine article" or "the real thing." R2-D2 only wants to play the video for the real, authentic Obi-Wan, not anyone who walks up and asks for it. To do that, we need identifiers and authenticators. *Spoofing threats* are violations of authenticity; you get someone or something that is not what

1

you're expecting. The Death Star fails to authenticate R2-D2 when he plugs in, a common flaw in the world of Star Wars. In our world, spoofed authentication codes are a common problem: we call them stolen passwords. But it's not just fake people; it's also fake websites for phishing and other scams.

Identifiers and Authentication

Authenticity first requires an identifier: a statement of who you are. This might be a name (Han Solo) or a role (Stormtrooper). Either might be true or false, and given the risk of impersonation, confusion, or lies, we look for authentication factors, such as an ID, a password, or a uniform, as we evaluate if the identifier is authentic and grant (or deny) authorization. This chapter will start with identifiers both human and technical. We'll naturally touch on authentication as we go through the various specific ways that human and technical identities are spoofed and then learn about it more in depth later in the chapter. There are many forms of authentication to consider, depending on if the authentication is *by* a person or a computer and *to* a person or a computer. From there, we'll look at spoofing in different scenarios, the mechanisms used, and the defenses. This chapter is longer than many that follow because spoofing manifests very differently when a person or a computer is impersonated, and the ways of checking are different when performed by people or computers.

As shown in Figure 1.1, the means of authentication differ, based on what sort of entity is trying to prove its identity and what sort of entity is checking.

Frankly, some of the methods shown in Figure 1.1 are not very reliable. For example, the computer in front of you is authenticated by its physical location: you trust it with your password because you're typing on it. Sometimes that weak authentication is OK, and other times the party checking the other entity wants the authentication to be stronger. See Figure 1.2.

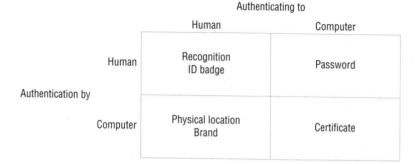

FIGURE 1.1 Ways of authenticating

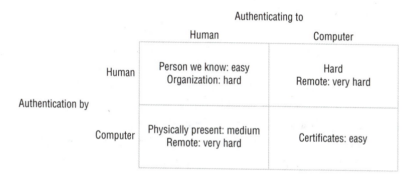

FIGURE 1.2 Difficulty of authenticating

Technical Identifiers

There are many types of technical identifiers including identifiers for services, machines, files, processes, and users. Some are designed for humans, such as `threatsbook.com`, others are designed for computers, such as 172.18.19.20. Of course, tools exist to map between them. These matter because each mapping is a looming opportunity for errors to creep in or for threats to impact your system.

In fact, any time there's a mapping from a real object to a representation of that object, there can be confusion. Calls like `listen(socket)` and `open(file)` are fraught with threats as you map from a filename to a file descriptor.

Machine or service identity involves a name, such as `rebelbase`
`.threatsbook.com`. Computer namespaces are usually unique for
some scope. Ideally, `rebelbase.threatsbook.com` will be globally
unique, but there can be many computers with a DNS name of
`rebelbase.local`—one on Yavin, one on Hoth, one on your
local network.

The service might be being spoofed with a lookalike name,
`rebelbase`. If it's a website and you give it a username and password,
its operators may log in to the real `rebelbase`, thus spoofing you.
Almost all connections that are vulnerable to spoofing have vulnerabilities in both directions, with the impact of an attack falling on different parties.

Computers will often have DNS names like `rebelbase.threatsbook`
`.com`. That address can refer to more than one physical machine, but
these are not the only names a physical computer can have. It can have a
UNC (Windows) name and other names. The name may refer to more
than one machine, via, say, DNS round-robin, and there may be layers
of mapping with cnames and other systems for indirection.

Similarly, files have both names and technical identifiers, such as
inode numbers, which the filesystem uses for efficiency.

The identity of a process can often be represented by a file or port,
or even an executable name. For example, someone might expect that
the thing listening on port 25 is a mail server, or the first process
named Chrome is our web browser. Processes can change their names
in the process table, and malicious code will often try to change process names to masquerade as something harmless.

Lastly, users have various sorts of usernames, display names, and
other identifiers, and understanding those brings in enough complexity that it's worth considering the very broad range of human identifiers and then how computers represent them.

Human Identifiers

In Star Wars, Luke and Han pretend to be Stormtroopers. One of them is apparently Stormtrooper TK-421. We never learn the other trooper's name, but it doesn't matter: he has a role, assigned guard, and that's enough for some authentication purposes. Ben Kenobi pretends not to be Obi-Wan Kenobi and, while doing, so lies to Luke about his father Anakin being killed by Darth Vader. Princess Leia pretends not to be a rebel leader, and we're less than 30 minutes into Star Wars.

Identifying people seems easy. That's Uncle Owen. That's Aunt Beru. Many people have more than one name that they use, without any malice.

Many people use more than one name. *The Simpsons* character can be Fat Tony or Marion D'Amico, and some people probably call him Uncle Tony. William becomes Bill. You and I mean someone different when we say Mom, and there are several people in the world named John Smith. People can usually handle this. Computers are not so flexible. They want unique, controlled namespaces for their identifiers and accounts. The Empire feels the same way, and so poor FN-2187 has no other name until Poe Dameron gives him the nickname Finn in *The Force Awakens*.

Faking human identifiers has a long and distinguished tradition, predating the Internet. Pretending to be who you are not, or not who you are, or pretending to a title or role you don't have is all in Shakespeare, but no one remembers Shakespeare. Importantly, these fakes predate technology. They're at the human level.

This variety matters because our technological designs need to interpret names and map them to identifiers: logins, email addresses, and more. Each interpretation may exist in an interplay between human and machine meaning, and as it does the discrepancies, discontinuities, or differences in interpretation may lead to unexpected outcomes.

Authenticating People to People

People are exceptionally good at identifying people they know well, even after a long time without seeing them. Not recognizing someone is awkward because we expect to be recognized. Recognizing those you're close to, such as friends and family, or even co-workers, is implicit and automatic. We don't need authenticators. But outside that circle, it gets rapidly harder. We use a lot of implicit identifiers such as uniforms, knowledge, patterns of speech, and we use explicit ones, such as ID cards.

Ben Kenobi leaps into action when someone he's never met sends a hologram saying, "You served my father in the clone wars." Shouldn't they have set up a passphrase?

If you're not trying to impersonate a specific person, it can be even easier. Anyone can portray themselves as a lawyer who's reached out to you to try to settle a distant relative's estate, as a customer support agent to ask for your credit card information, or as an attractive young person looking for companionship. The first is a classic con, while the last has a new facet—technology allows anyone to play an attractive young person in romance scams, where your new love interest needs money for a plane ticket to come visit you, or in catphishing where they wheedle knowledge or embarrassing photos out of classmates or famous people. This relates to the idea of authenticating to an organization, which is covered later in this chapter.

Authenticating People to Computers

Unlike Romeo and Juliet whose themes of identity and fakery end tragically in the human realm, Star Wars gives us examples of how people and technology interact: How does Ben Kenobi authenticate to R2-D2 to see the hologram of Leia? When R2-D2 plugs into the Death Star to find where she's being held, what UID gets used for his SQL request?

(By the way, your first answer, which was probably that R2-D2 is sentient, is insufficient. Leia does not know that this specific R2 unit knew Kenobi, so how can she write an access control rule?)

The first question of Ben Kenobi authenticating to a machine after 20 years is a hard problem. But even the simpler versions of the problems are hard. When you needed physical access to a computer, a password was usually sufficient to distinguish people. But those passwords were stolen, and access to machines became more and more available over networks, so authentication had to improve.

Different types of information can factor into an authentication decision. The following are the most commonly used factors and an example of each:

- **Knowledge:** The combination to a safe
- **An object you have:** The key to a safety deposit box or an ID card
- **A biometric:** Your physical being, measured or assessed in various ways (including a photograph)
- **Location:** In front of the computer
- **The channel you're using:** Internet, phone, in person
- **Who you know:** Trustees and designates

Factors also have strength: a passport is generally seen as a stronger proof of identity than a library card. The password "secret" is not very strong, while u8fdFN288jerfskla-#$d is pretty good.[1]

Using more than one type of factor is much better and is commonly referred to as *multifactor authentication*. The term *multistep* usually refers to the same thing and shifts the focus to the steps a person goes through, rather than their strength.

The traditional factors are labeled "what you know," "what you have," and "what you are." These were augmented by "where you are," "how you're communicating," and "who you know." "Where you are"

---

[1] Pushing for passwords to be more than pretty good is a waste. People can't remember many passwords that are meaningfully strong.

was implicit early in the history of computing (near the glass room with the mainframe), disappeared for a while, and reappeared recently, including the use of GPS signals and Apple using nanosecond timings for its watch to unlock an associated computer. The channel you're using may expose you to risk (in person) or be harder for an impersonator. Getting on the phone will expose that I don't speak Wookie.

"Who you know" can include your new password being given to your manager or social authentication systems, seeing if you know your friends to get back into Facebook, or having trustees authenticate you to get you back into some other account. These social authenticators are less common, but if you're interested, I discuss threats to them in Chapter 14, "Accounts and Identity," of my book *Threat Modeling: Designing for Security*.

The traditional authentication factors are often parodied as what you've forgotten, what you've lost, or what you were when you were younger and healthier. These challenges mean we need backup authentication techniques.

Backup authentication is variously called *forgot your password*, *password recovery*, or *account recovery*. The last is closest to accurate: No one cares about getting their password back; they care about getting into the account. I don't need to have ever known your password to use the feature, and in fact, it doesn't need to be my account at all. This isn't just nitpicking—understanding the problem is key to addressing it well. These backup authentication systems work best when they use secrets, known to as few people as possible. ("Where were the last three places you used your credit card?" is known only to you, your bank, the credit card processing networks, the merchants, and their marketing analytics firms, while "Where did you go to high school?" is known to all your Facebook friends and friends of friends.)

Sometimes, additional steps or factors are invoked as part of authorization: you may log in with a password, but adding a payee requires more. This pattern buys some usability at the price of confidential information, such as your most recent transactions, that might otherwise be used in that stronger authentication. Or in some cases, it's done at the expense of the security of the account, when that confidential information is used despite its exposure. We'll cover authority and authorization in more depth in Chapter 6, "Expansion of Authority and Isolation."

Malware increasingly emulates a person, and there is a new aspect to authenticating people, which is authentic gestures. These are captured by the local operating system at a low level and used to unlock password vaults and the like. They are designed to ensure that "commodity malware" can't emulate a person. However, they rely on hardware to be trustworthy, so an attacker that gives you a new mouse may be able to bypass them.

Authenticating Computers to People

It's hard to say when the first spoofed login screen was created, but it was probably around the time teletypes were replaced with electronic terminals. It was easy to write a program that would display `LOGIN:`, accept and store a name and password, display "Login incorrect," and log out, allowing the real login program to run.

This is why Ctrl+Alt+Delete helped keep your computer secure: it brought you to a real login screen. Similarly, the home button on your phone can't be intercepted by a program, and ideally the same is true of the gestures that replace the physical buttons. Phishing is a variation of this: the computer you're sending your authentication information to is just further away. Modern phishing scams will prompt you for the code texted to your phone or sent to your email. Similarly, fraudsters will fake caller ID information to make it appear that they're calling from an institution you trust: your bank or the Galactic Empire's Imperial Security Bureau.

It's hard for a person to authenticate remote computers. We usually trust that our local computer is doing a good job of understanding what we mean and communicating back in a way we'll interpret correctly. (I am even more skeptical of this than I sound, but the problem is incredibly difficult.)

Can we understand what computer we're talking to? Sure, from a certain point of view. Most websites we use have some combination of independently operated computer systems underlying them: the web server, a content distribution network, or various advertising, tracking, and analytic tools. When this is by design, we don't think of it as a problem, except perhaps for privacy, but I bring it up to illustrate that most people don't think deeply about what computer they're talking to. Having assurance of the identity of the remote computer is most important when it's asking for authentication information or other confidential data—we want our mental representation to be accurate enough, even if our understanding is limited.

We can recognize C3-PO because of the distinctive voice and mannerisms that Anthony Daniels created. Sadly, most computers are far less easy to recognize. There are many tools that try to make it easier for you to recognize a computer, and they change frequently to make it easier for attackers to confuse you about what you ought to expect today. Wait, I don't think that's the intended reason, but it is a real effect of the change. They change frequently in the hopes of handling new attacks. The way to protect yourself against all of these is to take control of the situation: press Ctrl+Alt+Delete, visit a bookmark for your bank, call the number on the back of your card. That works far better when organizations make it easy for you to reach the right person or a person with the right information when you do take control of the authentication process.

Authenticating Computers to Computers

Authentication is important anytime that you have a call like `listen(socket_id)`. The thing on the far side of that socket needs to be identified. When R2-D2 plugs into a socket, the Death Star allows all sorts of queries to be run, returning highly sensitive information about the location of prisoners. Given the sensitive data returned, we can only hope the account wasn't `guest` or `rebelscum`, but what was it, and how did R2-D2 prove the ability to use that account?

Each authentication may have some layered combination of technical and human identifiers. For example, the remote host probably has an IP address. It might have some form of client identifier like a cookie or an OAuth token. And it may have human or service identifiers.

When a client initiates a connection to a server, either side may require authentication. There are complexities when the act of connecting can be influenced by another computer or when that authentication is on behalf of a person. The simplest case might be using Telnet to connect to an IP address: it happens in response to a human typing a command, which is hard to influence. But only slightly more complex examples, like sending email, are subject to influence. If I try to send email to `luke@threatsbook.com`, my mail client will connect to my mail server, which will use DNS to look up the MX record for `threatsbook.com` and connect to that site. The DNS server for `threatsbook.com` can influence where my mail server will connect.

Spoofing can happen when your code calls `listen()` directly or indirectly. In the indirect case, perhaps a web server calls `listen()`, parses the TLS and HTTP messages, and passes in something more "refined." The code still needs to identify the caller. The web server may do some of that work, and even so, you may well need to map from the server's accounts table to one used in your databases. For example, I might log in as `adam@threatsbook.com` and may have a `customer_id` of 1234.

Computers identify each other, often using a mix of cryptographic certificates and human-readable identifiers. For example, if `darth vader@threatsbook.com` sends mail to `anakin@threatmodeling book.com`, then the `threatsbook` mail server needs to look up the `threatmodelingbook` domain and decide about using the TLS certificate it serves. The `threatmodelingbook` mail server needs to make decisions about the mail coming from `threatsbook` and decide if it's trustworthy. At many of the steps in this process, there's a cryptographic key, signed in what's called a *certificate*, and a tool that delivers a *policy* that this certificate should be trusted. These generally relate to either the *root authority* that's signed the certificate or to persistence. *Persistence* means the key was previously authorized to be used in conjunction with a hostname. SSH demonstrates a good pattern of prompting when a new key is presented, emphasizing if it's changed from what was previously presented.

Spoofing Attacks

This chapter introduced spoofing as a violation of authenticity. I want you to think about that broadly—think of spoofing attacks as breaking or confusing a link between an identifier and an object.

Many of these are where an attacker is injecting that confusion intentionally. But if we think of spoofing as violations of authenticity, we can end up in unexpected places. For example, if your mail client autocompletes an email address, that can be a mismatch between intent, action, and the authentic matching of that autocompletion to intent. It might seem like a strange thing to list under spoofing, but it's reasonable to do so in the context of authenticity.

Spoofing Files

Confusion about the exact file represented by a name can be the result of human imprecision or of an attacker substituting a file. And unlike C3-PO, most computers won't ask "What plans? What are you talking about?" Humans will give files the most awful names and save files under multiple directories, but the threats are where an attacker can substitute a file.

Opening Files

A file's identity is the name of the file. It can be spoofed when a file is underspecified (open "config.txt"). When a file contains a remote reference such as http://example.com/config.txt, the connection to example.com may be spoofed.

The simplest form of spoofed files is a failure to get the file you expect when you open it. For example, what file does fd = open ("./file.txt") open?

If you tell your computer to open("~/.ssh/id_rsa"), then what file you get back depends on the implementation of open() and either the effective or real UID of the process. It's a mistake to focus too much on the definition of the threat of spoofing here. Far more important is that your code handles these potential imprecisions or confusion in a safe, reliable, and secure way. More important is that if you're not sure precisely what resource you're going to get, or how it maps to your expectations and history with that file, there are security risks that your parser must handle.

A full pathname is a better statement of identity. You can be confident when you call open("/etc/passwd") or when you prepend a carefully validated prefix (/usr/local). But that won't always get you the file you expect!

For example, /tmp/file.txt can be owned by any user on the system and have surprising content. Appending random numbers doesn't protect you; open("/tmp/file2345.txt") only requires an attacker to create 10,000 files (or symlinks) to ensure that they control the file you open.

Opening an unexpected file becomes more distressing when the file opened is interpreted as code, such as when open is replaced by dlopen or LoadLibrary. (Opening a file and having it *unexpectedly* interpreted as code is even more distressing but is covered in Chapter 8, "Parsing and Corruption.") Each library loading function has a search path, and that search path can be influenced. On Unix systems, `LD_LIBRARY_PATH` and other environment variables influence what's opened, posing a problem, especially for setuid code. On Windows, the default library path has long included the current directory (.), and that creates problems for code run from an undifferentiated downloads directory. All an attacker needs to do is to find a library that not all systems have then get it downloaded to a downloads directory, and any programs run from there will dutifully use that library. This is frequently called a *drive-by download* problem, but it's really a spoofed library problem.

The introduction of a new library into "trusted" directories can alter the behavior of already installed programs. Of course, there are other ways to open a program, such as the `exec` family of calls, all of which can be invoked with nonspecific paths. There's a variant of this where the file to be obtained has a name like `npm:leftpad` or `BigBankValidationLibrary`. Many build systems also have a search path and so will look for `BigBankValidationLibrary` wherever it looks for packages, such as NPM or Maven. And it turns out that the answer is not persistent, so if yesterday that library was in a private repository and today there's a version in a public repository, well, we should get the public version, right? (Security researcher Alex Birsan created an impressive demonstration of this in 2021, with a variety of tricks to demonstrate that his libraries were being run so he could collect bug bounties. See (Montalbano, 2021 for the details.)

The nature of a path becomes even more fraught when the name is not rooted in the local machine. At one extreme of complexity are URLs, which are discussed in Chapter 8. It may be that specifying a file via a URL can make the pointer more specific, or it can add security via TLS. But it can also add parsing complexity, failure modes, or opportunities for attack, even when the URL is a static string in your code. Complexity is added because a library needs to take `file:///etc/passwd`, parse that it's a file URL, and follow the appropriate codepath. More failure modes appear when remote machines are invoked. If you refer to a file as `https://example.com/style.css`, there's a chance that that style file will be unavailable, or you'll get back either an old or cleverly inserted cached version. If you own the `example.com` domain and personally maintain it, that risk is lower and gets higher as those conditions are loosened. There are also malicious failure modes, also covered in more detail in Chapter 8. For now, imagine someone breaks into `www.example.com` and replaces the file that you rely on. It's reasonable to think this falls more cleanly under tampering, but examples where the host is spoofed are more complex to explain and are covered in the "Spoofing Machines" section.

Faking Files

Another way to spoof a file is to cause someone to open a file they think is authenticated. An attacker can do this by taking over a machine to offer up tampered files, altering digital signatures, or abusing weak authentication schemes. For example, perhaps when R2-D2 is opening files on the Death Star, those files are coming from a honeypot, and that's why it's so easy to find where Princess Leia is held.

Attacks on digital signature schemes can happen because the algorithm used for signing is weak or even broken, because the key is too short, poorly generated, stolen, or replaced, or because of encoding issues where parts of the file are not signed. They can also happen when a strong algorithm is used with a well-generated and well-protected key and the system verifying the signature displays insufficient information about the signature. That might be as minimal as saying "signature validated" or "signature validated as from Adam Shostack," rather than saying what key was used, when, and why that key is treated as trusted. (This can be a lot of information, and making that understandable can be tricky.)

It can also be possible to modify a file without breaking the signature scheme. This is more prevalent than you may expect. For example, in Windows it is possible to append additional information into a signed file and execute it. (The details are complex, but variants of the issue were issued the identifiers CVE-2012-0151 and CVE-2013-3900.)

Spoofing Processes

Files are not the only namespace on a computer. Processes also have names and ways of referring to them. Many local interprocess communication protocols assume that only the right code could listen on a specific port or file socket. Similarly, code often assumes that a remote process must be owned by root because it's listening on a port less than 1024.

After being kidnapped by Jawas, R2-D2 is able to evade the control of the "restraining bolt" they install and continue his mission to bring a message to Obi-Wan Kenobi. Perhaps he ran a virtual machine and allowed the restraining bolt to reconfigure it, not his main system? Or maybe I'm overthinking it. (The ambiguity was first pointed out by Jim Davies.)

Spoofing Machines

Let's start with a simple model of communication between two machines We'll call the source machine SRC and the destination machine DST, as shown in Figure 1.3. SRC sends a packet, and it arrives at DST. Magical, right? And as long as SRC and DST are in a threat-free network, easy! But there may be more than one machine named DST on the Internet. There might be DST.example.org and DST.example.com, and there may be other machines that send or receive packets pretending to be one or the other. That's a useful and common mental model of the way machines communicate, and like all models, it's wrong. An attacker can send packets, claiming in various ways that they're from a machine named SRC. Many of the systems that authorize based on IP address, like rsh, have been deprecated, but others, like firewalls, remain in common use.

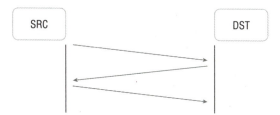

FIGURE 1.3 A simple model of communication

The names of machines are subject to spoofing at every layer of the network stack and at each interplay between such naming. Consider a "simple" request for dst.threatsbook.com/index.html, and let's get more specific about the data flows that support that request. As shown in Figure 1.4, there are many connections being made, each of which is subject to spoofing.

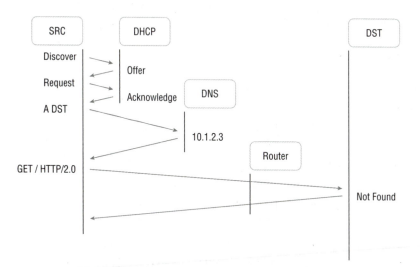

FIGURE 1.4 Many connections to support a request

At each layer and at each hop, an attacker can fake a from address to make a packet appear it's coming from an authorized machine. Perhaps the spoofed machine is authorized to send mail or to allow a login without multifactor authentication. Fake source addresses often abuse the authorization associated with the sources, or they can be used to provide additional layers of authentication failure. When the faked message is an IP or UDP packet, you can spoof "blindly." The fake source will get responses, but you don't have a need to manage sequence numbers or other things. That's getting harder to pull off if you're many network hops away, as many networks now implement source address filtering and will not forward packets that should not have originated within their networks.

We'll assume that this is a newly booted laptop, connected to a physical Ethernet. Each layer is subject to threats. For example, perhaps the DHCP server has given us a bad DNS server, or perhaps it's been manually configured poorly. Causes are marked with a capital, their effects with a lowercase letter. Thus, *D* means threats that misdirect IP packets, and *d* is packets being sent to the wrong place. See Table 1.1.

TABLE 1.1 Actions and Threats

Action	Threat
PC makes DHCP request	DHCP response with bad IP (A), DNS (B), or router (C) (either a bad server or a fake response).
PC uses bad IP for self (a)	Can't get responses—switch sends responses elsewhere.
PC uses bad DNS (b)	DNS provides faulty information—bad IP for DST (D).
Uses bad router (c)	Router either drops packets or engages in monkey-in-the-middle (MITM) attacks (D).
Sends packets to wrong IP address (d)	The other IP address can do what it wants.

You might think of a TCP frame containing the string GET http:// dst.threatsbook.com/index.html HTTP/2.0. But that frame doesn't transport itself. It's encapsulated in IP, which might go over

Wi-Fi for the first hop, cable modem for the next, and who knows what over the backbone. We usually ignore the encapsulations and decapsulation, but it can matter, because threats are possible at each layer of the stack and by each system that adds, removes, or changes a layer. Figure 1.4 shows a message going from SRC to DST, with a router in the middle, and this is often a useful model. And that model makes it easy to forget that at each hop, the packet is translated. Perhaps the first hop is Wi-Fi, and the access point accepts the packet and adds an Ethernet header to send it to a cable modem. The cable modem discards the Ethernet frame and adds a docsys header, and so it goes on its way. As shown in Figure 1.5, the IP datagram is the same per hop, but the local encapsulation changes. Each of these systems is a machine in the middle, and we either hope it does its job faithfully or we add defenses to ensure it does.

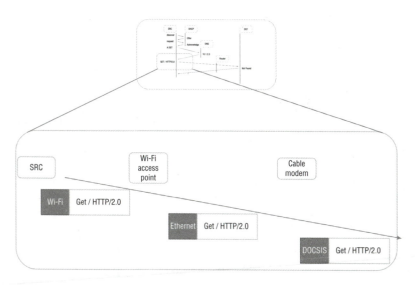

FIGURE 1.5 Packet encapsulation, hops

So, for any of the D threats from Table 1.1, the router can send packets (IP, TCP, HTTP) to the actual `spoofed.example.com` and modify the responses, or it can send packets to an alternate machine, configured to pretend it's `spoofed.example.com`. Other infrastructure along the route has the same ability, and some of it, such as load balancers, is put there to execute precisely this technical fakery, often with good intent.

Extending this set of attacks to the HTTPS variation with a stolen certificate or one issued to the wrong requestor or a self-signed certificate that's accepted by the verifier is left as an exercise for the reader.

Spoofing in Specific Scenarios

Spoofing threats don't go away because your device is small. There are both threats as the devices authenticate and opportunities to exploit integrated sensors. Mobile phones can be a locus of hopeful thinking replacing rigorous analysis, and so we'll cover a few common problems. Lastly, we'll cover spoofing around blockchain technology.

Internet of Things

Designers have to consider who legitimate users are and how they'll authenticate to the device. We also need to consider how to authenticate the device to others, including Wi-Fi, cloud servers, etc.

Many simple devices have a single user, and simple presence may be enough authentication. For example, televisions have a single user, who's local, and TV remote controls used infrared light, which was nice because walls blocked it. Even if you don't think your device will need multiple accounts, having more than one account will probably come in handy, and having code not run as root is an important application of the principle of least privilege and is easy if you apply it from the start.

The world is often surprisingly complex. For example, we put that TV in a hotel with adult content for sale, and it suddenly needs a way to control access to that content for some users and not others, and the hotel needs a way to reset the PIN when a guest checks out.

Similarly, some phones now have work accounts and kid accounts. Fancy cars come with valet keys.

Some devices, especially those deployed at businesses, need to integrate with directory services. Conference room tooling is a good example. You'll need to decide on a secure initialization flow, remembering that an attacker may be able to reset the device.

Safely authenticating to a new device can be tricky. For many devices, a password has been easily found with Google, because it's common to all devices made by a manufacturer, or worse, it's something like *admin* and works across manufacturers. This is the electronic equivalent of a lockless door with an "authorized staff only" sign. Attackers have lists of common passwords in their heads and tools to try thousands of default passwords, which are collected and published. For other devices, the password is something like the device's Ethernet address, available to anyone on the local network. In many jurisdictions, this is no longer allowable, and each device needs a unique password. You'll need to decide if this is visible to guests, waitstaff, and others who might have access to the device.

Voice access means physical location is less bounded than you may think. Open windows are like open doors, or you can ask Siri to open them for you. (We'll consider voice cloning in the "Attacks on 'What You Are'" section later in this chapter.) Devices may not be deployed in homes and private offices, but in shops where staff or customers may be motivated to attack it, or in an Airbnb, where the attacker has substantial time to attack it should they so choose.

Today's many voice-controlled devices have no accounts or authentication. When they do, it's likely they'll be set up to be forgiving to reduce frustration. It won't be like the movie *Sneakers* where much effort was required to tape (!) Robert Redford saying, "My voice is my password; verify me." Rather, your voice will probably be your username and password, rolled into one, and likely eminently spoofable.

Small devices tend to have limited user interfaces, which makes it hard to input secrets like passwords. Some devices overcome this by authenticating the device to the cloud and the user to the cloud and giving them tools to associate the user account to the device account. In this architecture, there are two important authentications and an important and tricky set of authorizations. The authorizations must include both adding an account and removing them. Good scenarios to consider include a valet parking your car, an Airbnb guest, a device sold at a yard sale, and an ugly divorce.

Those limited user interfaces also make it hard to display security indicators or data that might be used in a security decision, including URLs. There's a good argument that asking people to parse URLs is a waste of time and effort (Herley, 2010), and the argument is strengthened by the constraints of both IoT and mobile phones.

Mobile Phones

The problem of small user interfaces also shows up on phones, where screen real estate is limited and provenance of UI elements is hard. Intuitively, it would make sense for apps to be able to send a message to an app store app. For example, a game might send a message to the app store, and the app store could charge me a few dollars for the magic sword. How do I know that I'm in the app store and not a fake UI that looks like it? How do I know I am giving my credit card to the right app, rather than a spoofed one? I expect similar spoofing threats with voice apps and voice-controlled devices.

A couple of common bad beliefs are that phones are mapped one to one to people and that phone numbers are good authenticators. Many people believe in the deeply democratic principle of "one person, one phone," but it's wrong. Some people have more than one phone or more than one SIM, especially outside of the United States.

Some phones are used by more than one person; think about parents loaning their phone to their kid or partners picking up each other's phone. Couples (especially elderly ones) may share a phone, while younger ones may have full access to each other's phones. There are also people who don't have phones because of their life circumstances. Poor people (especially those in less developed countries) may not be able to afford a modern mobile phone with plenty of bandwidth. Older people may give up on phones because of trouble hearing; young people may not yet have phones.

On the other side of the scarcity-plenty spectrum, phone numbers are easy to come by in small quantities and not particularly hard to get in bulk. For the former, stop at any big-box store, and for the latter, set up a business and buy lines in bulk.

Mobile phones also have many of the issues of other small things, especially when it comes to entering secrets such as passwords or keys. They have also become crucial to many authentications and are thus tempting targets for attackers to either exploit the technology or trick a person into revealing authentication information.

Cloud

Many cloud systems support complex, layered delegation of authority. One cloud provider's "Organizations terminology and concepts" starts by discussing a "a *basic organization* that consists of five accounts that are organized into four organizational units under the root." There's a management account, which has a great deal of authority, and then the ability to assign permissions to those accounts in policies. If there's more than one account that a person is expected to regularly use, confusion is a likely result. (Emphasis added—the complexity grows rapidly.)

If a machine image contains either passwords or cryptographic keys, then each running instance will have the same authenticators, and anyone who steals the machine image will have copies as well. Modern practice is generally to have the machine request or register random keys in a secret store of some form. Each major cloud provider has guidance on bootstrapping these keys safely.

Considerations in Authenticating to Organizations

We regularly need to authenticate ourselves to organizations, including our banks, schools, utility companies, and the like. We also need to prove properties about ourselves such as creditworthiness, ability to work, or age to buy alcohol.

When people are responsible for checking details about strangers, it is surprisingly hard to define what "good" is and to execute on that well. It's hard to match a person to a small photograph taken years ago and printed as part of an ID card. When the property is "fellow employee of a large organization," the social pressure to say OK can feel high. Attackers will study manuals for a targeted organization so they can talk like their victims. Luke and Han know that they have no good answer for "What's your operator number?" when pretending to be Stormtroopers, so they pantomime that their radios are malfunctioning.

There are many nuances. For example, my state university ID card is a "government-issued ID," but it's probably not going to get me on an airplane. The level of required proof generally must balance security and business—good enough to say "We made an honest effort to comply with the rules" without turning away too much business. Many properties of these authentications are shared with authenticating to computers; people generally handle these exceptions, but the computer is less flexible, for good and ill. Similarly, demands for extensive documentation must be balanced with the customers who might feel it's overly intrusive. Security is one of several important properties in this calculation.

We also regularly need to authenticate that someone who's contacted us really represents the organization they claim to represent. Your bank, the IRS, a store with delivery problems…how do we know who they are? My advice to you is to take control of the conversation by initiating a new one to a trustworthy address. In other words, call the phone number on your card, log in using a bookmark to reach the authentic bank, or otherwise ensure that you're reaching the right place. Often, it's hard to get to the person who knows about your problem. Most organizations could deal with this much better.

Mechanisms for Spoofing Attacks

We've talked about spoofing files and processes on a computer, spoofing between nodes in a network, and spoofing people. I want to turn your attention next to some commonalities in the mechanics, not in the victim.

The mechanisms used include misrepresentation, theft, takeover, namespace confusion, exploiting mapping between layers, and confusion by deputies. There are also an extensive set of attacks on authentication techniques.

Misrepresentation

Misrepresentation is simply asserting a different identity. I might set the display name on an email to Luke Skywalker, but, by itself, no one would confuse me with the Jedi Master. After all, Jedi don't have email. But I am not putting forward an accurate representation. I might have an account "threat modeling instructor," which is accurate but not the name on my ID. I don't usually count that as misrepresentation. People should be able to call themselves what they want, as long as they're not doing it to deceive, and rules to try to constrain them to "real names" almost always cause more trouble than they're worth.

There are layers in which misrepresentation can take place. I might set my display name to Bill Gates; I might get the email address billg59@example.com. I might register a domain, gatesfoundation.com or gatesfoundat1on.com, that someone might think represents the Gates Foundation (and its nonexistent lottery).

Sometimes what happens is direct misrepresentation: "I am a Nigerian Prince," while other times the claims are implied. Still other times, the claim may be true and misleading: there's more than one Gates with a foundation, but only one who springs to mind.

There is also misrepresentation where text does not show what you think it shows. For example, the easily recognized string Υoda does not match the seemingly identical string Yoda. If you look at Figure 1.6, you'll see the following characters (identified here with their Unicode numbers). The top line consists of a Greek capital upsilon (03a5), Greek small omicron (03Bf), Cyrillic small letter komi di (0501), and what the heck, I used a Latin small *a* (0061). The bottom string uses a capital Y (0059), a small *o* (006F), a small *d* (0064), and a small *a* (0061). Unicode calls these *confusables* and has a nice tool to generate a list of confusable text. But the fun doesn't stop there.

Yoda ≠ Yoda

FIGURE 1.6 Spoofing Yoda

As you read this, you're reading left to right, but not all languages work that way. Many languages are read right to left, and so text processors often need a way to indicate a change of direction. Adding this to those confusables (to produce decoy text) means that the source code an editor displays may not be the code that the compiler parses. Ways to exploit these include an early `return` call, making apparently executable code into comments, and more (Anderson, 2021).

Theft

Either static authenticators (passwords, single-use URLs) or cryptographic keys can be stolen and used by an attacker.

Fake sites often use stolen HTML code. Even if the spoofer doesn't update their version of your site, people cannot avoid being trusting: they've learned that the world of the Web involves nearly constant minor changes, and so minor discrepancies are indistinguishable from the latest edits your brand team has implemented.

Takeover

I might not need to misrepresent myself, if I can use your account to do things that people attribute to you or that you are authorized to do. To do this, I bypass the authentication factors that protect your account or violate the integrity of the system that you use to log in. I can do that with malware, with systems management tools, or with other code or scripts.

Names, Mapping, and Canonicalization

A rose by any other name might smell as sweet, but you can't call the florist, order by some other name, and expect them all to show up roses. We use names to refer to things, and commonality between the names you and I use is a useful and difficult property. The names of people are freeform, not intended to be unique. In computers, names are often controlled by some authority whose goal is to ensure uniqueness for everyone who accepts the namespace. Some namespaces are local; /etc/passwd refers to a different file on each machine. Others such as IP address, email, or domain names are global. But not all addresses are global, and not all routing systems will respect the global nature of an address. The IP address space is generally global, until you get to addresses like 10.0.0.2, but that doesn't mean that every router will route 1.2.3.4 to the same place. If I control your router, I can easily write special-purpose routing tables that send packets to that machine to any place I'd like. Odds are I'll send them to a proxy of some form, which will tell you it's 1.2.3.4 and pretend to be you to that machine.

Email addresses, intuitively, have the property that an email address maps to a person, but that's not actually the case. Consider noreply@bank.com or support@bank.com. We think domain names map to an IP address, which maps to a machine, so everyone referring to www.google.com gets to the same place. What we really get differs from what we expect, and attackers often sit in those differences. This mapping between layers is another source of confusion and attack. If we return to the earlier example of the dst.threatsbook.com in the "Spoofing Machines" section, we can see that many of the attacks happen at the point of mapping, but, as you'll discover, a great deal depends on your point of view.

We hope that canonicalization reduces these problems. Intuitively, the simplest form of a name is better. If you canonicalize until the output of the canonicalization function is the same as the input you gave it, you are far less likely to have problems. But let's say you're making a canonical form of file://../../.././///./etc/passwd, which should simplify to file:/etc/passwd. You can do that before checking whether you want to allow it, and that is helpful. But it may not be sufficient for safety. Let's say that you simplify to file:///10.0.0.1:/etc/passwd. Is that OK access? Your canonical friends cannot save you now.

Attacks on Authentication Mechanisms

From Ben Kenobi telling Stormtroopers that they don't need to see Luke's identification to modern mind tricks of phishing or printing fake fingerprints, authentication mechanisms come under attack. They come under attack because if an attacker can impersonate, they can do all sorts of things the spoofee is authorized to do. Let's look at the mechanisms that recur.

Replay

There are many attacks that rely on an authenticator being static and thus reusable. If the string "stink,TheSithDo" authenticates Yoda's login, then an attacker can replay that string if a system isn't carefully designed to prevent replay attacks. This is the case if Yoda uses the same password on multiple systems, and it can even be a concern if the string is encrypted. Surprisingly, that's the case even if it's encrypted with a good cryptographic algorithm, but in a way that allows an attacker to replay the encrypted packet or message. For example, if the login sequence is always the same (login, password), then if I have the encrypted password for Yoda, I can just replay it. The defenses start with sending *nonces* (random numbers) that are incorporated into the messages.

Reflection

When adding cryptography to a system, even if there's good use of public key algorithms, messages tend to be encrypted with a symmetric algorithm. An effect of that efficiency choice is that packets can be decrypted by any endpoint of a protocol.

Attacks that reflect messages back to the party that sent them used to be remarkably effective, especially when encodings were either very tightly packed to work over slow connections, when the protocols are complex, or when decoders were designed to be liberal in what they accepted. Today's encodings tend to label data. To be concrete, a tightly packed encoding might be `1,Leia,16,74`, while a labeled one would be `{"id":1,"name":"Leia","role":"princess", "role":"general"}`.

Confused People

People are easily confused. We make mistakes and get distracted even when we're not being attacked. These problems are exploited by attackers in many, many ways, and highly relevant to multifactor authentication is how people can be tricked into helpfully bypassing such systems.

The same sort of attack works against many familiar forms of enhanced authentication, such as authenticator apps or text messages with a code. A person will happily enter the extra code on a phishing website. Attackers also have success saying "Oops, I entered the wrong phone number; can you send me the code you just got from my bank?" These approaches do require an attacker to be attacking live, rather than storing credentials and using them later.

People will also instruct their password managers that `github.com` and `github.io` are equivalent. They're not. Take a moment to think about why not and why the difference matters to security. Most people will guess that they're operated by different entities, which isn't true. Both are operated by GitHub. The `io` domain is used for user content. So, entering your password is very different (Burnett, 2017).

Confused Deputy Attacks

A *deputy* is a program that works on your behalf in some way, as a proxy. A "confused deputy" is when a program uses those privileges of a user on behalf of an attacker, who doesn't have those privileges. For example, a website directs your browser to request a resource in a cross-site request forgery, for example, `<img src="//192.168.1.1/password.cgi?change=secret'>`. Your browser is your deputy, and it's acting, confused, on behalf of an attacker who redirects it to change the password on your local router.

Threats Against Authentication Types

Each type of authentication factor (what you have, what you know, and the others) can be threatened in ways that are unique to that factor. Additionally, many authentication systems rely on sensors. Those sensors can be attacked separately from the attacks on the various factors or mechanisms. Sensors are the computers or peripherals that measure some physical properties, such as a fingerprint scanner or a GPS chip. Sensors are often remote relative to those who trust them and are subject to attacks such as tampering with the real sensor or spoofing it (claiming that some other computer or device is the sensor). For example, I might tamper with a fingerprint scanner in my laptop or attach my own device via USB. The way the biometric system's database storage maps from factor to account is subject to information disclosure, tampering, and denial of service. Those attacks vary by type of sensor, and the economics of sensor deployment often mean that the resistant sensors, or the sensor packages that may be harder to trick, are replaced with more vulnerable ones.

Attacks on "What You Know"

Passwords are the most traditional form of what you know, but there's been a rise in alternate forms, including a variety of systems that are intended to address the reality that humans frequently forget passwords.

"What you know" is attacked in two ways, guessing and theft, but it fails in more ways. There are innocent failures of such systems, where preferences change, memory fails, spelling doesn't match, etc. There are also failures where there are no passwords, default passwords, well-known passwords, or predictable passwords. Predictable passwords include using the username, date of birth, Ethernet address, an IMEI, a passport number, or similar elements that are "widely shared secrets."

Guessing

Guessing works because memorizing random strings is hard, so people want memorable passwords, and there's a short list of approaches. They include memorable words or keyboard sequences and techniques to appease the password edicts—appending a 1 or !, the month, the name of the site, and the like.

Attackers build dictionaries of likely passwords: *secret*, *letmein*, *qwertyui*, and *password* are all perennial favorite passwords. They can also be likely relative to a particular target. That likelihood can be informed by either password leaks or personal information about the target. Personal information used in passwords includes birthdays, kids' names, sports team preferences, Star Wars references, and more.

There are knowledge-based authentication systems that restrict the list of possible answers to a very small set, such as "What color are your eyes?" or "What's your favorite pizza topping?" While these systems may slow attackers (at the expense of customers needing to call and probably use yet another bad authentication system), a persistent attacker, such as a stalker, who keeps notes can still exhaust the search space. If you're breaking into Lando Calrissian's account, you can bet his favorite bird is probably a falcon, not an eagle or a hawk.

Attacks against each authentication factor can be split into online and offline attacks. Online means the attack is against the live system, including defenses that detect and respond to problems, for example, by getting exponentially slower at responding to login attempts within the same TCP session. A common aspiration is that you can rate-limit attacks testing passwords by IP address. It turns out that there is code available that will detect your rate limits and tune the attacks to come in just underneath them.

Offline attacks are those that disconnect some of those defenses, say using a stolen copy of an authentication database or a disconnected instance like a laptop with its Wi-Fi off. We'll revisit offline and offline attacks in Chapter 7.

Theft

Attackers can steal the answers from anyone who knows them. For a password, that includes your own site or other sites where a person uses the same password. For secret questions, it's anyone with access to the same data. (In this sense, use of the SSN as an authenticator is a success catastrophe.) The people who know the answers include the person whose data it is, who can be tricked into handing it out with "games" like "your Harry Potter name" asking about the street you grew up on. Attackers are also setting up sites that offer value for free registration. They mirror the secret questions of more popular sites and thus collect answers from those who answer honestly. Carleton University Professor Paul van Oorschot calls this variant an *interleave* attack in his excellent *Internet Security: Tools and Jewels* (Oorschot, 2019). These interleave attacks are an extension of a classic MITM attack but are less tied to being classically "in the middle." Credentials can also be stolen when people are tricked into providing their credentials to a program that shouldn't have them. This can be phishing, local copies of `ssh` or `sudo`, or a fake login screen. Thus, there's a strong relationship between spoofing and information disclosure.

Credentials can be stolen in transit, when they are being changed or federated, or from storage at a server, a client, a key distribution or directory server, or a third party where credentials are also used. Cryptographic credential schemes can reduce vulnerability by keeping a secret on a local machine, and a validator on remote ones. These schemes are great for those cases where you don't have to support arbitrary people on arbitrary devices with arbitrary software, which means you need passwords.

One particularly failure-rich transit is the mobile phone system, where "what you know" is interpreted as "what was sent to your phone number." This is so full of fails that words nearly fail me. There are all sorts of attacks, including attacks on routing and attacks that exploit convenience tools. Routing attacks include *number porting*, where someone convinces a phone company that you want to move your number to them. Then all the messages (and calls) get routed to "your" new phone company. Closely related are *SIM swapping* attacks, where someone convinces your phone company that they're you and need a new SIM. Those work within a phone company. Even if your phone company or SIM doesn't change, someone who can convince your mobile phone company that you're roaming can get your messages. That's less common. Additionally, modern communications tools want to make it easy to read your text messages, and so Outlook, iMessage, Google Voice, and others will pull your text messages into your email, so anyone who can read your email can read your texts.

Attacks on "What You Are"

Using "what you are" to authenticate you requires not only you but some stored information about you that is used for later authentication. These can be as simple as a photograph or as complex to measure as DNA. This is called *biometrics*, either from the Latin for "life measurements" or the Dutch for "gummy bear." Overall, there are threats to the enrollment process, where either the wrong person is measured or the wrong measurements are recorded. There are threats to the storage of the measured data, most importantly including tampering and denial of service, but depending on the data or who is holding it, information disclosure might matter. ("Do explain to me, Mr. Corleone, why the Polezia were so excited by your fingerprints?") Lastly, there are threats to checking a biometric, either fooling the instruments or fooling the evaluator. Of course, the evaluator can lie.

Let's make a few of these concrete. Looking at photographs first, people are bad at matching a photograph to the face of a stranger in front of them. Even if we are excellent at recognizing the faces of people we know, matching the faces of strangers to small pictures of them is hard, and the vast majority of the people you look at will have a matching ID, which makes it hard to maintain vigilance, and claiming that a person doesn't match is a socially awkward interaction even in structured systems like border control.

Somewhat surprisingly, no one in Star Wars ever seems to fake a hologram. But in our world today, there's voice cloning and deepfakes. Voice cloning is just what it sounds like: a computer takes a sample of a voice and says things in that voice. You can buy a teddy bear that talks like grandpa. And deepfakes are the video equivalent. Today, the tools are complex, slow to use, and don't work perfectly. Attacks only get better, those weaknesses in the attack code are being worked on, and our ability to use phone calls or video calls to distinguish the real you from a fake you at a distance will diminish.

Technological attempts to replace the person with a system may address the issue of boredom but are still terrifyingly imperfect. There are credible reports of people passing border control even when iris scans are in use (Youssef, 2010). Border control is useful as an example because it's a system where we can expect the technology to be at its most effective. Many interesting threats can be better managed, including fake equipment, tampering with the signal from real equipment, prostheses, and lazy, friendly, or bribed staff. So, biometric systems should operate around their peak of reliability.

Recently, there were claims that a set of generated master fingerprints could fool phone fingerprint scanners 65 percent of the time (Ross, 2017). There are questions about the research, but attacks only get better. The Chaos Computer Club (ccc) has demonstrated going from photographs taken at 5 meters to iris prints that fool the iris sensor on a high-end smartphone (ccc, 2017).

Physical attacks to steal body parts are not just the stuff of *Minority Report*; such have been reported in the real world. And while I don't want to get ahead of myself, we must face the possibility that we'll be up to our necks in biometrics like FaceID.

Voice systems are in increasing use, in part because they can be used surreptitiously. Systems to create synthetic audio of a person speaking in real time are on the near horizon. It's not just computers that may be confused. Link one of these systems to a phone call, and you can confuse another person into thinking that you're someone else. This will confound many call centers, whose operators want to move to voice authentication, because it has the potential to be used secretly (or perhaps unobtrusively) in the background. It seems likely the voice authentication system will detect some voice cloning tools, and attackers will search for or build tools that allow them to impersonate.

Attacks on "What You Have"

Things that you have can be lost, stolen, or duplicated. If the answer to what you have is a physical token for multifactor authentication and you want to outsource your job to a programmer in China, you can point a webcam at it so they can do your job.

Also, what you have might be a device, with device identifiers. It might be an IP address at which you can receive packets. The word *receive* is very important—it is far easier to spoof a sending address than to get packets to come back to you. There have been TCP spoofing attacks that have leveraged predictable identifiers and sequence numbers so they didn't need to receive responses.

Attacks on "Where You Are"

Location can be a helpful addition to other authentication factors. Physical location is hard. Most systems do not have sufficient timing resolution and reliability to determine how far radio signals have moved; radio travels at a foot per nanosecond, so if your timing is "merely" microseconds, you have accuracy on the order of 2,000 feet. (If you're unlucky signals are sent at the very start of a microsecond and received at the very end of the next.) As of 2022, the Linux `time(7)` man page still says "microsecond accuracy is typical of modern hardware."

If you are translating an IP address into a physical location, don't forget that IP addresses are flexible. The geolocation of an IP address is tricky; many mobile devices silently connect through complex proxy systems designed to improve performance. People often want to appear to be coming from somewhere else to watch television (!), so the tools for spoofing are easily available.

Attacks on Authentication Chains

Closely related to the attacks on who you know are attacks on chained authentication.

Many systems are moving to make it easy to send either a one-time code or a password reset to the email associated with your account. This is a practical recognition that as we all have too many accounts, it's easy to forget or lose your password. This means that those other email providers become or are acknowledged as a crucial part of the security of those systems.

This requires that the person still has access to the email account they used when setting up the account. Systems that have rare communication with customers, such as banks with retirement accounts, need to be careful that the account may be reassigned. This differs from a confused deputy because your email provider is not your deputy for account security (or at least perceptions about this differ.)

Defenses

Authentication is one of the tasks most frequently demanded of people through their day, so even your real, cooperative users or customers may find themselves worn down. It's important to design defenses that authenticate well without unduly burdening people.

Authenticating People

No single factor works well for authenticating people, and using more than one factor is the best way to overcome those weaknesses. (By this, I mean more than one type of factor, such as what you have and what you know, not many iterations or variations of what you know.) We discussed the factors overall above in Authenticating People to Computers, and I'd like to revisit "what you know."

"What You Know"

Defending password systems includes managing what people select as their password, dealing with the reality that people will reuse their passwords, understanding that other sites will leak them, and storing the passwords safely.

Defenders can expect, detect, and respond to dictionary-driven attacks. It's useful to include common passwords and to update the list each year. I'm reasonably certain we saw an uptick in *murderhornet* in 2020 and *covid* in 2021.

Offline attacks against what you know rely on direct access to a copy of the authentication database. Well-designed authentication databases use many iterations of a cryptographic hash to store not the password, but its hashed value. The hash function is designed so there's no way to go from the output to its input. (This is called a *pre-image* attack on the hashing function.) If your framework has features for password setting and checking, they probably do this for you. The nuances of defending stored authenticators are very educational if you want to go deeper into defense, but the simple answer is use Argon2, the winner of the Password Hashing Competition. You'll also need to use a salt (a random value per password, stored in cleartext) so that two users using the same password will have different stored authentication information. (See Chapter 7 for details.)

If you're using other secrets ("the street you grew up on"), then an irreversible hash imposes a requirement of precise matches. You might adjust people's answers before checking (changing *Street* or *St.* to *street*) as an alternative to storing the answers in plaintext.

Authentic Gestures—What You've Done

Desktop operating systems used to treat all software that was running "as the logged-in user" as equivalent. A program could read or write all your files. Ransomware loves this type of feature. That's evolved, and the way it's evolved, with a focus on "authentic gestures," is covered in Chapter 6. If you're developing a platform, consider if it's helpful to distinguish physical input from virtual.

Authenticating Computers

The ability to address spoofing varies with the type of software. If your clients use a web browser, you cannot control where that browser goes. Creators of connected devices often have more control. Their devices may need to connect to only a small number of destinations, and those destinations may be within the control of the device maker. That control allows you to specify the certificates or certificate authority (CA) that is trusted. (Doing so carries the risk of breaking things if the certificates are lost or the CA is unavailable.) Spoofing of local files that only your application accesses is relatively easy but gets harder as those files are accessed over a network.

Conclusion

Let's return to the question of how R2-D2 knows to play the hologram of Princess Leia saying, "Help me, Obi-Wan Kenobi." Perhaps as a high-level operative, the droid maintains a biometric database of trusted participants in the resistance? In that case, getting him off the ship and away from the Empire really is crucial—if captured, his storage might be retrieved by forensic specialists, and the entire resistance might be unmasked at once. Privacy is important to many people. Keeping customer lists or membership lists confidential matters even when you're not fighting a galactic empire.

More generally, because we allow action based on which account is being used and what authority it's granted, we must ensure that people and computers are sufficiently well-authenticated.

2

Tampering and Integrity

When the Millennium Falcon escapes from the Death Star, Han is right to worry that it's too easy. There are two reasons for that: Obi-Wan has tampered with the power supply to a tractor beam, and the Falcon itself has been tampered with: a homing beacon has been placed onboard.

Introduction

Tampering, where the data you get is not what was stored or sent, is a threat to the integrity of that data. The most common ways tampering manifests are failures of storage integrity and failures of communication integrity, but there are also many ways to tamper with the integrity of a process or with the physical integrity of a device. There's tampering with systems after an attack has succeeded. There also are questions of integrity in distributed systems and issues of atomicity in database systems. Integrity protections can protect you from both intentional tampering and reliability failures, caused by cosmic rays, mechanical or logical failures, or other random processes.

There are situations where the integrity of either storage or communication fails because you're talking to the wrong file or the wrong server. When that's enemy action, rather than a mistake, each of those can be a spoofing problem, which leads to the same problems as an integrity failure, but the actual files are intact or the right server would provide you with the right response. Integrity also bleeds into availability when the attack is to delete a file.

Targets of Tampering

When the Millennium Falcon was hiding in an asteroid field, creatures known as mynocks attached to it, threatening the integrity of the ship's power systems and hull. All tampering takes place in some context. Something is being tampered with, and the thing being targeted may be storage, communication, or time. There's also tampering with a process, which is a little different.

Tampering with Storage

When you open a file on your local computer, you expect that file to be as you left it. You'd like that to be the case even if something crashed. If you find garbage in it, that's an accidental integrity failure. For files you own and have locked, only you can make changes (well, you and root). Of course, there are files that are intentionally writable by more than one person or account.

You might consider using digital signatures to protect important files, such as binaries, which is a lovely defense. You'll need to check at least who signed the file, and you may need to check that the signature or date are what you expect. If you don't, you're subject to roll-forward or rollback attack. That is, if you have a signature for Microsoft Word 11.2 that is fully patched and someone can replace it with 11.1, then the integrity check of "is this the file we want?" is underspecified.

Data stores include shared memory, databases, filesystems, cloud storage, archival systems such as tapes or CD-ROMs, and sticky notes. Attacks are less dependent on the type of store, except that the type of store is correlated with how strongly it's attached to a system. Data stores are attached with various degrees of firmness to a particular computer. Filesystems are often on disks inside a computer, but sometimes on removable media or attached over a network. Tapes are stored in R2-D2 and transported through the most wretched hives of scum and villainy. (It's frankly shocking that the Rebel systems used to analyze the Death Star plans aren't running ransomware.) More often, tapes are stored on the very edge of a truck, poised to fall off, or in the mail, where they go missing.

When an attacker has physical possession of a data store, they can bypass operating system protections. But even if they don't, they may be able to bypass the kernel by accessing raw memory or devices, bypass the integrity checks, or convince a confused deputy to write for them. If your data store is in the cloud, then your integrity depends on isolation relative to other cloud customers.

Storage has limits, including capacity. When a disk is full, you can discard either the earliest or latest information. (I suppose you could get creative and throw away data randomly, or in the middle.) If you're going to constrain storage use algorithmically, consider that the decision to store N weeks of logs was last revisited for both Windows and Linux in the 1990s, when disks cost dollars per megabyte.

Distributed systems can prioritize write integrity (for example, Amazon really wants to make sure that "add to cart" is highly reliable) or read integrity (any "Alice's account is locked" flag will be seen by any read by every bank application), and they can prioritize either speed of convergence or speed of action, accepting some inconsistency.

Tampering with Communications

Messages flow through channels; email messages flow through an SMTP channel, and HTML pages go through an HTTP channel (and often also through a TLS channel). In today's world, we are accustomed to TCP transparently giving us reliable and ordered delivery of TCP segments over the unreliable IP backbone. You can tamper with the message or the channel, and the means and effects of doing so are different. Tampering with a message is generally easier to imagine before or after it is in a particular channel, especially when the channel has protection like TLS. (See Figure 2.1.)

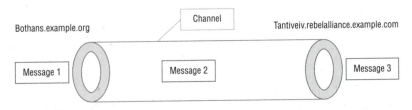

FIGURE 2.1 Channels and messages

Princess Leia's ship is the Tantive IV, and it's one of the two hosts shown in Figure 2.1. For some reason, it's communicating with some Bothans. There's a channel, shown as a tube, and messages that flow through it. (There are important privacy threats with this design, and we'll talk about them in Chapter 4, "Information Disclosure and Confidentiality.") A Bothan communications staffer can tamper with message 1 as it's being prepared, the Empire can tamper with message 2, and an Imperial spy working for the Rebels can alter message 3 before it gets to Leia.

Sometimes messages have integrity protection, such as a digital signature. Sometimes channels have integrity protection, such as each message being protected by a keyed hash.

If your messages have no integrity protection, nothing prevents tampering or helps you detect it. If you have integrity in a messaging system, you likely have a tricky process of selecting which headers are included in the integrity protection. With email messages, for example, you can't include the "Signature" header(s), but more interestingly, you can't predict the route the messages will take and therefore can't include the `Received` lines that are added along the way. And so many such schemes will be vulnerable to header injection. Header injection is the addition of new headers in ways that are not parsed properly by receivers.

Header injection attacks may take advantage of duplicate headers, depending on how the code is written. Human and automated parsers will likely interpret things differently, or worse, signature verification might be separate from display parsing, and an unsigned header might be displayed to the user because it's first or last or whatever the UI code decides to show in this revision. More on this attack is in Chapter 8, "Parsing and Corruption."

Of course, when you're signing or authenticating messages, you have to store and manage keys. The key storage can be threatened by tampering or information disclosure, and the management code is subject to tampering, information disclosure, or expansion of authority threats. These can result in keys being stolen or used outside their normal path. Either will break message integrity. Exception handling is hard, which is why, after the Rebel Alliance steals authentication codes, an assault team can land on a small moon of Endor. How to deal with expired keys is an infuriating problem; see Chapter 3, "Repudiation and Proof."

Channel integrity can be important as a system property, protecting a group of messages as a set, or as a backstop, making it harder to tamper with particular messages. For example, it might be useful to protect the information that a Bothan sent three messages to a rebel, even if you have no information about their contents. If you want to tamper with a channel, you can do so because the integrity protections are nonexistent or poor or because the keys are not managed well. Metadata about messages that a channel might protect from tampering include time, size, direction, participant entry and exit, and/or mappings between participants and system or display names. For example, if you protect information about the IP addresses associated with a channel, you might also capture and protect information about how those IP addresses map to domain names, SMB names, or other naming systems at other layers. Systems management software will often modify these mappings over time and may not maintain the logs you want, maintain them for as long as you want, or be in sync with your timings. These modifications are a feature, and thus we say "modify," but attackers may do the same, in which case we call it tampering. Also, the mapping between the names your system uses and other identifiers such as email or phone number is often information that at least some people will want to keep private.

When you are focused on integrity, it can be easy to ignore intermediates, historically labeled *man in the middle* (MITM). MITM also stands for monkeys in the middle. Assuming you can get set up as a MITM, there are ways to monkey around beyond adding or deleting messages. These ways include replaying signed messages, reflecting them back (which is more often interesting in the context of symmetric authentication such as message authentication codes), or sending bad messages with apparently good sequence numbers. If you're handling sequence numbers before message authentication has succeeded, then you may treat future valid messages as invalid because you've already parsed that sequence number.

Also, if you have a channel from point A to point B, how good are the endpoint guards? Can someone insert a message into one side and have it come out the other? When it does, will it be treated as a message from A by B or C? This can be a confused deputy or one who's accepted a bribe.

Tampering with Time

Most systems have at least several opinions about the meaning of "now," and disagreements, misunderstandings, or even attacks on time are either a hindrance to operations or a building block to an attack. There's the system time, which is either set to wall time or to UTC, and a display time, which likely takes time zones into account. Phones and laptops are often physically moved to new time zones, and the abomination of daylight saving time means that time doesn't always increase one second at a time.

When you rely on time, it's important to understand that it can change for both malicious and well-intentioned reasons. The motivation doesn't change the problem, and the defensive design and implementation patterns that you'll want to use to protect you from malicious changes can also help your systems be more reliable.

Sometimes a system time second is longer than an hour, like when a virtual machine goes to sleep. Other times, wall time can shift in unpredictable ways. The government of Samoa once decided that a particular Friday was not essential as they relocated to the far side of the date line, meaning that the time difference between Samoa and everywhere else except the island of Tokelau changed. (Yes, Samoa really did this in 2011 to bring their time zones closer to important trading partners [Mydans, 2011; Sussman, 2012]). Keeping system time in UTC, rather than local wall time, means that you have fewer concerns created by changes to local wall time. So unless you're on an intergalactic mission, keep system time in UTC. (This also applies for shorter-range spacecraft—Mars rovers get an exception.)

Most system time is managed by an onboard clock, with corrections from time servers, often via NTP or GPS, or maybe from a cell tower. Clock drift is a problem for log correlation even absent an attacker. Attackers take advantage of this design to tamper with system time. Many systems will implicitly trust a DHCP's direction of what NTP server to use. A remote attacker who can forge NTP packets, GPS signals, or cell signals can use those tools to alter a system's idea of what time it is. Similarly, a local user may be able to alter the system's idea of time offset (wall time to system time), time zone, or system time. This may or may not require administrator rights.

Attackers can take advantage of time by changing the time. Moving it back may lead to a certificate, license key, or other data being treated as valid after its expiration date, or invalid because it's before the go-live date. Moving it forward can have similar effects. On the local computer, this might let you use expensive software longer, block access to a site because the system sees that site's certificate as no longer valid, or play extra Star Wars games because parental controls aren't working as planned. If you can adjust a server's idea of the time, you might be able to buy concert tickets before they go on sale or prevent your procrastinating rivals from submitting by closing a submission window early. Similarly, you might trade stocks when the market is closed. Each place where there's a window of allowed activity, tampering with time can help you, hurt your rivals, or both.

Process Tampering

In all but the simplest cases, processes can rely on the operating system to protect them from processes owned by other users. (Bootloaders such as MS-DOS, smartcards, and the other low-end systems of the day usually fail to provide these protections.) This isolation functionality sometimes has two modes: protection against processes from other users and a weaker protection against processes running as the same user. At the stronger end, an operating system should provide controls as to which process can read or write the memory of another process. Historically, this was weakened in the context of processes running as the same user: you want to be able to debug your own processes and influence them to behave in different ways. Apple declared a different set of defaults in IoS, and while certain functionality was hard to add, it was also harder to write malware.

Network Attacks Against Processes

An operating system mediates access to hardware, including network hardware, and provides an interface to streams or packets, which can contain anything that passes the (very minimalistic) limits of the network stack. Processes must protect themselves from what these attackers might do. For example, a remote client might tamper with a nonce that you've provided or tamper with the value of `admin=no`, add a token `admin=yes`, or even remove the token `rebel_sympathizer`. They might also attempt to tamper with your inputs that are coming in via remote file systems or generate confusion between code and data or otherwise damage the integrity of your process. The attacks on process integrity are covered in Chapter 6, "Expansion of Authority and Isolation," and Chapter 8.

Tampering by Other Users

An operating system creates channels that allow communication and interference between different user IDs, including file access, signals, and shared memory. For tampering, it is write permissions that matter most. Usually, these protections are quite strong for what they intend to protect against. For example, if your operating system or cloud provider has an append-only mode for logs, you can likely rely on it working, and only the authorized log reaper is able to delete logs.

Protecting your process against tampering by root, admin, or the hypervisor is hard, and trying or worrying about it is a waste of effort if you don't have hardware support. With hardware support, such as Intel SGX or Apple's Secure Execution Environment, there are explicit authorization paths that control what the operating system administrator can do and that provide strong integrity protections. The specifics are beyond the scope of this book, but recall that all code has bugs, bugs in security code are often security bugs, and this hardware requires unusual skills and access to test.

Tampering by the Same User ID

When a process is invoked, a great many things about its environment can be controlled by the caller and possibly tampered with later by the creator. Most prominently under the caller's control are environmental things like working directory and environment variables, including environment variables that control the behavior of the dynamic library loader. Less conspicuous, but no less important are open file descriptors for input or output.

Convincing a person to tamper with their own computer is an interesting and perhaps unexpected form of attack. As computers become ever less scrutable, "Google the error message" is not only a frequent response, but a reasonable one. There are sites that are rife with advice that will leave you insecure, sometimes by accident and sometimes because people seem to be filling them with bad advice, such as "Download this software and run it as administrator." These attacks may seem hard to target, and many of them are likely harvesting low-value targets. But if you make heavy use of TB-65B X-Wing Fighters and your opponent knows that, then they might use a starship mechanic website to convince your mechanics to adjust the in-flight radios in a way that makes the fighters easier to track over long distances.

Library Tampering

There are three interesting cases of tampering via libraries. The first is library load paths, such as the Downloads directory or the LD_LOAD_LIBRARY environment variable; the second is libraries loaded via a package manager; and the last is libraries loaded via the Web.

The Downloads directory is used to store lots of downloads. If someone downloads an installer and that installer is imprecise about what DLLs it wants, then downloaded copies of those DLLs can be loaded into the installer. Of course, this applies to any code, not just installers, but installers are a common victim of this form of tampering, since running them in downloads seems reasonable and normal (Lawrence, 2019). The best fix for application vendors is to ship an installer package, such as an .app, MSI, or .dmg, rather than an executable. Operating system vendors should also use special-case directories, such as Downloads and tmp, and require special build flags to load dependencies from such directories. A variant on this is checking that a library is in a trusted directory, such as system32, which has untrusted and writable subdirectories such as Tasks (Forshaw, 2017). As tempting as it is to mock Microsoft for this, all systems have variants of this.

Modern package management systems make it easy to manage dependencies. In fact, it's so easy that developers often add the same library repeatedly to web pages. They add both the same and different versions (Lauinger, 2018). There's a problem, which is that calls to the versions will be imprecise, and the result is accidental library tampering. One common fix to this is to version-lock dependencies to help manage compatibility. That leads to old versions, full of software vulnerabilities being locked in (Morszczyzna 2017, Pieczul, 2017).

The web approach to library tampering builds on the Web's use of libraries included from other sites. There's more than one way to do it, but `<script src=URI>` is common. An attacker who breaks into the site serving the URI can tamper with all the sites that depend on it. For example, in November 2018, someone broke into Statcounter, an audience measurement site whose code was used on 2 million sites at the time (Faou, 2018). The attackers inserted six lines of JavaScript, which triggered if the loading page URL included `/myaccount/withdraw/BTC`. That URL was probably only present on cryptocurrency site `gate.io`. If the URL matched, additional code was loaded. As an aside, this represents either a wasted opportunity to attack 1,999,999 other sites, or good tradecraft, making the attack less likely to be detected on another site.

Input and Tampering

Lastly, you need to protect the integrity of your code and control flow against corruption by your input. Attacks that exploit this are covered in Chapter 8.

Tampering in Specific Technologies

When Luke removes the restraining bolt from R2-D2, that's droid-specific tampering. (Let's not worry about how that bolt interacts with the rest of the droid technology.) Although most readers are not producing droids, many are working with specific technologies, and so it's worth exploring how tampering manifests in devices, AI/ML, and the cloud.

Tampering with Devices

Many software people think that attacks on devices are "out of scope." Microsoft, in its "10 immutable laws of computer security," says, "If a bad guy has unrestricted physical access to your computer, it's not your computer anymore." Operations people often put a cage around the computers they care about, because the locks on most commodity PCs and servers can be easily opened with a paperclip.

Building solid tamper resistance into devices is expensive. A decent safe you buy to hold valuables at home resists attackers due to its mass and an expectation that there are easier pickings elsewhere. Safes that are tested and rated to resist a skilled attacker with tools for 15 minutes will cost upward of $1,000. (The ones you buy for hundreds lack that "TL15" certification.)

Of course, safes are not the only smart devices, and many of them are far more exposed to random passers-by. There are Bluetooth-enabled padlocks, doorbells with cameras and Wi-Fi, and security cameras that are designed to be outside and thus outside (or on) your perimeter. Building defenses into these devices isn't cheap, and the hardware limits often converge on some special screwhead and sometimes a tamper sensor. Devices are exposed to retailers, installers, housecleaners, landlords, and guests, including the nice people your teenagers bring home. You as a system designer or end user should expect that your device is subject to physical tampering.

If you care, and are not targeting the hobbyist market where that's encouraged, you should consider identifying weaknesses in your system by tampering with hardware and especially tampering with your storage (often on an SD card) or tampering with RAM. Cooling RAM with a can of compressed air allows an attacker to remove it from power, connect it to a new system, and read its contents. This is easier when the RAM isn't soldered. There's also an important recurrent problem with "JTAG" interfaces. JTAG stands for Joint Test Action Group and refers to a specific interface for debugging and testing electronics. JTAG interfaces are often left available after devices leave the factory, and this allows attackers all sorts of access.

The case of Jedi Knights is interesting—is it fair to critique the Death Star engineers for not better locking down the tractor beam controls? Having given this question more thought than it deserves, I think it's unfair. The Death Star was a controlled military installation, and there's a potential need for emergency maintenance when the tractor beam is pulling something in too quickly.

Tampering with AI/ML

Attackers who can influence the selection or storage of training data can do all sorts of things from that vantage point. Some systems attempt to update their models by learning from data in the field. These systems come under attack. Sometimes that's very public, as in the case of Microsoft's Tay AI, who, when exposed to Twitter, rapidly started spewing racist garbage gibberish. Other times it's less publicly visible. Microsoft has spoken publicly about malware uploads that seem engineered to influence the machine learning systems they use to improve detection. (Parikh, 2018) Training models are subject to tampering where they are fielded. When a learning system is decentralized, or federated, it can become vulnerable for attack. These federated learning models may be subject to either false inputs or false reports between collaborators.

Tampering with the Cloud

Cloud systems like Gmail or Facebook have the interesting property that they allow logins from anywhere. Attackers who manage to authenticate into an account will routinely tamper with the controls, including security and operational controls. For example, they'll add an email they control to account recovery, and in a mail service, they'll add rules that cause replies to their messages to be forwarded off and not shown to you.

There are new venues for tampering in the cloud. These include both the code you get from others, and the code you create yourself. Code you get from others includes possibly public virtual machine images, Docker containers, and other software you use. Then there's the code you create. Both are combined as part of your own deployment pipeline. Both the public and private storage can be tampered with. For example, when you get a prebuilt Amazon Machine Image, how sure are you that the people who built it and stored it are giving you what you expect? Least likely but most powerful would be an attacker getting some admin rights within the cloud provider. Don't focus too much on this—your ability to influence it is low, and the cloud provider knows how damaging it would be to their business.

Mechanisms for Tampering

Having discussed tampering with storage, communication, time, and processes, as well as how these manifest in the cloud, IoT, and AI/ML, let's turn our attention to some of the mechanics involved.

Location for Tampering

There are many mechanisms by which people can tamper, and each of them requires authority of one sort or another.[1] In the classical computing world, the most important privileges were to run code, to do so as the administrator or domain administrator, or to be attached to a corporate or physical network. Being attached to a corporate network meant being "behind the firewall" in the quaint phrase of the days when there was a single firewall. It also meant you could freely connect to all sorts of resources that were private-ish. Being attached

---

[1]Sometimes that authority is granted freely, as on Wikipedia. But Wikipedia does not allow anyone to edit it; they have blocked access to those using the Tor privacy system.

to a physical network meant you could see all the packets that went by because they were broadcast to everyone on the wire. Being able to see them, you might also be able to modify them at least enough to break a checksum and then send a fake version in their place. Wired networks that once used coaxial cable have generally been replaced by direct-run Ethernet over twisted pair, with broadcasts tamped down at a switch. Of course, if you control the switch or router, you can modify anything that goes through it.

It may seem quaint to be talking about wired networks in today's age of mobile phones and computers, but wires are still very much in use in dense environments like data centers, and in those installations, like embassies, where the risk of wireless eavesdropping (or tampering) is sufficiently important. For these networks and for many IOT devices, physical access is an important privilege required for tampering. Physical access is traditionally defended via fences, walls, and sometimes even the enclosures of the device. These are often augmented by guards and dogs. (Sometimes those dogs are dedicated to guarding, perhaps like a Doberman Pinscher; other times they're family pets like Cocker Spaniels.) Those controls are effective to various degrees and also porous in surprising ways. Universities, coffee shops, hotels, churches, and other welcoming spaces are shockingly open if you're paranoid, and our homes are open during neighborhood socials, sales, or when rented out as Airbnbs.

Our homes and businesses are also usually open to radios, and radios are often surprisingly powerful. (Radios are another example of perversity in security: when you want the wireless to work, the range is surprisingly short, and when you're worried about attackers, surprisingly far.)

Lastly, there is tampering in the supply chain. The people who design, fabricate, assemble, or ship physical things can deliver products that are not quite what you expect, and there's not a great deal most software developers and security engineers will do about that. See *The Huawei and Snowden Questions* (Lysne, 2018) if you think you'll do something about it; otherwise, move along. Our general inability to build software that's secure even when we want to means that most attackers don't need to bother.

There is also tampering in software. If a compiler designer wants to insert a backdoor into the machine code their compiler produces, they can do so. They can even write a version of their compiler that recognizes that it's compiling a compiler and insert the extra code into the output compiler. Having done so, they can delete the trojan code. But have you ever looked at the code for GCC? You could hide a Sandcrawler in there and no one would ever see it. So, you almost don't need to delete it, except for deniability. Ken Thompson talked about this in his Turing Award Lecture, "Reflections on Trusting Trust" (Thompson, 1984).

Tools for Tampering

The mechanisms by which someone tampers intentionally range from general tools to specialized ones. If I'm logged in and can write a file, I can simply open it in a text editor. This works even if the file isn't text, although it might be tricky to make the alterations you want, and your editor might "fix" irregularities in the file. That is, it might tamper with your tampering. Such chutzpah! Such trouble can be avoided by using the standard clients: a database client for a database file, Word for `.docx`, emacs for `.html`, or `gdb` or `windbg` for a process. There are also specialized clients for both analysis and modification of local files, some of which are fairly nifty, such as the Veles file visualizer or a code obfuscator. (What's that you say, an obfuscator isn't there to modify the file but to prevent someone from understanding it? Of course it is, and it does that through tampering with its contents. Believe those modifications are authorized? Listen to the developer swear a gray streak while debugging.) A great many of these tools now work in a web browser, which makes them no less specialized but does reduce the installation and configuration burden.

Modifying a network connection usually requires specialized tools of some form. There are tools that are designed to modify network connections you control and to modify networks as an attacker. You modify your own network connections to gain capabilities such as recording or easily modifying complex streams like web sessions using the OWASP Zed Attack Proxy (ZAP). Someone might want to noncooperatively modify your network connections, as happens most times you stay at a hotel, or modify the network by sending routing commands to reroute all traffic through their system.

One interesting tampering technique is the rowhammer family of attacks. If you think of RAM as lots of tightly packed cells, with each cell holding either a zero or a one, you're spot on—and it's a very tiny spot. As RAM density increases, current can leak from one cell to an adjacent one and actually cause a bit to flip, because as that philosopher of engineering Martin Gore has pointed out, everything counts in large amounts.[2] And with large amounts of writing to adjacent memory, bits can be flipped, which is to say tampered with. After rowhammer was announced, memory makers added a technique called *target row refresh* to protect against it (Ducklin, 2021). If you are working with standard PC components, this is likely not an issue for you, but if you are implementing hardware, it's worth ensuring your components protect against this and other, related attacks.

Another interesting tampering technique is via Internet advice pages. This technique exploits a very confused deputy, the human owner of some system, who is trying to solve some problem. Even great "user-generated content" can include insecure steps, but these sites can also be overwhelmed by attackers who provide bad advice either intentionally or accidentally. Links from these sites can be bad from the start, or the targets of the links can rot away and be replaced by attackers distributing malware.

---

[2] He also commented insightfully on the impact of latency issues in 'People are People.'

Defenses

Integrity is provided by preventative and detective controls. Either can work cryptographically or by relying on something with more authority: a security kernel, a cloud provider, or hardware. The security kernel approach works only when all access to files goes through it, which usually means the local machine or a cloud service that intermediates all access to its storage.

Cryptography

Cryptography can prevent tampering by either malicious storage or network attackers. Malicious storage includes any storage that might be controlled by an attacker. A simple example is a USB drive that's plugged into an attacker's computer. You can no longer trust the operating system to protect you. And over a network, there's no operating system to protect the packets.

Crypto defenses include both asymmetric and symmetric techniques. Symmetric cryptographic techniques, where both parties share a key, can be used to protect messages. For example, keyed hash techniques can protect messages from tampering. The asymmetric (public key) techniques allow one-to-many integrity protection; for example, everyone can see that this file was signed by this key, which is associated with Adobe and used for signing software updates. So, asymmetric techniques can also be used for authenticating files to yourself after they've been through possibly untrustworthy storage or between different systems under your control while keeping the private portion of a public key pair on a single machine.

The Kernel

The kernel—the part of the operating system that runs all user-level code—is the canonical example of something with more authority. Today, a fuller list includes not only "the kernel," but a hypervisor, a security chip, a corporate Identity and Access Management (IAM) tool, and more. Whichever it is, as long as it really controls all access to your data, it can provide integrity protection.

Regardless of how it's implemented, it's important to tell it what you want to have happen, and to be sure that your intent is clear, via permissions. Your local operating system has a security kernel, as does your mobile phone and your cloud provider. Each has unique and important properties.

Mobile operating systems (iOS, Android) generally protect apps from tampering with each other when running, protect them from tampering with other apps' storage, and limit app installation to an app store. They will also check the app store signature before loading an app, protecting it against tampering on the device.

Cloud services have layers of administration, help desk, and "enterprise" administration. Providers of Infrastructure or Platforms as a Service, which encourage their customers to upload powerful and flexible code, are exposed to tampering by those customers. (This relates to expansion of authority and other concepts discussed in more detail in Chapter 6.)

Telling the kernel what to do can be harder than you expect when permissions are inherited in various ways, when multiple roles can set permissions (for example, you and your Office Applications administrator), and when the permissions that the kernel grants change. Debugging or fixing permissions quickly will often result in "it works now," even if what works is permissions that were more open than intended.

Hardware is not made of magic security dust. From read-only memory to cordoned-execution, encrypted memory, or even a separate chip, hardware can offer security at a more trusted level of execution to protect you against tampering and other threats. Read-only memory can be hard-coded ROMs, or it can be protected in various ways, ranging from a switch that must be moved, a wire that must be cut, or simply RAM to which only a special chip has write access. It is worth considering threats to each of these when you are able to specify them, for example if you're designing a connected device where you integrate the hardware, software, and perhaps cloud service into a single package. Security people often recoil from the idea of accepting a defense whose quality we're not sure of. This uncertainty is common in dealing with hardware. It's difficult and expensive to inspect, even when that JTAG port is left open. It's reasonable to depend on the hardware, even when you can't specify exactly what the hardware will be. It's likely harder to attack than the higher levels you're working on.

When there is no kernel to rely upon, for example if an attacker can tamper with local storage either at or underneath the OS level, it is hard to defend against them. It's tempting to sprinkle magic crypto dust, but an attacker who can modify files can likely alter your verification routines, your user interface, or other bits that will fool you. In other words, a kernel that would allow your files to get twiddled would also twiddle your code. So, it is likely not worth worrying about within an operating system or application, but at an enterprise or system level, it might be worth examining files now and again via forensic imaging, remote integrity checks, or other such mechanisms. It's much more rewarding to defend storage that is over a network or cloud. Such storage can be checked cryptographically.

Detection

When they are detected, failures of integrity can be addressed by throwing away the bad bits and getting a clean copy, say, by re-downloading a file or restoring it from backup. Bits that are corrupted can rarely be cleaned up. Detection can also lead to investigation of why the corruption happened, and that can reveal either accidents or attacks.

Detection can also be an adjunct to preventative controls. It can be hard to get the rules exactly the way you want them, and the permissions granted to an account will be exploited by an unauthorized user of that account. Such detection can be done by audit logs or cryptography. Cryptographic defenses are sometimes rolled into "file integrity management" tools.

Conclusion

When your opponent has unfettered access to a large, complex system like the Millennium Falcon, detecting a small homing beacon that they've planted there can be like finding a needle in a haystack. This is the case even if the system were regularly and properly maintained. If the subsystems were each individually protected, the job would be easier, and that's why you should ensure that each component has appropriate integrity.

3 Repudiation and Proof

Lando Calrissian: "You said they'd be left in the city under my supervision!"

Darth Vader: "I am altering the deal. Pray I do not alter it…any further."

Here we see Darth Vader reneging on a deal he made. He doesn't claim that he didn't make the deal. He just repudiates it, then threatens Lando.

Introduction

Repudiation is the threat that some party will refute or deny some responsibility. The merchandise didn't arrive; the payment didn't go through. The claim that they aren't responsible may or may not be true. The word *repudiate* can provoke broader thinking about refusal, rejection, and even words that don't start with *re*.

Repudiation is an unusual word. If I could, I'd repudiate its inclusion in the STRIDE mnemonic, but the replacements are no better, so we'll start with definitions. Repudiation is a specific form of denial or rejection. Here are some examples, inspired by dictionary definitions:

- **Refuse to accept or be associated with:** She has repudiated policies associated with the Jedi Council.
- **Deny the truth or validity of:** The Moff repudiated claims that Alderaan was a peaceful planet.
- **Decide that an agreement is no longer effective:** The Emperor has repudiated the Senate and swept away the last vestiges of the old Republic.
- **Refuse to fulfill or discharge an agreement, obligation, or debt:** Darth Vader repudiated his agreement to leave Cloud City neutral.

It's helpful to understand that the concept of repudiation overlaps with fraud. Not all fraud is repudiation, and not all repudiation is fraud. For example, I can sell you a fake Gucci bag, which is fraud, and if I claim I didn't know it was fake, that's me repudiating the merchandise. Where they overlap, eventually, society's rules about fraud, misrepresentation, or theft can come into play. An important stage in such processes is often that someone complains to the police. This can be a fine ending point for your technical designs. A long time ago, a friend wrote that "'and then the cops show up' is a rotten step to include in your protocols." This is a true statement; to the extent that you can design and operate systems in which fraud can't happen or there's no need to call the cops, then those systems are probably more resilient and secure than others where the police are regularly involved to resolve disputes. Also, you're front-loading the cost of security, which may be more expensive than back-loading and securing a smaller number of transactions. Also, "going to the police" has many important properties, including that lying to police is usually a crime and that police are trained to investigate: to establish facts, to assess the credibility of witnesses, etc. Thus, a police report is an authoritative repudiation of many debts that stem from identity theft. Vader's repudiation of his deal with Lando is simply reneging, not a fraud.

In this chapter, we're going to focus primarily on repudiation as a threat to security, but I'd like to mention two other facets of the word.

One can repudiate past action: "I'm no longer going to get drunk and yell." (Here the repudiation is implicit, and of course, it matters more if someone goes beyond just repudiation and apologizes for such behavior.) Second, repudiation is also a philosophically interesting threat because in security, the threat is repudiation, but in privacy, non-repudiation is a threat. That is, to preserve our privacy, we want to be able to disavow words, actions, associations, and other aspects of our selves or our social milieus. We want our association with the Rebel Alliance to remain private. Lastly, because repudiation is an unusual word, it can be awkward to work it into a sentence. To help you see the collection of threats, I'll sometimes use another word to clarify what's being repudiated (argued with) and put one or the other in parentheses.

This chapter starts with message repudiation, including denying either sending or receiving those messages ("That wasn't from me!"). From there, we'll consider fraud by sellers and buyers, issues with intermediaries, and account takeover, a hall of mirrors from which some never escape. Each of these is important both because fraud often leads to repudiation and because the defenses are similar. We'll look at voice cloning and deepfakes. These make it more plausible to repudiate recordings. Someone can say "I never said that; it was a deepfake." We then move to the back and forth chess game of attacks on logs, attacks via logs, and attacks that exploit responses to fraud and repudiation. We'll look at how repudiation interacts with various technologies, especially the cloud and AI and, specific to this chapter, the special issues with cryptography and blockchains. We'll close with defenses.

The Threat: Repudiation

Repudiation of past behavior can happen between people:

Grand Moff Tarkin: Since you are reluctant to provide us with the location of the rebel base, I have chosen to test this station's destructive power on your home planet of Alderaan.

Princess Leia Organa: No! Alderaan is peaceful. We have no weapons. You can't possibly…

Tarkin: You would prefer another target? A military target? Then name the system. I grow tired of asking this, so it will be the last time. Where is the rebel base?

Leia:…Dantooine. They're on Dantooine.

Tarkin: There. You see, Lord Vader, she can be reasonable. Continue with the operation; you may fire when ready.

Leia: WHAT?

Tarkin: You're far too trusting. Dantooine is too remote to make an effective demonstration, but don't worry; we will deal with your rebel friends soon enough.

Here, we see Tarkin offer a deal: name another system. He proceeds to immediately repudiate the deal he just made, demonstrating that he's evil. We don't repudiate our judgment of his nature when we—and he—learns Leia lied.

Repudiation can also happen between a person and an organization, often through the organization's customer support channels. The customer can repudiate receipt of the product or argue that it wasn't what they expected.

There's an interesting variant of repudiation in development and operations, around the question of what code was in production. For example, someone might say, "That shouldn't be happening with the new rev of that library." Part of the value we get from DevOps is that changes go through a change control system, and so the accuracy of someone saying "I didn't do that" becomes far easier to check. Failure to commit a configuration file becomes easier to note.

More frequent are message repudiation and fraud, and we'll examine each in depth. Many of these schemes have crazy labels and names associated with them, like brushing or the Spanish Prisoner…a Jedi troubles themselves not with such things.

Message Repudiation

Perhaps today's most common lie is "I didn't see your email." It's common because people frequently do overlook messages, so it's believable. Even if you have a "read receipt," perhaps the recipient was distracted?

Closely related but less frequent is "I didn't mean to copy everyone" after a snarky reply. The first is repudiation of receipt, the later repudiation of intent to copy everyone or, perhaps, implicitly of the snarky tone or a hope to evade (repudiate) accountability.

Messages can be lost or eaten by a spam filter. The check may have been in the mail and lost by a sorting machine or gust of wind. (Such problems are incredibly rare, but at scale, a one-in-a-million event happens regularly.)

More subtle than claims about delivery are claims that data was tampered with, which is repudiation of a message's contents or integrity. Each copy of a message, document, or file may or may not reflect the state in which they were created. Some messages are digitally signed by various intermediaries to help manage spam. For example, most email today is signed by DKIM (it stands for Domain Key Identified Mail, and that will not be on my exam). DKIM is a standard that's used to reduce email spam. So most email today is signed, but verifying those signatures requires a perfect copy of the email as sent, including message headers that many systems don't display by default. So, a copy printed by your mail client can't have the digital signature checked. Preserving evidence is surprisingly hard.

An attacker can create messages and simply attribute them to someone else, requiring that someone else to say "it wasn't me," repudiating the attribution. But sometimes it's possible for them to re-send a real message, such as "I saw your message, and let's go ahead," or "You're fired" in a way that it's read out of context. If that message is digitally signed, then what the original sender wants to repudiate is the context in which their words are misleadingly presented. This context elimination is also easy to do with screenshots from a phone. Many modern cryptographic protocols include cryptographic digests of all previous messages as a way to mitigate this sort of problem.

Common as these claims are, they become more meaningful when the message is a package or a check: "I didn't get your package" or "The check is in the mail." The latter was a denial of nonpayment or a denial that other actions or bills took precedence. In email, Microsoft Exchange has a feature, message recall, which does not work once your message has gone to another mail server. (That second mail server may be outside your domain. Maybe other Exchange servers respect it, but I'm not looking up the answer because you have no idea what a mail server is really doing with your message, and I'd hate to have to repudiate my answer when Microsoft changes the behavior of Exchange servers.)

Fraud

Fraud is a large, complex topic, and it's tempting to keep it simple by restricting this section to fraud against retailers, but there are other forms of fraud that are instructive and, more important, in the space of what every engineer should know. Those other forms include fraud against an employer. That fraud can either be simple, against accounting systems (that's where the money is), or abuse or misuse of the duties, expectations, or responsibilities of a position. Sometimes these will involve an accomplice, such a fake vendor. The heart of fraud exploits our belief that people are generally decent and that *they wouldn't do that.*

Responding to fraud involves various parties like a merchant or customer producing evidence, often contradictory, which bolsters their view of the situation and challenges (repudiates) that of another participant.

In dealing with fraud, some participants are directly involved, either as the one complaining or as the one perpetrating the fraud. Others are involved as providers of evidence. The role of a participant may shift as the story unfolds. For example, I might go from thinking that a merchant on an auction site never shipped me the package to thinking that the package was stolen by a delivery driver.

As moving money by apps becomes increasingly popular, there are newish frauds involving it. Many take advantage of the new apps trying to reduce friction (the amount of work involved in adding a payee or sending money) or round-trips (the back and forth over "Do you really want to do this?"). "Send money to any phone number" may be based in part on the silly idea that phone numbers are tied to people, so if there's fraud, it's easy to track down the perpetrator.

Fraud by Sellers

Sellers will lie about what they're selling. They'll take the money and run. They'll send fake goods or goods that match a carefully misleading description. (There was a rash of sales of "Mac boxes," which were literally just the cardboard box in which the Mac came. Perhaps that's useful if you're moving and need to pack your expensive computer? Usually, sending an empty box is a different fraud.) Each of these will lead to the buyer wanting to repudiate the transaction to get their money back.

Con artists may sell things—from the Brooklyn Bridge to droids—that aren't even theirs! Factories make fake products in quantity. This is both in facilities making their own versions of "designer" bags for sale at flea markets and in authorized factories running an unauthorized midnight production line. The maker of the authentic bags, say, Gucci, would want to repudiate both. In one case, the fakes may cause people to question the quality of the real bag; in the other, the profits are going to someone else.

It's important to remember that fraud can happen early in the supply chain, and sellers may be unaware that they are selling counterfeit goods. Is that real Bantha milk, or something else with blue food coloring?

Fraud can also happen when a buyer sells or gifts a Trojan horse. Luke falsely represents that R2-D2 and C3-PO are gifts to Jabba the Hutt to help him smuggle in his lightsaber.

Fraud by Buyers

Buyers, too, will commit all sorts of repudiations. I didn't buy this, I didn't consent to that, I didn't get the package, the package didn't contain what I ordered or expected, I returned it, etc. Many times these claims are truthful.

Buyers will often leave reviews, and some of them will relate to the product they bought. Others will relate to the seller's moral character, gender, ancestry, or sexual predilections.

More broadly than just buyers, customers will leave reviews for all sorts of reasons. One of those reasons is that they are paid to leave reviews. When you detect or suspect that this has happened, you might want ways to repudiate (remove) all their reviews rapidly.

Issues with Intermediaries

Retail intermediaries like eBay or Etsy are in a complex place where both buyer and seller may cheat, or buyers may use dispute resolution systems to express dissatisfaction with a product, for example, claiming that they didn't get the product as advertised. Beyond the bounds of repudiation, intermediaries make choices on what they will carry. Amazon is not the everything store: it restricts a wide and sometimes surprising range of items including alcohol, animals, drugs, fine art, explosives, human parts, offensive or controversial materials, pesticides, postage meters, and surveillance equipment (Amazon, 2022).

App stores have some control over content, which means in addition to buyer repudiation fake apps are a problem they want to control. And there needs to be a way for eBay (or others) to repudiate an app that claims to be eBay, probably having it removed from the app store. The app store needs to be able to flow the effects through to my account, and eBay might want those logs to bring to the police. If you're selling software on an app store, you don't care about fraud (by you), but the app store operators do care about the refund requests (repudiations) by your buyers, including reviews claiming that the software doesn't work or demands to get their money back. You might care about fraud by people who've sold you an advertising system. Such fraud could include sending bots to visit pages to drive up view counts, sending bots to follow links to drive up "click counts," presenting ads to badly matched visitors, changing affiliate links so they collect fees that should go elsewhere, and more.

Shippers end up in repudiation disputes: Was the package shipped? Was it left in a mailroom or on a porch? How much did it weigh? Shippers also divert or replace expensive goods or notify thieves of shipments. In a publicized case, a delivery contractor was taking cell phone pictures of packages on people's porches and then picking up the packages and taking them to pawn shops. In another, the UK's Royal Mail had a delivery tracking service that tracked only the postcode to which a package is delivered. Fraudsters would Photoshop the delivery address and send an empty package. In 2020, there was a well-publicized spate of packages of seeds being delivered from China, with a customs label claiming they were earrings or something similar. There were even claims that the seeds were a "bioweapon" (Saldana, 2020; WSDA, 2020).

There are several plausible explanations for these seed shipments, including review fraud and shipment fraud. A review fraud would involve two conspirators: a seller and a buyer via a marketplace site like Amazon or Etsy. The buyer buys something (probably expensive), the seller ships a package of seeds, and the reviewer leaves a glowing review. The package is shown as shipped by the post office. This review scenario sets the stage for future fraud. Shipment fraud would be an innocent buyer who gets a package of seeds rather than their expensive item. The buyer complains, repudiating that they got what they were supposed to get. The seller claims to have shipped the real item, and look! Here's the shipping receipt! Someone might also put a bag of sand in place of the treasure, but this is a Star Wars book, and no one who appears in Star Wars would do such a thing.

Payment processors can also be pulled into repudiation, most obviously of credit cards. That a payment was sent, delivered, or charged back is relevant to the transaction. The flow of money can also be influenced by laws, and that may be information that you can't reveal to one party or another. Laws about bribery, money laundering, or export-restricted countries or people can all cause a payment processor to delay, deny, or hold funds for payment. For example, news reports in 2019 indicated that although medical equipment was exempted from sanctions on Iran, banks wouldn't process any payments from Iran (Inskeep, 2019). Any of these can lead to repudiation-like issues, and some preventative controls can ensnare legitimate buyers engaged in behaviors that look strange.

Games that allow you to trade cash for goods have to deal with buyer fraud ("I paid, but the sword never arrived!"), and multiplayer games have to deal with all the frauds outlined here, carried out in-game.

Other Fraud

Accounting fraud is, in many ways, far from repudiation, but the mechanisms that are used to manage accounting fraud can inform defenses that allow proper repudiation and manage false ones. For example, the process of one company paying another starts when the buyer issues a purchase order. Eventually, the seller generates an invoice, and each is numbered to allow for cross-reference, a job that is assigned to someone and audited. Expenses are cross-checked against receipts, but the cost of getting, tracking, sending, and checking receipts is high enough that systems are often designed with slop, such as "receipts are only required for amounts over $50." Often there are additional controls in the background, such as noticing that a particular employee seems to lose a lot of receipts, which can trigger additional analysis of their spending. The Imperial answer, force-choking those who lose receipts, is probably not a good one.

Account Takeover

Attackers who steal your credentials can log in to your account. Once there, they can do the things you can do: send messages, post, buy magic swords or diamond rings…the only limits are the same limits to what you can do with your account on a given service (or all the services where you use the same username and password). If the account taken over is a bank account, money can be moved, and if the account is a credit card, then the thief can spend money that the account holder is expected to pay back. (That expectation may be influenced by consumer-protection law or card-issuer business practice. Because these are common, there's a clear workflow for an account holder to repudiate the charges.) If it's a social media account and you were drunk tweeting, an easy out is to claim the account was hacked.

The ease and frequency of credit card theft have led to it being given a name, identity theft, and there are several important variants, including account takeover and new account setup.

Real Account Takeover

When Princess Leia presents herself at Jabba's Palace, she masquerades as the real bounty hunter Boushh to insinuate herself as a known criminal. As far as we know, Boushh never finds out.

For us to react to a takeover, it must be detected, either by the service or by the customer. If the detection is by the customer, they have to convince the service that the account was hacked, re-authenticate, and break the attacker's ability to authenticate. If the service detects it, they need to inform the real customer and get their cooperation (in either case, repudiating the change of control of the account). Then the account needs to be remediated both at a technical and business level. Attackers will add extra applications with access to an account, extra recovery options such as new secret questions, or new backup authentication mechanisms. Attackers will also take specific actions based on the account type. For example, attackers engaged in business email compromise will add email processing rules to hide their activity.

Whether an account takeover can be remediated in a business sense, and the person who is responsible for the fixes, is dependent on the type of account. An attacker has your emails; who knows where they've gone? The diamond ring shipped to New York has to be paid for by someone. Attackers will transfer magic swords in-game for dollars outside of it, complicating the work game operators must do to address the problem. If Alice's account was compromised and the attackers bought a magic sword with her credit card and then sold it in-game to Lancelot, do you take the sword from Lancelot? What happens if the player behind Lancelot says she sent bitcoins to Alice? Let's count the possible repudiations: Alice is repudiating her purchase of the sword and possibly lying. Lancelot will certainly claim to be an innocent victim, repudiating his part in the fraud. If you take his toy away, he may attempt to repudiate the payment. You might want a vorpal blade to try to cut through the complexity, but the vorpal blade is no lightsaber, it just goes snicker-snicker.

False Claims of Account Takeover

Since accounts can be taken over, people can falsely claim their accounts were taken over as a way of repudiating its actions. It is difficult for either party to conclusively prove fault. System operators like to believe that bad security (malware, bad passwords) were at fault. People like to believe there was nothing else they could have done.

Account takeover is a frequent problem, and so false claims of account takeover can be credible. Such takeovers lead to the need for repudiation and mechanisms for asserting and managing those claims. It's also possible to create a real account that doesn't tie to the real person and produce messages that must be repudiated by the real person.

Someone who wants to engage in defamation, pranking, catphishing, or other mischief can simply create a new account with a name or label that's plausibly related to that of their victim. That victim must repudiate both the messages and the account.

Identity Theft

The term *identity theft* has many overlapping meanings including account takeover and new account fraud. Critics have pointed out that these are simply fraud, and the term *identity theft* is used to shift blame to victims who have little influence over the information used to commit the crime or the mechanisms exploited to commit these frauds. This is an important point, but incomplete. Certainly, the best way to deal with fraud is to assign costs to those who have the ability to prevent it.

The incompleteness of the argument that "identity theft is simply fraud" overlooks the damage to people whose "identity is stolen." They must spend time going to the police and repudiating claims by creditors. (As mentioned earlier, police reports are treated as authoritative.) However, the problems are exacerbated by aspects of the American credit reporting system. Credit reporting agencies will combine information that is only weakly linked (for example, the same name and SSN with a different address or similar name and addresses, such as Will Smith and Willow Smith).

Bad information in credit reports is excluded from libel laws and addressed by arcane, difficult to use "dispute systems," designed and operated by the credit reporting agencies. In at least one major breach, those dispute systems turned out to be insecure (Bomey, 2020).

The Identity Theft Resource Center points out that the long-term damage to some victims is a form of trauma, where victims become averse to applying for or using credit because they fear having to again deal with the red tape. In this sense, their good name is stolen from them.

Fake Account Creation

While it's not the same as account takeover, on many systems, it's easy to set up an account with any name you want. You can use these for impersonation either one on one or in some social space. For example, after creating the account Darthvader57, you could send email to Imperial contractors asking for secrets. Or you could set up an account for Yoda900 on a website, and use it to "confess" to false claims about the Jedi. Do, or do not. There is no try, because it's so easy.

Deepfakes

Voice cloning or deepfake video may portray someone saying words they never said or doing things they didn't do. When the person really didn't do it, they want to repudiate the deepfake. When they did, they can claim that the video was faked. The ease of creating such fakes makes repudiation more complex. Is it really a deepfake or a false claim to distract from the real content? Voice cloning, deepfake video, and similar attacks on "what you are" are discussed further in Chapter 1, "Spoofing and Authenticity."

Logging Threats

Logs are a primary tool for incident discovery and response. Incident discovery and response go far beyond repudiation, and if you think about repudiating the belief that "No one has broken into our systems" or "This fully armed and operational battle station," then logs are primary tools for response to incidents. ("You think this battle station is fully operational? Nobody noticed the ransomware on the main gun control computers!") These include repudiation "incidents," when someone requests a refund through your call center, initiates a card chargeback, or rages on social media. All these logs are attacked in a variety of ways. There are attacks against the logs themselves, there are attacks that are carried into the logs, and there are attacks via response systems.

Attacks Against Logs

Because logs help defenders investigate attacks—including repudiation attacks—attackers try to corrupt or destroy them or introduce false evidence. This leads to attacks on how logs are created, transmitted, received, routed, and stored.

Log creation can be attacked by tampering with the logging client library or by turning off logging features at the client. There's a battle there between people who want privacy and advertisers. The technical implementation means that a similar conflict plays out over and over in different contexts. Those contexts include browsers and privacy plugins, enterprises that can block log transmission, and mobile apps. In each, log creation or collection is being attacked. (This shines a light on an important question of "security against whom?" If you move from delivering *secure* systems to delivering *security* systems, you must grapple with this. The ACM Code of Ethics is a fine place to start, even if you're not an ACM member.) If the software offers a feature to stop sending logs, then there's no threat. The same effect can be caused by someone tampering with the software, DNS, or routing.

Log transmission can be attacked, say, with firewall rules. Transmitted logs can be attacked in transit, either by an unexpected MITM inserted by an attacker or by software that's designed into the path, like a web application firewall or an API gateway. Those attacks can be intentional, by someone who's taken over such a system, or accidental, as they "helpfully" alter the messages. The log receiver can be overwhelmed with input so it drops log messages. And log storage can be overwhelmed. This depends on storage being expensive, and so it manifests more in cheap devices than in larger systems. Of course, if you keep enough data, disk space eventually gets expensive.

Attacks via Logs

Useful logs contain lots of data supplied by outsiders, some small fraction of whom are attackers. Data in logs is often in a raw form—logging sanitized or canonicalized data limits the usefulness of a log. We often forget to treat logs as hostile.

The log4shell family of attacks was where a popular Java log parsing library had "remote code execution by design." It will likely be the canonical example of attacks via logs for quite some time.

Some other examples of attacks that come through logs include attempts to log in as `</td>root` or `/table`. They can include invocations such as a backtick for a shell, or commands or string terminators (`` ` `` `;` `\0`) that lead to the next characters being read as a new command. Another powerful attack is the regexp exploder, a regular expression with backreferences or complex matches that slow the regexp parser. Each stage in a log processing routine (often a series of shell scripts) can come under attack. For more discussion of these issues, see Chapter 8, "Parsing and Corruption," but remember logs are radioactive by design: they're full of attacker-influenced data and possibly personal data.

Attacks via Response Systems

Luke Skywalker leaves his Jedi training because he senses his friends are in danger. Many of us would give our right hand for a detection system that's so well-tuned, but here I'd like to focus on Darth Vader's abuse of the response system. Luke is tricked into acting in a way Vader has planned, and that is a problem with many response systems.

We must also think about how attacks are carried by logs through to analysis and presentation systems and how automatic defenses can be triggered by attackers. For example, we might deter sellers from buying glowing and false reviews of themselves by closing their account. If we do, those same companies will then simply buy false glowing reviews for their competitors, goading us to close the account of that competitor. Naturally, that competitor will repudiate the reviews and claim they have no idea how they got there. Here the platform is detecting (repudiating) the false review, responding by closing the merchant's account (repudiating the relationship).

Social media and other platform companies see floods of attacks via their "report a problem" links. These are often in response to unpopular or even reprehensible things people say or do either on those sites or elsewhere, but sometimes they're used to report a problem with someone drawing attention to that first offensive statement.

Copyright management systems have also been attacked by people playing copyrighted music so that videos taken of them will be taken down. An early example that came to public attention involved a police officer playing Beatles music.

For intermediaries, like an online store or payment system, responses to repudiation attacks usually involve either increasing fees or terminating a relationship. Credit card companies will increase merchant fees (and often demand manual effort) for merchants with an abnormally high chargeback rate. Business relationships can also be terminated or curtailed. That might be an Amazon shop being closed, a startup forbidden from distributing via Apple's App Store, or, more personally, the end of a Gmail account.

Any response system can be tricked, and response systems are often kept confidential, leading to situations that can fairly be described as Orwellian. People who violate your rules, intentionally or not, maliciously or not, may use social media or news outlets to attack your repudiation system's responses. It's enough to make a droid's head spin.

Repudiation in Specific Technologies

While repudiation often starts with humans saying something, the particular nature of systems can influence how it plays out. This seems as good a place as any to note that as the world is more and more controlled by algorithms, it's also possible for a repudiation to be started by a bot, managed by bots, and never noticed by a human who's paying attention.

Internet of Things (Including Phones)

Some devices, like security cameras, can provide information that informs repudiation claims. We tend to trust videos, but deepfakes are getting easier, and if the goal is to show a package being stolen, it might be reasonable that faces are obscured. So look for real video showing a fake theft to support a fraudulent repudiation claim. (I might ask a friend to walk onto my porch, pick up an expensive package, and walk away. I then send the security video to the merchant to show that the package has been stolen and ask for my money back. The video shows all the facts and none of the motivations or connections.)

Devices will come under attack to either support or prevent repudiation. If I think a device logs locally, perhaps destroying it will prevent it from ever revealing those logs.

More generally, inexpensive IoT devices usually have simpler user interfaces than a traditional computer. The opportunity for a person to repudiate, to say "I didn't mean to do that," is higher, and the opportunity for a normal person to dig into logs is lower.

Cloud

Issues of log integrity and availability to end users used to be a bigger deal with the big IaaS cloud providers, and they may still happen with smaller ones. With a SaaS provider, you may or may not get the logs you want, and it's important to test that you get sufficient logs for your needs. You'll also need to understand how long those logs are kept.

Cloud services can provide "third-party" attestation as to what they saw at certain times. If you are trusting them for non-repudiation, you should consider what happens if a company providing such services goes out of business, or even changes their business model. For example, if all of your contracts are stored in DocuSign and it quadruples its prices, do you need to keep paying them to get access to those validated signatures? (I believe they add a cryptographic signature to the PDF file and lock the document to prevent editing.) Perhaps their competitors do this as well, and it's important that you know.

AI/ML

One of the best aspects of machine learning systems is that they can find hidden patterns and surprise you with their insights and their willingness to select random correlates of the things you care about. The story about an AI learning to detect tanks based on them being photographed on a grassy field is probably apocryphal (worth repudiating), but it carries truthiness in that we all suspect ML systems act weird sometimes.

That suspicion makes AI a great scapegoat for inexplicable, embarrassing, or otherwise hard-to-defend systematic errors. Unfortunately, until ML systems develop the ability to explain themselves, this trend is likely to continue. And so "The AI made us do it" is a "great" repudiation of responsibility by an organization.

At a more technical level, we cannot predict what systems should do; updates to the models may be made outside more rigorous software development processes, and we cannot tell if the files in the model were the ones we intended. These potential tampering problems exacerbate repudiation.

Crypto and Blockchain

Cryptographic tools including digital signatures, message authentication codes, and hash trees can provide exceptionally strong evidence that something has not been tampered with and thus support the security property of *non-repudiation*. As good as those technologies are, they are stronger when they are interlocked, and that's a key to the distributed ledger aspect of blockchains.

Key Expiration and Repudiation

As the Rebels approach the second Death Star in a stolen shuttle, they're challenged for an authentication code. Admiral Piett tells Darth Vader, "It's an older code, sir, but it checks out." It's enough to make a Grand Moff tear his hair out. Keys are vulnerable to theft, and so you want to expire them. After you expire them, you don't want to trust them, but you must. For example, if you rotate keys annually, then you must use an expired key to validate a digital signature generated years ago. You use expired keys to decrypt old backup tapes. By their nature, these older keys cannot be discarded, but they also should not be used for new material. The expiration is analogous to repudiation: we'd like a clean break, but we may have to apply judgment.

The difficulty of generating, distributing, and managing key material led Soviet spies to reuse one-time pad key material. A one-time pad uses keys that are as long as the messages and, used properly, are "information-theoretically secure." The sender and the receiver each xor a message with the key. If you reuse the key, the xor of the two messages is the xor of the plaintext. (The key is effectively xor'd with itself, resulting in a key of all zeros, and what remains is the xor'd plaintext.) The United States took advantage of this failure in a project called VENONA. Exploiting stolen or misused keys is not limited to intelligence agencies; attackers stealing data routinely look in configuration files, code directories, and anywhere they can reach to get copies of the keys for the data you were trying to protect. When the keys are used for encryption, then the result is a confidentiality failure. When used for digital signatures, the result can be repudiation or integrity attacks.

Blockchains

One of the most salient aspects of blockchains is their wholesale rejection of repudiation mechanisms. A key technological innovation of Bitcoin was a way to generate and maintain a distributed consensus ledger. Data that is on a blockchain is there for as long as the blockchain is maintained. Bitcoin has no way to repudiate a transaction, which is either a bug or a feature, depending on who you ask.

Repudiation Mechanisms

You've seen a large set of ways in which repudiation can happen, and I'd like to now help you organize those into a more useful framework. We'll cover denial and misdirection, destruction, social media, and a particular case that incident response folks call "loss of view."

Denial and Misdirection

The first step in a repudiation is some statement that X didn't happen or something that shouldn't have happened did. Claims are made, and someone eventually makes a judgment of some form. The exact steps are extremely scenario dependent, but they usually start with "Where's the email/package/money I was expecting?" (They rarely continue with "Tell Jabba I have his money!")

Destruction

Destruction of logs or evidence can be an important part of a repudiation and are generally, but not always, done by an attacker, rather than by a business partner or customer. This can be physical destruction by destroying the media, logical destruction by deleting or overwriting files, or destroying comprehensibility by deleting a cryptographic key.

Social Media

Increasingly, people use the power of social media as part of a repudiation or customer service escalation. These seem unfair to the people who designed the customer service mechanisms that reasonably optimize costs by making customers wait on hold for half an hour to talk to a person with no authority. Less sarcastically, social media is being used to rebalance power and the perception of power, and when thinking about business processes to manage repudiation, it can help to ask "What would we do if a B-list celebrity with 100,000 followers complains about this?"

Loss of View

One approach to repudiation is to cause a loss of view: the inability to see the state of a system, or the prior states. This is done by attackers to incident responders. Attackers can tamper with monitoring or analysis tools; or they can destroy logs or tamper with the logs or log analysis systems. Destruction of evidence is narrower than the idea of "loss of view." The evidence might be present, in many different systems, with timestamps that don't make sense. This might be seen as "failure to develop view."

"Loss of view" is a framing in common use by incident response teams to describe a situation where they're having trouble figuring out what's happening. Loss of view happens at a technical level and, more important, at an operational level. When an oxygen tank on Apollo 13 blew up, there was no "oxygen tank exploded" indicator. It took nearly 15 minutes before anyone looked outside and noticed a cloud of gas and longer before Mission Control accepted the report from astronauts.

These failures to observe or failures to believe probably don't rise to the level of repudiation, but repudiation may be a convenient place to consider them.

Defenses

The key to defense is to have ways to understand what has happened in the past and to be able to use the evidence to convince others of your perspective. That can be cryptographic proof, logs, or other tools. Star Wars stores such evidence in "holocrons" and asks that Jedi Knights search their feelings for answers. This doesn't turn out very well, and I recommend more modern defenses.

Cryptography

One of the first uses of public key cryptography is to create digital signatures: testable bindings between some cryptographic key and some document. The signature is a mathematical operation performed with a document and the private part of a keypair. Anyone with the public part of the keypair can check that the signature was applied to the document. There are a number of caveats: the document is usually represented by a cryptographic hash for efficiency reasons. The signature is created and tested by software, which might lie.

Digital signatures are not the only way to use cryptography to authenticate bits. Hash trees are a specific subset of the classic tree data structure, where each lead node is hashes of documents; the parents are a hash of the children. Thus, inserting a new node only requires calculating hashes equal to the log of the size of the tree. This tree was invented by cryptographer Ralph Merkle and is often called a Merkle tree. If you both store changelogs and publish the root of the tree in a trusted place (such as a physical newspaper), then you can demonstrate that certain hashes were in the tree at that time, and thus the documents associated with those hashes existed then.

At the opposite end of the efficiency spectrum, various blockchains provide distributed consensus and ways to ensure that all parties will come to a convergent view. The mechanisms are labeled "mining" and involve some hard to perform and rewarded calculation. That calculation might be finding a partial hash collision for a new block and the previous block. This collision is hard to find, requiring possibly billions of hash calculations, but easy to verify, requiring just one. The block is a set of hashes of documents, often treated as transactions. The hash "commits" the block, consisting of that set of transactions, to the chain. Anyone who validates the chain can see that a block, and the associated hashes, was committed at a specific time.

Keeping Logs

Generating logs is incredibly helpful for many goals, including debugging, handling repudiations, and detecting attacks. If you're writing code, make sure you include logging options. If you're operating the code, make sure you turn logging on. Without logs, it's hard to establish what happened in the past. So you want logs.

Lots and lots of logs. But lots of logs are not enough. You need the right logs to deal with the problems you'll face. This chapter, along with some threat modeling and use and abuse cases, can help you think through many ways in which repudiation attacks might take place. Test them and see if the logs give you enough to find the attacks and satisfy yourself about what happened. This chapter is focused on repudiation, but logs are also used in responses to attacks. So as you engineer your log generation, analysis, and access, it's helpful to think about both, so I'll cover both here.

What to Log

While it's important to have lots and lots of logs, it's also important for the logs to be useful, and "log everything" is not useful advice. The signal would get lost in the noise. So, choosing what to log when you're writing software is hard. The best logging tends to relate to code with strange bugs or obvious failure modes.

As a set of principles, log three things: input, actions, and decisions. Log the context that informs them. Log who, what, why, when, and where. Log both successes and failures, and think about how your logs will be used by an investigator asking who, what, how, and when. They'll also be asking why, and your logs can help them answer why your software did something.

When I say log the who, that means a collection of identifiers (what you did to authenticate each is covered under why). This includes the following:

- The remote machine and all the names it currently has. (Machines have at least an IP address and a DNS name; oftentimes they'll have other names, such as WINS names, Zigbee names, Bluetooth names, MAC addresses, and the like.)
- The account can be one or more of an account name and an application-centered name, or bank or credit card numbers. (For example, I log in as `shostack` and invoke `mysql -user wordpress`.)
- Who created the log. (This means what machine and application created the log, because log aggregation means that "localhost"

may not be very meaningful to the person or system reading a log message.)

"Log the what" means log what the other side sent or did. For a human, that will be the input, including text, mouse, voice, gestures, and brainwaves. Log the commands and the arguments, and if the responses are from somewhere else, maybe log those too. For a remote machine, capturing complete communication is useful for debugging but too verbose to store long.

"Logging the what" also means what outside input your code is taking and from where. That might include files, URLs, or IP addresses. Logging full file paths and perhaps even hashes can be very helpful to investigators.

"Logging why" means logging your decisions: Where did your software branch, and why? What authentication or authorization decisions is your code making, and why? If you checked a password, log "password success," not "password1 was used to successfully authenticate." If you give up the ghost, say so.

"Log when" means log events that happen. As we discuss in Chapter 7, "Predictability and Randomness," keep your logs in UTC.

There is an approach to logging called *canonical logs* that involves augmenting "in-the-moment" messages with a summary log message containing all the useful information in a single message to save operators the work of reconstructing and correlating it. That shouldn't prevent you from emitting logs as you go, especially if your code is attacked and never reaches the function that emits a canonical log.

The "who" and the "why" will be heavily used in responding to a repudiation. If a consumer says, "I didn't make that transaction," then we can go back and check: were there factors that stood out as unusual? If there were many (different IP or geolocation, different browser), we are more likely to believe them. Who and why are also heavily used in responding to more complex attacks. If an attacker is able to authenticate as Han with the right password, we probably want to look at each place Han uses that password.

All of this can lead to chatty logs. Apply judgment to what gets logged at what debug levels, but set thoughtful defaults. Writing deeply sensitive information (passwords, cryptographic keys, social security numbers) might require a special debug option.

Operational Logging

You have to consider where the logs are created, where they end up, and who has what access to them. Maybe your software is a local application, and the logs stay on that system. Perhaps the logs go to the cloud or to a log aggregation service.

Access to raw logs, or the ability to run arbitrary code on logs, is powerful (and risky if there's confidential information in those logs). When the logs contain personal information, being able to track who's accessed them will be important. So generally, you'll want to build tools that support the common use cases. Repudiation will be the most common use case when you have human customers, and auto-matically collecting and analyzing the relevant information speeds up responses and makes them more consistent. Those tools will never quite replace raw log access for dealing with new or different attack patterns. (More on this in the section "Who Sees What Evidence?")

Having your logs around for a long time is sensible but can be expensive. You'll need to consider how long you hold what informa-tion. There are regulatory and operational needs. Operational needs vary, but it's not infrequent to hear of a break-in being discovered years after the fact, and being able to discover what the attacker did can save you from having to tell your customers, "We don't know if the attacker accessed the private information you entrusted to us because we have no logs."

While repudiation by a consumer is often immediate, attacks are often detected after years. Unfortunately, today's operating systems have log rotation policies that were designed when disks cost dollars per megabyte, and those policies haven't been updated. Your operat-ing systems are throwing out logs before your intrusion detection catches an attacker. Generally, rotation and regulation lead to moving logs to some central store.

Lastly, the UK's National Computer Security Centre has some solid guidance in a page titled "Introduction to logging for security purposes" (NCSC, 2018).

Personal Information in Logs

Logs will include personal information and need to be treated carefully as a result. Careful treatment includes managing permissions of who can read them, possibly splitting data into several logs, tokenizing data, or writing tools to extract data from the logs at various levels of detail.

It's generally a good practice to tokenize all personal information. That means replacing the sensitive data with a random string and keeping a map from tokens to the protected values. Sometimes tokenization is conflated with cryptographic techniques such as hashing or encryption. Hashing is subject to a dictionary attack. The attacker creates a dictionary of, say, all possible phone numbers or SSNs and then hashes each. They now have a dictionary of all the plaintext and hashed values, and for small lists, like billions of phone numbers, it's pretty fast. Also, if you tokenize, it may be that deleting the link from the token to identifiable information can help satisfy obligations under "right to be forgotten" rules.

Responding to consumer repudiations of transactions can check the tokenized information, rather than the raw information. Similarly, exercising that right to be forgotten is like repudiating a customer's relationship with you. (The implementation may even be identical, but this book is not legal advice.)

Also, you may need to log that you've deleted all the information about a person. (Don't look at me; look at European law!) Ironically, this may require that you log what you once knew. Storing field names, rather than values, is probably a good start. You might also store a hash of an index key, like an email or phone number in that particular circumstance when you cannot keep the map.

Third-Party Logs

There are many reasons to have third parties keep logs. It's not trivial to serve lots of transparent 1-pixel GIFs quickly to track when people view emails, open documents, or display web pages. Why not let someone else do it and own the attack surface and scaling?

Also useful is that an independent third party who generates logs can act as a bulwark against false repudiations. Records kept in the ordinary course of doing business are treated as reliable, at least in the United States. (There are limits. I have not magically become a lawyer since you started this book, and even if I were, this would not be legal advice.) Thus, companies like DocuSign not only can help manage the signing process but also maintain logs or cryptographically sign the documents. (I don't know what DocuSign actually does; this is just a hypothetical example.)

Logging vs. Audit System

Microsoft calls the Windows logging system the *audit system* (Microsoft, 2017). This can lead to confusion about what an audit is, as shown by statements like "We have audit enabled." An audit is an inspection or examination to see if you're keeping appropriate records and that the actions you're taking match your commitments. Audits can be enabled by logs or inhibited by their absence or insufficiency.

Using Logs

By themselves, logs do nothing. Repudiation is handled by technological systems that gather logs for people to use. That can be simple, in the case of "Here's a screenshot of your email in my spam folder," or far more complex in the case of a credit card chargeback.

Visibility is implicit in how we address repudiation, account takeover, and fraud. The claim in "I'm sorry I didn't respond to your email;

I didn't get it" is simply bizarre absent someone saying "Why didn't you respond to my email?" Similarly, someone needs to investigate to look into a claim of account takeover or fraud.

Some uses of logs will be more frequent than others. Requests that are frequent and consistent should be automated, for efficiency and accuracy. Other log uses will require bespoke queries and analysis.

Frequent Views

Let's use account takeover as a lens into what might require frequent and repetitive analysis. If you run a large system accessible by the public, you will face account takeovers. These are exacerbated by weak authentication (see Chapter 1, "Spoofing and Authenticity"), but for high-value accounts, like those with access to lots of crypto-currency, attackers will dedicate weeks of background research.

When dealing with repudiation in the form of a claim of account takeover, you'll want to marshal evidence and evaluate it. You want to check the various elements both for themselves and in combination. Does the person typically log in from the same IP address? Same client? Do they have a regular pattern? You'll also want to look for abnormalities that might inform your judgment. Were there hundreds of login attempts from that IP address? Millions of attempts to log in with that username or password? Is there a history of complaints by the account owner?

Another way to say that is you should actively look for evidence that either bolsters or undermines the claim, rather than one or the other. And when you do this regularly, the factors that play into your decisions can be standardized, and decisions can be handed off to systems. Such systems can be designed to avoid the various cognitive biases that influence people. There are entire jobs where a person is still in the loop because someone fantasizes that they might notice something strange through mind-numbing tedious repetition. But I wouldn't bet on it. I would bet there are better ways to bring them in, such as audit or analysis, rather than having them click OK all day. (Airport luggage screeners are presented with fake weapons and bombs, because the job is so tedious that system designers expect them to miss the very rare real ones. We should learn from that—if log analysis is incredibly boring, people trying to do it will become uncomfortably numb.)

What makes a frequent view frequent is that the same evidence needs to be marshalled each time, making these excellent candidates for automation.

Less Frequent Views

There are other situations, such as when a human attacker takes over a corporate Windows box, where the steps that they take and the investigation involve both standard steps like asking what tools were installed or run or what did they connect to, and less standard like looking at the output of those tools, looking at RAR files of data to be extracted, or following the trail through additional compromised accounts or machines.

These situations, where investigation cannot be as automated, happen more frequently in investigation or audit than they do in repudiation.

Predictable vs. Frequent

It's easy to fall into talking about "predictable" and "unpredictable" use cases. Frankly, all use cases are predictable to some degree. We run into problems when we forget there's a spectrum, rather than a binary choice. Details may differ, but that makes them less common, not unpredictable. (Also, as you increase detail, things become less common. It is less likely that someone is both tall *and* a basketball player than simply tall, because not every tall person plays. But, in study after study, people routinely describe the combination as more likely.)

Sharing Logs

Who gets to see what evidence? There is a strong argument that good system security should not depend on anything that is hard to change, so you ought to be able to expose the decisions your system has made. (For more on security by obscurity and Kerckhoffs' principle, about things that are hard to change, see Chapter 7, "Predictability and Randomness.")

Consider this: A customer has disputed that a package ever arrived. You've reviewed the shipping company logs, and someone signed for it at their address. It's easy to show them that log. But many organizations use heuristics that they believe block amateur fraudsters. And while these are often anecdotal or unsubstantiated, those who maintain them may argue against sharing logs that show those factors that you keep secret to help prevent fraud.

When your service bans a bunch of accounts, do you share that with your competitors? A sharing agreement can keep everyone safer, sooner. Well, except for the customers caught in a Kafka-esque shutdown of their accounts when you or your competitors have banned them, and they can't find out why.

Who trusts whom to maintain the evidence? This can be an advantage of logs generated or stored by a third party or of using blockchains or Merkle trees to provide evidence of what was logged when.

Antifraud Tools

There are a lot of commercial antifraud tools available that fit neatly into antirepudiation tooling. Cybersource publishes a useful survey, which it characterizes as validation services, your proprietary data, multimerchant data, and purchase device tracking. Validation tools include checking cards and checking phone numbers or addresses for validity. Your data includes what the customer has bought, order velocity, and website behavior. Device tracking are tools like fingerprinting and geolocation. Using these can reduce fraudulent orders substantially while minimizing impact on real orders and real customers.

Conclusion

Repudiation threats matter in all systems that involve humans. These threats can involve truth or lies, and as engineers, our job is to ensure that we can establish the facts.

Returning to the dialogue from the beginning of the chapter, Darth Vader doesn't merely alter a few terms of the deal—he repudiates it entirely. The deal was supposed to be trading "somebody called Skywalker" for the Empire turning a blind eye to Cloud City. By the end, it's Luke, Leia, and Chewie taken away by the Empire, and Han given to Boba Fett, with the threat of an Imperial garrison left behind.

Another example of repudiation occurs when Luke Skywalker confronts Obi-Wan Kenobi, saying, "You told me that Darth Vader betrayed and murdered my father!" Obi-Wan's response is, at its heart: "So, what I told you was true...from a certain point of view." The exchange ties to a deeper truth, which is that in many repudiations trust has already frayed. Dead Jedi are not alone in twisting things to try to appear consistent. Having signatures or logs and software to search them consistently can save you from trying to fall back to searching your feelings. While that may arguably work for Jedi, it's a poor form of proof.

4 Information Disclosure and Confidentiality

The very first scene of Star Wars shows Princess Leia's ship being pursued, and we quickly learn that the Empire is hoping to recover the stolen Death Star plans. From the opening scene through the climax, *Star Wars: A New Hope* is the story of information disclosure and its consequences. I have no idea why people say it's about Luke's journey to adulthood, his relationship to his father, or anything else. Of course, throughout Star Wars there's plenty of undisclosed information, such as what happened to Luke's father, where the Rebel base is really located, or the Empire's plan to destroy Alderaan to demonstrate the awesome power of the Death Star.

An important attribute of information disclosure is that the information is someone's secret. Breaches of confidentiality can be a disclosure to a select few, the public, or any set beyond those who are supposed to be "in the know."

Information disclosure can be from one account on a system to another; information can be disclosed to those who observe the network your packets traverse, and there can be disclosure to unaffiliated entities, those who aren't along the expected network path.

Confidential information is often about the data itself, but sometimes it's information about data, or *metadata*. This can also include information about who is talking to whom. Information about files, even the existence of the Manhattan Project, needs to be concealed (hey, come on, I have to move off Star Wars occasionally).

Threats to Confidentiality

The US National Security Agency (NSA) has a model of the data they steal: they either get it when it's *at rest* or when it's *in motion*. We'll follow that here in part because how we protect data can depend on the attack we're concerned about. In STRIDE-per-element threat modeling, this theft manifests as information disclosure against a data store or a data flow. There are also threats of data leakage by a process, including side effects of computation, which often result in covert channels that someone can use to communicate stealthily, and information about human connections. These data leakage, side effects, and data about human relationships don't cleanly fit the model of data at rest/data in motion. That's OK—we care more about the threat than the model.

Incidentally, while we often use words like *theft*, the threat is usually about making copies or having access, not taking it away from its owner.

Information Disclosure, at Rest

Data "at rest" usually has authorization checks that protect it, implemented by the operating system, database, or cloud provider. Data at rest is data in files, in memory, or in databases. It can be physically tied to a computer—inside a processor, on disk, or even on removable media like backup tape. It can be stolen by an attacker, discarded by its owner, leaked by an unhappy or insufficiently careful employee, or dropped off the back of a truck. Entertainingly, we consider the moving box of tapes to be data at rest, because the best protection will be storage encryption.

Of all the files in the world, only a very small set of them are truly intended to be world-readable, although that proportion may be changing as the Web makes more files available to everyone. Some of that change is accidental. Amazon's customers had enough trouble locking their S3 that Amazon built new features to draw attention to "buckets" that were public and to help find sensitive data in those buckets (Barr, 2017; Macie, 2017).

Of course, not all file access is intentionally authorized. There's a set of failures based on confusing the reference monitor about canonical filenames (which are discussed in Chapter 1, "Spoofing and Authenticity.") There's also a set of failures based on access control failures, either the explicit ones provided by an operating system or the ones implied by an email address. Most systems that encrypt an email do not harangue the sender for independent confirmation of the addressee's email address and cryptographic key identifier. Such confirmation might, now and then, reveal that the person has accidentally selected two different identifiers, and we could even envision a UI to learn which is correct, such as buttons labeled with the two identifiers. However, the extra effort needed would likely be infuriating—"I've already told you where the email is going!"

The issues with data exposure don't require a lot more explanation. Metadata can be much more subtle.

Metadata

You might think that metadata is when an android locks all the humans out of the holodeck and makes a fantasy world that's just duplicates of himself. And you'd be in the wrong fictional world. In a galaxy far, far away—and in ours—metadata is data about data. For example, the fact that Brent Spinner was on *Star Trek: The Next Generation* is data. That he played Data is data…OK, I'll stop.

Data can rest in files or in databases, and each has associated metadata, like file names or path. Many people are likely interested in the content of `JuneLayoffs.xlsx`. The content of `staffing/Alice JuneLayoff.docx` is implied, but it might be a letter saying "Alice, your job is safe." The file `Junelayoffs/Alice.docx` is more interesting because of a combination of metadata: the directory and name are each less interesting on their own.

Information can be disclosed about any of the following:

- The contents of a file
- The file's name
- The pathname where the file is stored (full or partial)
- If file or path exists or not
- The size of a file
- The permissions on a file
- Access or modification time on disk or in a version control system
- Tags

If there's no file `staffing/DarthJuneLayoff.docx`, then the nonexistence of the file is information that someone might really want. (As an aside, I wouldn't want to be the one tasked with informing Darth Vader that his job as a Sith Lord has been eliminated.)

Even hard-to-understand names can provide information. For example, if you spot a file `EgotisticalGiraffe.txt` on a system and later discover the existence of a secret program called Egotistical Giraffe, you might suspect that the files are related. Similarly, size, format, and access times are metadata that may be interesting.

All of these are generally accessible to an authorized user of a classic operating system, and many of these—and analogous metadata—are exposed in modern SaaS or cloud systems.

Metadata is often subject to interpretation. There was an interesting tiff between Tesla Motors and the *New York Times* (Bishop, 2013). The undisputed fact is that a reporter drove a Tesla around a parking lot until the battery ran out. He panned the car in his review but did not mention driving around the lot in his initial story. Tesla claimed in a press release that he was "looking to run down the battery." He claimed that he was looking for a charging station. My take? Data can be cast in many lights, and metadata is even more subject to interpretation.

You can tie yourself into an intellectual knot over the question of "is a cryptographic key a form of metadata?" On the one hand, it's not the data itself that anyone cares about; but because of what it enables, you care deeply about its confidentiality (or integrity, in the case of a public key). The right answer is that it's the wrong question. You need to protect the keys to protect the data. That's easier because they're smaller and because you can treat them with greater care.

Databases may use a file system provided by the OS or one they provide themselves. This "raw disk mode" of course has abstractions like those of the OS, but optimized for the database's usage.

While metadata that exists is often easily found, there is also plenty of information that's present but hard to see.

Obscured Data

Files can contain data that's explicitly hidden—just use the "hide columns" feature in a spreadsheet. They can also contain data that's "occluded," which is to say hidden or obscured. For example, if you make the highlighter in Word black, you can obscure information.[1] If you distribute the file as a Microsoft Word document, then anyone with the file can change the color of the highlight and read what you'd redacted. There are less silly versions of this, from looking at change history to using the Unix strings utility to unzipping the file and examining its constituent parts. If you draw a black box and then "print" to PDF, you might be surprised to learn that the PDF format has layers. American intelligence agencies will often release printed and scanned versions of documents, which is a reasonable way to avoid these problems, even if it does make the documents less useful.

---

[1] The Onion's "CIA Realizes It's Been Using Black Highlighters All These Years" is a classic.

Modern, variable-width font rendering means the precise length of a phrase can also reveal information about the words that are covered. This is easier with shorter strings, such as names, rather than sentences or even paragraphs.

There's also a set of attacks where you get an authorized party to gather data on your behalf. For example, if I tell your browser that there's an image at `file://etc/passwd`, then will your browser read it? Will it make the content of the image available to the DOM (the way a browser represents a web page in memory)? These "confused deputy" attacks bypass authorization and can result in information disclosure, tampering, and other effects, and are covered in their own subsection in Chapter 6, "Expansion of Authority and Isolation."

Physical Storage

It's easy to forget that storage eventually requires a physical device that can be attacked. An attacker who bypasses the authorization checks imposed by the system has tremendous power to access not only the data that is currently there but also the data that was previously there. Data that is supposedly destroyed may still be present but not easily found. For example, memory that you've freed is probably not overwritten with zeros. Removing in-memory secrets that you no longer need takes only a few lines of code and, often, instructions to the compiler to not optimize away the cleaning.

When storage is designed to be long term, this problem is bigger. An attacker with physical access or low-level logical access may still find data on disk. We can replace the contents of the file with random data and then unlink the fit. We can do similar things to the files or free space on a filesystem or to filesystem indexes, although that can be more complex. Unfortunately, flash storage devices started implementing leveling algorithms that carefully wrote data in different places to reduce wear on the device, reducing assurance that the data is really gone. Reputedly, Apple removed the `srm` command (secure rm) around the time of macOS Sierra (Harris, 2016) because of the difficulties involved in secure deletion.

Once you dispose of a disk, you no longer care if the files on it are tampered with, but confidential data is still subject to information disclosure. Encrypting hard drives and other data storage is a solid start at a defense and is a very solid defense if done carefully.

Offsite backups are the ultimate version of data at rest. Getting assurance that the tapes have been kept safe or destroyed can be tricky, so encrypting tapes means destroying (or losing) the key is technically as good as destroying the tape. Designing cryptographic key storage that is assuredly as reliable as the underlying backup mechanisms is tricky. This complexity, not the demands of the plot, were what really caused the Empire to store data unencrypted in the archives at Scarif.

The NSA's longstanding practice of physical device destruction seems more prescient every year.

Information Disclosure, in Motion

Data in motion is data that is transmitted by radio, over a wire, or by some other means, like on a tape, a truck, or an escape pod. (A droid in an escape pod is still just data in motion.) However the data is moving, you cannot rely on an operating system or other program to protect it. Data carried by a courier can also be seen as data in motion, and protection for the data in motion may be less. Princess Leia's ship, the Tantive IV, is less protected than a base. A courier with a briefcase full of cryptographic keys has to maintain discipline for an extended period to keep the keys safe.

Data in motion can be disclosed because it's sent in cleartext, because of a failure in the crypto, or because of a failure in the routing. There's disclosure because the channel isn't protected and disclosure because the messages aren't protected. (See Chapter 2, "Tampering and Integrity," for more on channels and messages.) You can also think about the exposure of metadata of several types: existence and timing of communication, addresses, quantity (volume and frequency), and even tooling. An easy-to-understand example of tool metadata is that Twitter exposes the operating system and tool used to tweet. At least one maker of Android phones has disciplined an employee for tweeting from an iPhone.

As discussed in Chapter 2, the difference between a channel and a message is important. A channel carries messages. For example, email messages are carried over an SMTP channel. You can encrypt the messages with PGP, S/MIME, or other email encryption tools, and you can encrypt the SMTP channel with StartTLS. You should do both, because the channel is protecting the headers and the content as messages move between servers, while the message encryption protects the content at rest on those servers. Similarly, Chapter 1 presented the idea of a monkey-in-the-middle (MITM) threat, where messages are routed to an attacker, and the attacker may choose to simply observe, rather than tamper. Authentications are a particularly important type of message to protect—sending passwords unprotected is so 1990s.

There are a few common reasons data is generally not encrypted. Sometimes the engineer doesn't even think about it. Other times the engineer believes that the receivers are too expensive or tricky to build or install. Compatibility or operations can also make deploying hard. (Remarkably, as late as 2014, video from Predator drones was not encrypted [Schactman, 2012; Pocock, 2015].) Crypto failures are from bad algorithm choice or evaluation. During the Second World War, there were several German evaluations of the strength of the Enigma cryptosystem. All of those evaluations arrived at the wrong answer. They attributed to coincidence what was in fact the Allied invention of the computer. Your adversaries probably spend less, and while they certainly don't have Alan Turing, they might have someone almost as brilliant. More frequent than bad algorithms are bad key management practices. Keys are subject to all the disclosure threats in this chapter and are far easier to sneak out than other information. For example, a 2048-bit key can easily be encoded in two old-style tweets[2]; if you encode 8 bytes per DNS lookup, then it's just 32 lookups for domains like `ifgdnexp.threatsbook.com`. With more lookups, the names can look even less suspicious. Those channels are less useful if you want to steal a copy of the plaintext.

Shockingly, not all information flows over the Internet. There are other systems that still use radios or cables. Sometimes people confuse the "private" nature of the network with "privacy" features. There is a long history of faulty assumptions that receivers (or transmitters) would be too challenging to build or install. This has impacted cell phones, global positioning systems, submarine cables, and more.

Metadata that can be captured when data is well-encrypted with well-managed keys exposes the fact of communication. No amount of encryption will help a Bothan who's trading daily emails with Rebel leader Mon Mothma. Of course, those large files may be pictures of the grandkids or otherwise be entirely innocent. That's the trouble with metadata.

Communications metadata is subject to interpretation. Why is someone repeatedly calling a drug abuse hotline? Are they addicted, getting help for a loved one, or establishing a help program for their employer? The ability of different observers or participants to describe the same set of observations very differently is often called the Rashomon effect, after a beautiful 1950 movie of that name. Some observers even claim that Rashomon is a better film than Star Wars or that its director, Kurosawa, was a major influence on George Lucas. It would all be a matter of interpretation—except Lucas has explicitly acknowledged Kurosawa's influence.

If you think concern about metadata is overblown, I'll leave you with a quote from Michael Hayden, former head of the NSA: "We kill people based on metadata" (Ferran, 2014).

---

[2]The 140 byte ones.

Limits of "At Rest/In Motion"

A box of backup tapes falling off a truck. An email stored on disk. Is each data at rest or data in motion? It's important that you not get caught up in that sort of question. You have a concern—metadata in a tweet led to an issue. You want to be thinking about where data exists in your system, where it's transmitted, and what that can mean. My book on threat modeling opens with this quote from statistician George Box: "All models are wrong, but some models are useful" (*Threat Modeling: Designing for Security* [Wiley, 2014]).

Information Disclosure from a Process

Processes tell the world about themselves in a variety of ways. Processes that listen on the network often emit a banner saying something like "Sendmail 4.6.2 running on a 32-bit OpenVMS Alpha, vulnerable to CVE-2002-1234." OK, that's a very slight exaggeration. You need to do a lookup on a banner to get a list of known vulnerabilities, some of which might be patched without a change to the version number. Even if your process doesn't emit a true banner, it probably has headers that evolve with version changes.

The behavior of the process will often be enough to identify it. For example, perhaps it responds to "HELO" and "helo" in the same way, but not ELHO and elho. Perhaps your firewall drops connections silently, or perhaps it sends back a FIN or RST packet. Attackers will catalog such changes to use in fingerprinting, that is, using these behaviors to identify the software, and to use that identification to focus the next stage of an attack.

Processes contain data. You use Word to open the layoff documents, and you use EmpireCAD to read the plans for the Death Star.

Having done so, those processes obviously have a copy of the data, but processes also contain security-relevant data, including the following:

- Cryptographic keys
- Random numbers
- Memory layout information
- Authorized file or socket handles

Each of these should remain secret. Memory layout is important when the layout is randomized as a defense against attacks (for example, Address Space Layout Randomization, explained further in Chapter 7, "Predictability and Randomness") or when the end of the stack contains canaries to prevent overwriting. Authorized file handles may be kept open when a process forks and execs another process or may otherwise be made available to another entity.

There are also threats of information disclosure when the process intentionally sends data to logs or debug files. Simple examples include passwords entered as usernames, but connection data (by IP address, username, or machine name) is commonly logged. Different systems have different approaches to system log confidentiality. Windows has a separate security log, which is *writable* only by processes with the SeAuditPrivilege, and the SeSecurityPrivilege is needed to read it (Microsoft, 2017). Unix has a variety of log files with various permissions. At the application level, thought must be brought to the questions of what's logged where and who needs to access it for what.

There are also ways that a process can accidentally send information to storage, including dumping core, swapping, or using a chunk of its own memory to overwrite confidential data. Swapping is a strategy used by operating systems to pretend that slow disk is really RAM and that the machine has more memory than it actually does. It was more noticeable when memory was expensive, disk was slow, and swap algorithms were less cleverly optimized, most of which means this is probably still happening on cheap devices. If your operating system doesn't allow you to mark memory as "unsuitable for swapping," then secrets like crypto keys may end up in the swap files when the machine loses power.

There are also attacks that cause a process to emit information. Sometimes this is just badly designed error messages: "`cannot connect to database with username dba and password secret1!`." Sometimes the information is influenced by an attacker. The Heartbleed bug allowed a client to ask for a message of a certain size to be returned, and the code copied that much data from memory (rather than filling the memory with zeros, a counter, or 0xdeadbeef). The memory copied could include secrets such as crypto keys, username and password combinations, or other arbitrary information. On the positive side, it was hard for an attacker to predict or influence what would come back. On the negative side, the attack allowed a practically unlimited number of requests.

Human Connections

There is a tremendous amount of information in who talks to whom and who's listening. What accounts do you follow on Twitter? What groups have you joined on Facebook? Even if you don't interact or post, your choices can be used to make inferences. Those may be good inferences or bad ones, but since this is a threats book, we're going to focus on Luke Skywalker's active participation in the Rebellion and his willingness to talk about his desire to join the rebellion and fight the Empire. Additionally, his social circle includes a suspected radical he calls "Old Ben," a fugitive religious fanatic formerly known as Obi-Wan Kenobi. (I'm drawing here on the insight of a blogger writing under the name "Comfortably Smug" (Smug, 2015).)

Data Linkages

Data gets linked in a wide variety of ways. For example, from a street address, I can look up a list of who lives at that location. The address can be used to infer race, income, and other demographic factors. I can infer relationships between the residents based on name and age. I might be wrong, but I am unlikely to be penalized for being wrong, unless I'm doing so in a country with privacy laws that have been updated this century. The stream of interesting things that might be inferred can seem never ending.

You can make decisions about what is exposed and what is not. For example, Twitter exposes usernames but not phone numbers. But anyone with a Twitter account can search for users by phone number and link them with people whose phone numbers they have. If the API for this function allows you to upload a list of contacts, then it also allows you to search by phone number. If you upload a lot of contacts, you can create a list of "cell phone to Twitter handle" mappings. For people who keep their cell number private, this information disclosure would be a privacy breach.

Side Effects and Covert Channels

Processing information requires energy. Monitoring the energy consumed or emitted by a computer or its components is a never-ending source of exciting information disclosures. These range from learning about the exponents of public keys to tracking phones through battery levels after someone clears their cookies. (Each 1 bit in the exponent requires computation, but the zero bits do not, so having more 1 bits consumes more energy.) You can monitor energy use directly, by plugging the computer into a device designed to monitor power usage (with either your own or a smart meter that samples at thousands of samples per second) or just by asking it, "Hey, web browser, how much battery do you have left? I'd like all the significant figures, please" (Fleishman, 2016).

Technology also emits energy in other forms, frequently heat and sound. Monitors are designed to emit information in the visual spectrum, and the guy next to me on the plane keeps glancing at what I'm writing. But the attack works from farther away. Monitors draw and refresh pixels sequentially, and so each line displayed can be reconstructed with a photovoltaic cell looking through a telescope. Monitors also emit radiation outside the visual spectrum, and intelligence agencies care a lot about this, which implies that they take advantage of it. Hobbyists and academics have built systems to reconstruct displays from hundreds of meters away. As attacks always get better, the ability to reconstruct the contents of a display is probably commercially available. Monitors probably also emit sound in interesting ways, but I am not aware of anyone who's reconstructed it. The CPU and its enclosure also emit light and sound. The sound has been used to reconstruct cryptographic keys. These attacks have been shown to work both in labs and in noisy environments like data centers.

Our computers are getting much smaller, and designers are including sensors including compasses, location, gyroscopes, microphones and cameras, and radios including (in rough order of increasing transmission power) near-field, Bluetooth, Wi-Fi, and the cellular protocols. Sensors are going to get much better and much more pervasive over the next couple of years. In 2019, there was a case of a Japanese pop star who was kidnapped. The kidnapper was able to read a bus sign that was reflected in her eye from a news photo, use this information to determine where she lived, and then kidnap her. (Fortunately, she was not physically harmed.) Sensors are far better than we expect.

These side effects are all accidental. When they are intentionally used to communicate, they are called *covert channels*. A covert channel is a connection between two parties that's designed to be unnoticed and even unnoticeable. The first public analysis of this possibility was in nuclear test treaty verification. The United States and Soviet Union agreed to the placement of very sensitive instruments in their respective territory, with the ability to send messages back home. The problem arose, how to ensure that the messages that the sensors sent were *only* about nuclear tests?[3] Obviously, that creates a requirement that the message be in cleartext, but then it can be spoofed or tampered with.

Digital signatures are perfect for this! To ensure that each signature is unique, we usually prepend a random *initialization vector* (IV). Imagine a sensor that creates signed messages, where each message is a message, s, and $s=rsa_k$ (IV, message, padding). If IV, the initialization vector, is supposed to be random, then how do you demonstrate that it's not really a secret encrypted message? You can't accept an IV from the outside without serious security problems, and we certainly don't want the Russians sending encrypted messages to their sensors, hidden in IVs or signatures! The covert channel problem is unsolved, and it seems unlikely to be solvable. (Publishing source code doesn't guarantee that that code is what's in an executable, even if you compile it yourself. Unix creator Ken Thompson explains why in his Turing Award lecture [1984].)

You Call It a Cable, I Call It an Antenna

Robert Morris (Senior) said that, over and over. His point was that at the time, many devices used cables to send data from one point to another, and all those cables (and their connectors) acted as antennas. Today, we've replaced many cables with transmitters, moving from implicit side effects of wires to explicit Bluetooth, and we rarely stop to consider all the ways this goes wrong.

Not only is the signal broadcast, but as your body moves through the fields, you divert them by enough to produce measurable effects;

---

[3] I suspect that this problem only really arose because it was an argument against the treaty, but that's beside the point.

both your gestures and your typing can be measured from the data coming off the antennae and transmitters in the environment.

All Will Be Revealed in "Do" Time

The time a computation takes is often data dependent. Skilled poker players will often count seconds before making a move, because betting or folding quickly can leak information.

Several classic technology examples include password checking. One early example was a 1960s algorithm that performed a character-by-character comparison of entered passwords and stored passwords, and it returned a failure message when the passwords didn't match, exposing the number of correctly matched characters. A variant of this problem is mentioned in Morris and Thompson's classic paper, "Password Security: A Case History" (1979). They said "The encryption was done only if the username was valid, because otherwise there was no encrypted password to compare with the supplied password. The result was that the response was delayed by about one-half second if the name was valid but was immediate if invalid. The bad guy could find out whether a particular username was valid." Another classic example is when the time that it takes to exponentiate is "obviously" dependent on the data. You can optimize out the time it takes to shift bits when the exponent has a zero-bit, and thus, the time for exponentiation is dependent on the Hamming weight of the exponent. (The "Hamming weight" is the count of 1 bits in a string. As mentioned in the "Side Effects and Covert Channels" section, each 1 bit in the exponent requires computation [Kocher, 1996].) Timing attacks over a network have more jitter than when the measurements are local. On a LAN, that jitter can be as low as nanoseconds and "over the Internet" on the order of microseconds (Crosby 2009, Hale, 2009).

Thus, processing of sensitive data should return after a set time, and then you're safe, right? Not so fast. If an attacker can run code on the same processor as yours, perhaps in a cloud data center, then they can count cycles available to them and thus infer how many you're using (processors, not virtual machines [Sinan, 2015]). Similarly, attacks like Spectre exploit branch prediction to learn about various caches.

Information Disclosure Mechanisms

The simplest way to get information is to look for it. Information is often broadcast. It's put on "obscure" fileshares or websites (and then browsers tell Google about this exciting new URL). You can search for "Company Confidential Information" in many places, not just Google.

If the information isn't broadcast, you might have to ask for it, either directly or indirectly. A direct request is of the form open (file), select * from SSNs, or GET /rest/API/customer/fullinfo/. Given the difficulty in setting access control rules, this often works. Indirect requests include asking another program to make a request on your behalf or exploiting a vulnerability or misconfiguration that allows reading storage that shouldn't be read.

Developers often engage in information disclosure by storing secrets in source code or binaries. The source code is checked into GitHub; the binary is not treated as a secret. It would be better to ask the OS to store the secret for you.

If the information an attacker wants to see is protected, they may be able to guess at it and check their guesses. For example, if you think my password is "darthvader," you can try to log in to my account using it. You might also try "Darthvader" and "DarthVader," and if you're typing each, you might stop there. It's easy to write code to permute these guesses, and we call that *brute force*.

There's a close relationship between the direct mechanism of "just look" and the indirect mechanism of guessing. That relationship leads to this chapter having many callouts to Chapter 7. As you might guess, predictability as a threat can lead to more than just information disclosure, which is why it gets its own chapter.

Information Disclosure with Specific Scenarios

Smart devices are smart because they gather information from the physical world, and those sensors are often surprisingly good. They also often have radios, and those radios have real implications for privacy that we've barely begun to grapple with—and privacy more generally strongly intertwines with information disclosure. Sending information to the cloud always entails disclosing it, except when we use encryption. Machine learning (ML) is threatened by information disclosure from training data and data sources through the models themselves and to their outcomes. Blockchains are tools for consensus, and the information contained within them cannot be private, but it can be hard to interpret. We'll cover each of these in this section.

Internet of Things

It isn't just nannycams that have hidden cameras; it's all sorts of things. They also have microphones, pressure sensors, and barometers.

These sensors in things are far better than we expect. Phone cameras can resolve the text on folded papers from dozens of feet away. Microphones pick up ultrasonic signals in stores or TV ads. Gyroscopes reveal where on the screen someone tapped, thus revealing their passwords (Schmitt, 2020). GPS data from exercise trackers reveals the location of special forces bases and running paths. The sensors make inferences: what you typed, what you were watching, where you were, sometimes despite explicit preference settings. (It is unclear to me why it is not considered deceptive to collect location information when an app has been told it has been denied access to location data, or when the FTC or European Data Commissioners will prosecute such a case.) The inferences and raw data are transmitted to places we don't expect.

There is an argument that such data is governed by consent in EULAs or terms of service. However, that argument doesn't credibly address devices used in public, or places open to the public like stores. It also doesn't address devices deployed in other people's homes, devices in hotels, or even smart locks installed in apartment buildings, giving landlords insight into when you enter or leave in a way that mechanical keys did not. This issue is not limited to these devices. Most jobs these days, even low-paying ones, require you to have a smart phone and to run employer-selected apps. You have to use devices and software they select, and the legalese gives the creators unlimited ability to change those terms in the future.

The intrusive nature of these systems came into ironic focus when Examplify blocked future lawyers from taking the 2022 bar exam. Examplify is software marketed to prevent cheating. It attempts to ensure it's not running in a virtual machine, and that makes it incompatible with Windows on Intel's latest CPUs (Roth, 2022).

As an engineer, it is important to understand the impacts of the software we build and to design so that we can live in the world we build.

Sometimes devices have more sensors than we think. Microphones are now so cheap that manufacturers will include them against potential future use cases (Fussell, 2019). Apple phones have included barometers since the iPhone 6.

Mobile Phones

In addition to the excellent sensors already discussed, mobile phones have a set of radios that can be triangulated to an accuracy of as little as a few feet. Technologies such as Ultrawideband hope to improve that to a few centimeters.

Combining location data and movement data with compass data allows marketers to assess who in a crowd is talking to whom. The only way to limit that tracking is to put the phone into airplane mode (which may no longer turn off the Wi-Fi).

These tracking technologies are creating an increasingly detailed record of where roughly every person has been, and the data is being kept for years. In a brief to the Supreme Court that I was able to contribute to, we described how "cell site location information is becoming increasingly detailed, contemporaneous and precise," how it is collected without the knowledge or consent of people, how it "reveals an extraordinarily detailed picture of an individual's life, every bit as revealing as the content of their communications" (Soltani, 2017). I urge technologists to not accidentally create such surveillance technologies. We have very little idea of what they will do to our world and very little control over how the data is stored and used.

Cloud

If "the cloud is just someone else's computer," then your data, and your code, your cryptographic secrets, in the cloud, are in someone else's computer. That's information disclosure within the cloud. There's also information disclosure to cloud services that are integrated into your systems and the code that they run. URLs are subject to two information disclosure threats. First, they can contain confidential information, and second, they can point to such information. Each of these aspects of the cloud is covered in this section.

One other aspect of cloud and information disclosure is many backup systems send data to the cloud. Whether or not your backup system does, backups are often like the cloud in that they're offsite and outside of your control. I'm hopeful that at this point you can see the tampering and information disclosure threats to that, and you'll learn about denial-of-service threats in Chapter 5, "Denial of Service and Availability."

Information Disclosure Within a Cloud Platform

The word *platform* can be used either in its broad English sense or in the sense of platform as a service (PaaS). Using the term broadly, the owner of the platform, their employees, their attackers, and their other customers can all peek (or try to peek) at your data or metadata more easily than when the data is on your computer. There are defenses against this including contracts, particular types of cryptography such as homomorphic encryption, or technical features such as Intel's Software Guard Extensions, which provides an encrypted area of memory and protection for that memory down to very low levels of hardware. There are also systems that are labeled "Bring Your Own Key." The word "bring" is, well, crucial. Most of these systems disclose the key to the cloud provider, who promises to take substantial steps to control it.

One of the ways in which someone else who can run arbitrary code in the cloud can peek at your data is by using side channel attacks of various forms. Most notable recently are attacks such as SPECTRE and Rowhammer. Each of these attacks will expose the contents of memory, and the details are fascinating, especially to people who care about hardware architecture and optimization. There are other side channels, which include accessing a built-in microphone, which, being more effective than you might expect, collects the sound that the CPU makes as it executes different instructions.

Information Disclosure to or by Cloud Systems

Many people think of cloud as infrastructure as a service (IaaS) or software as a service (SaaS). Not precisely within that definition but also worth discussing are the various and sundry web toolkits, such as analysis providers, which, by design, are information disclosure to the analysis system. These often collect a great deal of detail, including full URLs, which might contain secrets.

More generally, information is disclosed by design far more broadly than analytics libraries: it's available to all the code you include. In fact, that's not all that's available, but information disclosure can be a very subtle attack. If the library tampers with your data, website, or app, you're more likely to notice.

These attacks by included code are not limited to the Web, of course. A great deal of modern development involves pulling in arbitrary libraries, all of which can steal your data.

Also in the world of modern development are cloud-driven development tools. Many of these, intentionally or accidentally, get information that you want kept secret. GitHub offers private repos, and it seems reasonable to think that at least some of those are accidentally more open than their owners intend.

URLs

There are two information disclosure threats associated with URLs. The first is direct information disclosure when someone shares a link or when a link is processed by a proxy, cache, or analytics software. Information in such a link (`&username=darth&password=youweremy friend`) is directly exposed. Anyone with the URL can simply click it. If the password is not replaced, they can attempt to log in as darth on any site they want. Replacing all potentially sensitive data with tokens reduces both risks.

The second threat is that the URL is used as a kind of "capability," replacing access control checks with an assumption that anyone with the URL is authorized to get to the data it refers to.

AI/ML

You may want to keep one or more of your training data, data sources, your models, or their analysis confidential.

An attacker who can read your training data may be able to reproduce your AI or find flaws that you're not aware of. The trained model is much smaller and may be much more valuable. It is also subject to disclosure by attackers.

All deep neural networks inevitably memorize information, and the better they're optimized, the more they need to memorize. So unfortunately, if you put your ML learning system in a haven with highly private data and then take the model out, you're taking some of that highly private data with the model (Feldman, 2021).

In 2019, the OpenAI institute created a very competent text generation tool (GPT-3). They worried that giving away the full model could lead to its abuse and released it in stages. They followed the same pattern for their image generator (DALL-E).

Blockchain

Information on a blockchain is public, by design, as is metadata about transactions. Putting a hash of non-public information allows you to use the non-repudiation features without revealing the information that was hashed. Unless the system has been specifically designed to prevent it, transactions are *linkable*: you can say that the same wallet executed transactions 1234 and 2345 because of metadata about the wallet. Because transactions are linkable, if any of them are *traceable* (namely, someone can connect them to a person), then all those transactions are traceable. As such, Obi-Wan Kenobi probably should get a new wallet when he ensconces on Tatooine and disappears.

Privacy

Tracking and using disclosed information are at the heart of many privacy issues. The information may be disclosed by the subject or by others. It may be inferred. Many people feel uncomfortable as the subject of scrutiny or judgment; some privacy scholars argue that public policy should focus on harm reduction. Many large security breaches are disclosed because of laws requiring that when a data custodian loses track of personal data they've collected. A full treatment of privacy is larger than the scope of this book.

Defenses

Defenses against information disclosure depend on if you can rely on an operating system to help, if you're designing your own program, or if you're communicating over a network. If you can leverage an operating system to protect data at rest, permissions are a useful place to start. Even if you can, you may want to use cryptography, and you'll need to do so while communicating. When writing your software, you'll need to consider metadata and the data it leaks.

Those new to security often want to use obscurity as a defense, and that's fine, if what's obscure is also protected. By way of example, major search engines will respect a website's /robots.txt file telling them what not to index. Curious attackers also respect this file, but as a great roadmap to the good stuff. Predictability also comes into play. There's been at least one prosecution of someone who predicted the URL for a company's earnings report and was able to access it early. The details of the legal case don't matter for our purposes—what matters is the defender relied on obscurity, and it didn't work. It's much better to rely on something stronger a topic we revisit in Chapter 7.

The rest of this section explores defenses related to operating systems, processes, and cryptography.

Operating System Defenses

One of the key jobs of an operating system is to intermediate between processes and control who can access what resource. Permissions are a primary tool for that. The operating system also produces, tracks, and manages metadata, and you may need to adjust your behavior or code to control what metadata is available to whom. Modern operating systems also include search functionality that you may need to consider if you're creating such a service, or more likely, if metadata is a concern.

Permissions (and ACLs)

The way permissions are handled depends on what you're working with. Unix and Windows have two fairly different access control models. One is very simple, the other quite complex, and with the benefit of hindsight, neither is "just right."

The Unix mechanism is that of files having a set of independent permissions (read, write, and execute) that can be set for the user, group, or "other," meaning all users of that system. Permissions are stored in 4 octets, with the 4th being used for special permissions: setuid, setgid, and a "sticky bit." When the sticky bit is set on a directory, deletion is restricted; thus shared directories can be somewhat protected against a user deleting (and possibly creating replacements for) another's files.

The Windows mechanism is an access control list (ACL). There are multiple entries in a list, and they're evaluated sequentially. Darth Vader is granted Read and Execute access to all objects. Princess Leia denies Read access to all members of the Imperial group. Which rule takes precedence? I honestly don't remember, and if I have to consult an expert to understand, most developers and users will get it right only by luck (Microsoft, 2021).

Setting permissions or ACLs gets difficult quickly. Assigning rights to some Unix groups is not particularly expressive, and the more expressive Windows model is so confusing that a colleague got their PhD researching how it breaks (Reeder, 2008). Respected security expert Dan Geer has made a strong case that openness, including accepting failures, is cheaper than carefully configuring permissions (Udell, 2004). Lastly, when troubleshooting, it's easy to set permissions to be very permissive, and noticing that permissions are set wide open requires diligence. Once "it works for me," who goes to look to see who else can get access to data?

The design of access control systems is a special subdiscipline of computer security. It gets complex very quickly as you deal with prioritization of rules and how to deal with groups. For example, what to do when an account is in groups with contradictory rules? This design challenge is well outside what every engineer needs to know—just know that it's not something to undertake lightly.

There are two additional design challenges when the permissions are for an online service: compatibility and usability. If I set my permissions today to enable read access by the "editors" group, what happens to those permissions when the service replaces groups with teams or separates "comments" as a specific thing that can be allowed or denied? Should editors have that new comment capability? Similarly, a service like Facebook that regularly adds permissions will eventually end up with a complex sprawl. They'll inevitably encounter these sorts of issues when they refactor, leading to either more usability or frustrated people, or both. (Google has a suggested search "why do my privacy settings on Facebook keep changing" [Cassidy, 2022; Coldewey, 2021].) You probably want to avoid emulating Facebook for this detail.

Metadata Management

Metadata including directory names and filenames can be protected by a level of folders. Create a directory called `private` that contains the `Junelayoffs` directory, and make sure that only authorized parties can read the contents of `private` and then apply this recursively. This works for local computers, cloud storage sites such as Dropbox, or websites that expose a directory structure.

If you provide a search service or indexer, then you need to ensure that the data it returns is what's authorized for the searcher to see. Returning the file "Order 66" when someone searches for "Jedi" is revealing even without being able to see the contents of the file.[4]

Timing can provide meta-metadata about what's in the index. Also, authorization can be tricky: if today Alice has set permissions on her

---

[4]Order 66 is the secret order that declared Jedi are traitors subject to summary execution.

bookmarks file to allow Bob to read it but tomorrow revokes those permissions, the indexer should stop revealing the contents of that file to Bob and no longer reveal that the contents match a given search string. But what if the indexer read in the file, checked the latest permissions, and then Alice changes them? Traversing every file to check its permissions will slow down a search function; traversing a subset might reveal information about the subset.

If the "confused deputy" way of thinking works for you, your search services can be easily confused. If not, it may be a good example that helps you grasp the concept.

As filesystems become more complex and add journaling features, protecting the metadata becomes practically impossible. Allegedly, the complexities of protecting files on NTFS (and WinFS) were part of the justification for Microsoft creating BitLocker as a full disk encryption product. (I'm repeating this claim not because I have evidence, but because I find it plausible.)

Defending Your Process

For code you create, it's important to consider what information it reveals. Your code will need to emit logs and error messages, and there may be secrets it needs to manage.

Well-Designed Logs and Error Handling

Secrets can often end up in error messages and logs. That's better than showing them to the end user, and when you put secrets in logs, you must consider who can see what logs and who's using what log analysis tool. In addition to secrets, personal data often ends up in logs, and thus those logs need protection under privacy laws. That personal data can be in unexpected places, like a machine named "Tim Cook's iPhone" or "Tim Cook's Wi-Fi."

To avoid putting sensitive data in too many places, there's a pattern called *tokenization*: replacing personal or sensitive data with a token. For example, you can display a GUID or other long string to the user and then include that GUID in the canonical log message so your support staff can find it. That's a lookup key approach to tokenization. You can also take an encryption approach. If you encrypt data, then information disclosure of the key can retroactively expose the data to anyone who has a copy of the logs. Additionally, if the information being encrypted is small (say, an SSN), then an attacker with a list of SSNs can encrypt them all and see if any match.

This sort of indirection is a time-honored technique. Spies use dead drops where they leave packages so they can avoid being seen with a handler. Mafia bosses have underlings talk to the hit man. If the metadata of concern is who's talking to whom, then publishing (or broadcasting) messages may be a valuable defense. Again, spies will broadcast messages to each other to avoid having to be in the same place. In the days of analog transmission, the messages were taped and played back at high speed so direction-finding had less time to work.

Careful Secrets Management

The Empire is careful with the plans for the Death Star. They're secret, so they're not scattered around or stored in many places. You need to be careful with your secrets, and you need to be careful with cryptographic keys: secrets that protect other secrets.

Secrets   Secrets include but are not limited to cryptographic keys. Highly sensitive data like Social Security numbers, medical records, or intimate partners should also be treated like secrets.

Secrets need to be handled carefully. That includes identifying them, using them for defined purposes, storing them properly, and overwriting them when they are no longer needed so they can't be revealed by accident.

Modern systems have APIs to store and retrieve secrets, and modern cloud systems have ways for newly running processes to get secrets from a service so that the secrets are not checked into version control or compiled into machine images.

It's generally a good idea to get rid of secrets you no longer need, and you'll be unsurprised to learn that it's hard to reliably delete a secret. Compilers and runtimes will often optimize away code like this:

```
for char in array[0..sizeof(secret)]
{ array[char]=0 ;
char++ ; }
free (array);
```

After all, who cares about the value of free memory? Not compiler designers. They're all about the optimizations. Your crypto library probably has a routine that is designed to carefully free memory, and the authors will worry about keeping that current.

Cryptographic Keys Cryptographic keys come under special attack because they are the keys to the kingdom, or at least whatever they protect. I'll take as a given that the entire system is known to the attacker, and the only unknown would be the cryptographic key. (If you question that assumption, see Chapter 7.) In some, very unusual circumstances, the attacker has to be online to test keys, in which case exponential backoff and attack detection can be helpful.

Cryptography

Cryptography is the very best way to protect confidentiality. With modern crypto, access to plaintext is conditioned on having both the ciphertext and the key. Ciphertext on disk? Safe. Ciphertext on the wire? Safe. Ciphertext installed as art at CIA headquarters? Safe. (Really! The Kryptos sculpture has stood undeciphered for more than 30 years.)

Ciphertext is the result of an encryption function, e, being fed a key and a plaintext message, m. This is usually written $c = e_k(p)$ because cryptographers are mathematicians, not programmers, and I have just made a thousand enemies. When the encryption function is symmetric, then there's a function d (decrypt), which takes the ciphertext, the same key k, and produces the message: $p = d_k(c)$. There are other cryptographic systems where the recipients have different keys, which is very cool mathematically and incredibly useful when you have more than a few participants, because each participant can have a small set of keys and communicate so that no other participant can eavesdrop. (If we have 100 people using the symmetric system and each has k, each can decrypt one another's messages.)

Many times, we analyze a system pretending that the goal of the attacker is to determine k. (That's not usually the attacker's goal, but it's an excellent stepping stone to real goals.) Also, for this section, let's focus our attacks on the key itself, rather than how Alice and Bob agree on it. See Chapter 7 for more on guessing keys.

It is, of course, important to use a modern cipher designed and analyzed by experts, with a well-protected random key, and probably a random initialization vector. Initialization vectors are important because otherwise similarities in plaintext can show through. In almost all cases, that means AES-256 using the right modes.

There are some remarkably interesting use cases that cryptographic tools can enable. There are schemes called *forward secrecy* that allow you to encrypt data so that even if someone steals the long term key you're using, they can't decrypt the messages. Some optimists are so optimistic that they call it *perfect forward secrecy*. There are other schemes like secret sharing that allow you to split a secret into m shares, of which you need any n to recover the secret. For example, 3 out of 5. In that case, n would be 3, m would be 5, and these are often called *n-of-m*.

There are attacks where what you know is the ciphertext and you want to recover the key. There are also important attacks where what you know is some plaintext and you want to know what ciphertext it will produce. There are many variants of chosen plaintext attacks. If you find yourself dealing with terms like known plaintext and chosen plaintext, you may well need a book on cryptography.

You also need a book on cryptography if you ever try to write cryptographic code yourself or use a cryptographic function in a funky or innovative way. The code is unforgiving, the implementation complexities are high, and there's no reason to not let someone else do the hard work.

Data at Rest

You can encrypt either individual files or entire disks, or both. Similarly, you can encrypt a database, columns, or cells. In each case, you need to manage the keys.

It can be useful to encrypt a volume with a key stored outside the disk so that on disposal, the key and the ciphertext are separated. There are lots of hard drives that will encrypt the data with a key stored inside the drive. This design allows drive owners to reliably block access to the filesystem, should they remember to do so when disposing of the disk. Modern operating systems also now come with full disk encryption.

Neither design protects against someone with logical access to the system, and the question of protecting against an attacker with physical access gets complex quickly. For example, if your Airbnb includes a guest computer, then a guest has some operating system access, and full disk encryption won't defend against that guest, or others who have the ability to run code on the computer. Many devices store secrets in a way that can easily be accessed in this scenario. Effective protection requires that the operating system have support for disk crypto with the keys stored securely. (To be precise, there may be some other component that manages the disk crypto, other than the hard drive.)

There are security models for encrypted database security that protect against an attacker who can execute queries, and those who can snapshot the encrypted data. There are also database security models where the data is supposed to be private, but queries against it are allowed. This is useful, for example, with census data. Differential privacy is an approach that measures the data that queries return and limits it in useful ways. Differential privacy is moving from academia to deployment at companies such as Apple and Uber.

Data in Motion

Data in motion, between systems, is only as safe as those wires or radio waves that carry it. Encrypting it protects you from attackers who can compromise those interconnections, but not from those who can compromise the cryptosystem.

Engineers tend to have a few mental models of how data gets from one system to another, and none are labeled "data in motion." So to be explicit, those mental models are often things like RPC, calling an API, or HTTP. Another mental model is that of network traffic, where we know that data is flowing from one system or cloud provider to another. For many of these, we now reflexively slap TLS onto those flows and assume it's good. And TLS is much better than not TLS. However, TLS relies on a system of "certificate authorities." You met certificate authorities (CAs) in Chapter 1.

Let's revisit those "authorities." They're the ones issuing identification, and in the digital world, a great many companies and a few governments issue them. My Mac has about 130 authorities that it will trust, including, as I look through the list, FNMT-RCM. Who are they? I think they're part of the Spanish government. Why does my Mac trust them? This is a tricky trade-off of usability. Without these roots of trust, how could my computer make a decision? Most of us, myself included, generally trust the folks who make our computers to make this call, and we accept the risk that these 130 authorities have a lot of power.

Let's assume that the Sith operate a CA, and my Mac trusts it. The threat is that SithCA will issue a certificate for threatsbook.com and install it on their fake version of my website. But my website usually gets its certificate from LetsEncrypt.

Smart folks at Google built a system to observe how they're using that power. It's called Certificate Transparency, and a lot of software, such as web browsers, report the certificates they see to the Certificate Transparency (CT) system, and CT points out anomalies. That acts as a deterrent to misuse of power.

In the previous paragraph, the words "a lot of software" are doing a lot of work. If your custom software trusts 130 certificate authorities, does it also participate in CT? You can configure either your computer or a particular program to trust a smaller set of CAs, participate in CT, or both. You can also "pin" your system to a particular CA. This turns out to be operationally risky—if you make a mistake in how you describe that pinning or need to switch CAs, you can deny service to your own systems.

Limits of Encryption

Managing keys is hard. It requires discipline and processes, and code is excellent at providing those. Managing keys is also easier than protecting everything that the keys protect. As an engineer, you must consider the life cycle of a key from creation to distribution to destruction.

If I have a database of math grades (A–F), each stored as an encrypted block next to the student's name, I can see that there are only five ciphertext values. I can guess that Albert Einstein got an A and probably also see which ciphertext means a C with some elementary statistics. Switching the grades is then trivial, and so integrity and binding are also important. I might encrypt ciphertext = e_k(IV, name, grade). Using nonces, times, and initialization vectors is a great start, as is using the right mode for encryption.

Cryptography protects the confidentiality of the communication, but the ciphertext itself might reveal things: for example, the number of students in the class. This doesn't seem super-interesting, but the size of ciphertext coming off a web server can also reveal what page someone is visiting (most obviously because of images of various sizes, but certainly not limited to that). More, simply visiting a website can be interpreted by others. You can "pad" the data so it's a standard size.

Perhaps you're visiting Planned Parenthood's website to gather information about healthcare choices for you or a friend, or you might be looking for things you can quote for political reasons. The art of analyzing encrypted communications to learn things is called *traffic analysis*, and it's remarkably powerful. There are well-studied cryptographic defenses against traffic analysis beyond the scope of this book. Those interested should study the design of Tor for protecting low-latency data, and Mixmaster for when higher latency is acceptable.

Steganography is the art of secret writing, and there are cryptographic techniques for hiding the existence of either communication in network traffic or content hidden in other files.

Information Disclosures in Star Wars

I've often said Star Wars is the story of information disclosure, and its consequences. To emphasize that, let me point out how often it's an important plot device. The computerized information disclosures in Star Wars include the following:

- *A New Hope*:
  - The Death Star plans stolen on tape.
  - Floor plans and prisoner locations when R2-D2 plugs into the Death Star.
- *The Empire Strikes Back*:
  - None spring to mind!
- *Return of the Jedi*:
  - The Bothan discovery of the location of the new Death Star appears to be information disclosure, but...it's a trap!

There is other information that is kept confidential: Leia withholds the location of the Rebel base, and Obi-Wan hides Darth Vader's true nature, but these are not computerized.

R2 playing the hologram is authorized (by R2) each time. In *The Empire Strikes Back*, Luke feels Han Solo being tortured, but that's by design.

Conclusion

Information can be disclosed to just one person or the whole galaxy; it can be small or voluminous. In the context of a galactic empire, Darth Vader's famous words "No, I am your father!" is a small piece of information, disclosed to just one person, but with tremendous consequences.

Information can be observed at rest or in motion. The data in motion reveals that the endpoints communicate, even if the contents of those communications are protected. Information can be disclosed digitally or as side effects of computation. Disclosing information about human relationships can have tremendous effects, even beyond family.

The mechanisms for information disclosure are relatively straight-forward, but guessing—and checking those guesses—can be surprisingly effective. Sensors have surprising and increasing power in both smart devices and phones. The cloud has information disclosure threats that range from incredibly obvious to very subtle or surprising. These can manifest or be seen as either security or privacy issues.

Defenses can sometimes be provided by an operating system, and sometimes they must be part of your code, or operational processes. Especially with logs, those operational processes are easiest when supported by good design. Similarly, good design makes effective use of a breadth of cryptographic defenses.

The Death Star plans are important not in and of themselves, but because of the risk they'll be used to plan an attack. Much data has this property: we keep it confidential because it's the best way of preventing its misuse, or even preserving an advantage we have. We don't need to fully predict or evaluate the chain of events that follow its disclosure to know that we want to keep things confidential.

5

Denial of Service and Availability

Resources are always finite and sometimes constrained. Denial-of-service attacks threaten availability by consuming some resource, slowing, crashing, or freezing things. Freezing Han Solo in carbonite was easy—heck, Luke Skywalker was nearly frozen just because he went outside on the ice planet Hoth. It's freezing in a way that allows recovery that requires cleverness. As an aside, Han was supposedly frozen to test the system, and it's not clear why Darth Vader doesn't demand that he be fully thawed out. The goal of full-cycle testing is especially important for denial of service.

Brute force is the easiest form of denial-of-service attacks. But there are plenty of clever denial-of-service attacks that use knowledge of (or assumptions about) what's expensive for a specific target. Denial of service is often focused on an organization, but not always. These attacks are used to disconnect opponents from games, to "split" IRC networks so someone can be given operator privileges), and for many other reasons.

Denial of service is often abbreviated DoS or DOS. (The latter is less confusing now that no one uses Microsoft's Disk Operating System.) These attacks often come from many small systems, leading to the acronym DDoS, for distributed denial of service.

Like an Ewok, each attacker can be smaller and weaker than its target, but with sheer numbers can overwhelm a well-defended target. This property is shared with many distributed denial-of-service attacks.

These distributed threats, like Ewoks, cascade in surprising ways. One of the most famous DDoS attacks was executed by the Mirai botnet against a DNS provider, Dyn. It was widely noticed because Dyn supported a lot of sites that people needed for work, reputedly including Office 365, Amazon, and Slack. The people who used Slack included a great many IT teams, some of whom had never heard of Dyn but were unable to collaborate to understand and remediate the problem. As Turing Award winner Leslie Lamport quipped long ago, "A distributed system is one in which the failure of a computer you didn't even know existed can render your own computer unusable" (ACM, 2013). The Mirai attack was also notable because most of the machines in the botnet were IoT security cameras that had been compromised. Lastly, most of the cascade was an accident. The perpetrators were looking for an advantage in Minecraft hosting, by damaging the reputation of a leading provider (Bours, 2017).

Resources Consumed by Denial-of-Service Threats

All denial of service depletes some resource to limit availability. Traditionally, when servers were plugged into a data center, these attacks targeted compute, storage, or network. More recently, they've been used against budgets and batteries.

Compute

R2-D2 is able to save our heroes from being squished in a garbage compactor because it's computer-controlled. Maybe he crashes the process, maybe he sends it a new command. And maybe it's just a movie, and so we don't need the precise mechanism. Either way, causing a process (or a whole computer) to crash breaks availability. These attacks are important, and most new low-level network protocols have these vulnerabilities until they're discovered, exploited, and patched. Examples have included teardrop, where faking a TCP SYN with the target's IP address as both source and destination could cause an entire system to crash. But more often, we hear about attacks that slow a system, rather than crashing it.

The simplest way to exhaust a service is to ask it to do a lot of what it's supposed to do. Do that enough and systems will get loaded. If a website will let you download videos in any size you want, asking for a video to be displayed in 2580 × 1480 will absorb compute cycles. (The QuadHD standard is 2560 × 1440.) Most websites will have a limited set of sizes and will cache results. Caching is a great resilience and performance strategy. It can be harder to apply defensively in features that search large datasets (especially when those queries can be made to invoke database joins).

The video coding example is one in which an attacker can ask you to do hard work without having done such themselves. They send a web request, you transcode video. The request is cheap, the response is expensive. TLS had this problem. A client shows up, and then the TCP handshake says, "Please do a cryptographic signature on this nonce." Cryptographic signatures were expensive in the 1990s, and a high-end server might do a thousand per second if it did nothing else. Of course, as it did that work, it was adding milliseconds to every other response it was trying to send. More recently, optimizations in TLS have reduced these costs substantially. Cryptocurrency mining is designed to be expensive in terms of compute, so getting someone else to do it is delectable: the victim spends money, the attacker claims it. That is, the victim is paying for compute cycles at a cloud provider, and the attacker whisks away any cryptocurrency that emerges. From the attacker's perspective, the worst case is they get nothing.

There are other ways to break a process, such as holding a mutex or other lock. Because these are designed to control what part of a process can run, holding them holds the process from proceeding. Additionally, accidents teach us a lot about various failure modes, and many of them can be caused by an attacker. If you have an accidental issue, it's worth asking what would have happened if an attacker had caused it and if variants might be possible. That can jolt you away from the "it was really unlikely" line of thinking.

"Proof of Work Proves Not to Work" Proven Wrong

In the early 2000s, there were a set of defensive proposals called *proof of work*. The idea was that you couldn't just walk up and ask for resources; you had to prove you'd done some work first. These schemes were going to solve spam and denial-of-service attacks.

A paper in 2004 was titled "Proof of Work Proves Not to Work," and it pointed out the trouble with these schemes was that if you had other people's computers, the proofs of work didn't do much good. Bitcoin, based in proof of work, showed that proof of work can be a useful building block, when the proofs are sufficiently expensive.

Storage

Much like compute, storage attacks can be simple or complex, and they can apply to any form of storage, including tape, disk, RAM, or cache. At the simple end, an attacker uploads a lot of files. You'd be right to think that we cared more when disk was dollars per megabyte, and the attacks were somewhat easier then, but the issues haven't gone away. If you provide storage and let people sign up for free accounts, someone who doesn't like you can sign up for a lot of accounts, store files, and walk away. Walking away also works great with USB drives.

More complexly, there are storage expansion attacks, where compressed files are designed to have surprising expansion. A feature of most compression algorithms is that they'll say, "and then one billion bytes of 0x40." That's amazing compression! Close to 100 million to one! And it's amazing decompression, too. Compressing files before they transit networks is increasingly common: Microsoft Office's 2007 file formats such as `.docx` and `.xlsx` are zipped XML. HTML is typically served compressed by modern servers. These implicit uses put decompression on more code execution paths, and so zip bombs will set off more reliably.

For most of the threats in this section, such as compute or electrical power, an application's limits are similar to the platform's limits. However, programs often implement storage limits in fixed-size buffers, queues, or lists. If an attacker can exploit your small storage limits, they don't need to overwhelm the platform's overall capabilities.

Until the late 1990s, the Unix TCP stack had room for exactly five "half-open" connections. A TCP request is half-open between the receipt of a SYN and the receipt of a SYN-ACK, when the connection becomes fully open. That was enough until the public execution of a SYN flood attack. The first fix, expanding the buffer, ate kernel memory and wasn't sufficient. The nature of the TCP handshake exacerbated the issue, because a forged IP source address could include the TCP SYN request, and the server would be left hanging. The more permanent fix included adding a clever authentication step: TCP sequence numbers were computed with a hash of a secret and a counter, and so TCP SYN-ACK packets could be tested for plausibility without storing the half-open connections.

If what you're working on is a cloud service, your denial of service will be very different from that which impacts a small smart device, where storage is quite constrained. Some devices implement fixed-sized buffers for things like "known devices." I recently rented a car where I had to figure out how to disassociate the previous set of cell phones before I could Bluetooth my music in. Fortunately, the denial of service on my attention as I careened down the highway wasn't too bad, because someone else was driving as I figured out the "entertaining" entertainment system.

As an aside, some compression libraries seem to pass full paths to indicate where the data should be stored. Most recently, these were re-discovered under the name zipslip (Snyk, 2018). These are yet another example of a confused deputy, where the unzipper is working for the person who created the zip, not the person who wanted the zip unpacked.

Networks

There are threats where someone sends a lot of data, often from a lot of their devices, and others where they send a little data and someone amplifies it. IP networks have features that can be used as amplifiers, such as pinging the broadcast address. These are covered in the "Amplification" section later in this chapter. Of course, these attacks are not limited to IP; token ring fails if you fail to give up the token.

In an age of abundant IP bandwidth such as "fiber to the home," we can forget that bandwidth is always constrained. Radio bandwidth is more constrained than communication over wires. In airplanes, where all the passengers share one radio, bandwidth is dramatically limited. Even local, lower-power radios have important constraints. As bandwidth use increases, so does contention. Ask anyone who's debugged Wi-Fi in a dense apartment building. Zigbee, Wave, and other very low-power systems can also be overwhelmed. In one demonstration, they were overwhelmed by (ahem) smart lightbulbs, which are a useful attack tool because their radios are plugged into a power source. Even without saying anything useful, they can flood the local network or interfere with message delivery. This interference is easiest to imagine with radio broadcasts, but a MITM can also interfere with delivery or alter messages in a way that causes them to fail integrity checks. That tampering can lead to denial of service as a side effect.

This current section of the chapter is named "Networks" rather than "Bandwidth" because a network denial of service can work by using either very large packets or very small ones. Very large ones consume bandwidth, while very small ones consume the processing power of routers and switches (Emmons, 2020).

Beyond attacks on network capacity, there are attacks on data flows. These include corrupting messages. If you have a good message integrity check, the corrupt packets may get thrown away. The resultant code path is probably less optimized, and there may be a cascade of compute or storage issues as you manage and log the strange packets.

Electrical Power

Most devices don't use as much power as a tractor beam. (It's worth asking—when an intruder turns off the power, is that a denial-of-service threat? It's certainly a threat to the availability of the system, even if it feels different than other threats we discuss.)

When electricity is provided by batteries, battery drain can be a substantial problem. Battery-powered devices can be subjected to computational attacks, because, of course, computation requires power, and they can be subjected to attacks on other power draws. Simply asking a device to wake up more often than planned can drain the battery, as does operating peripherals like screens, radios, or hard drives.

There are also batteries that are hard to reach. These might be in a security camera, high on a wall, or distant, detecting something deep in the wilderness, or even deep in outer space. And while we think of those as "painful" to reach, it's literally painful to open someone's chest to replace the battery in their pacemaker.

More frequently, electrical power comes from a socket, and most uses outside a data center won't change power draw enough to make for practical DoS attacks. As anyone who's worked in a data center knows, it gets complex quickly, and that complexity can lead to failures. Those failures, like those induced by storms, are generally managed by people building data centers.

Money

The cloud exposes a new resource to exhaustion, your budget. The cloud provider can take quite a bit of abuse on their pipes, spin up new compute nodes for you, and give you unimaginable amounts of storage, all for an unimaginable and probably unmanageable bill.

Cloud providers will happily sell you more cloud, and generally they're happy to sell you as much cloud as you want or can afford. That's great as long as your computers are doing money-making work. Your need to scale is, ideally, correlated with increases in business. But when your systems come under resource-intensive attacks, those attacks can transcend storage, compute, and bandwidth and hit you directly in the pocketbook.

When you're buying these resources in small chunks, what runs out first might not be the resources but your budget. As the bankrupt folks at Long-Term Capital Management remarked, "The market can remain irrational far longer than you can remain solvent," but the market wasn't even irrational; the firm succumbed to a coordinated attack on its budget.

Money, of course, is a great motivator. Attackers prefer taking your money to having you pay a cloud provider. So, if you use text messages for notifications, reminders, or the like, attackers can give you a premium-rate number. These are numbers where the sender is charged to send a message, like those used to charge per vote for reality TV. This attack is common enough that there's an acronym: IRSF (which stands for international revenue sharing fraud). This attack also applies to using text messages for authentication, which was always a bad idea, as discussed in Chapter 1, "Spoofing and Authenticity." It's made worse by these attacks. Setting a budget for sending texts can be a backstop defense (after checking area codes against a list or using a service that does so). If the budget stops texts, you likely should have real-time access to the state of your budget. Only discovering that your budget was entirely spent when your service is cut off or the monthly bill shows up is another kind of denial of service, this time executed by your defenses.

Many of those attacks might be more logically grouped under fraud and thus repudiation. But keep in mind that all models are ultimately wrong, and if thinking about "how would someone eat our budget" leads to good discoveries, you should run with them.

Other Resources

All systems have resource limits that can be run out, often in surprising ways. The five slots for SYNs (discussed earlier in the "Storage" section) was a surprising limit. There are limits on file descriptors, process IDs, and memory size, and most can be attacked. For example, a fork bomb is a simple program that repeatedly calls `fork()` to launch more copies of itself until no more processes can be created.

Triggering defenses as a means of denying service to someone else can be quite effective. Passwords that lock after five tries mean attackers can lock you out. In Chapter 3, "Repudiation and Proof," we learned about buying obviously fake reviews for competitors to get their accounts shut down. There are certainly defenses that can't be abused into denial of service, such as carefully controlled issuance of digital signatures, but they are less common than you might hope. It can be an effective trade-off to intentionally degrade service when under attack, when the trade-offs aren't accidents.

Not all denial-of-service attacks are against technical targets. All resources are finite. Some customers need way more handholding than others. Terrorists engage in multiple simultaneous attacks to strain the capacity of responders from ambulances or police through hospitals. Supply chain issues in 2021 and 2022 exposed many places where "optimization" assumed that everything would keep flowing smoothly, and when it didn't, factory capacity went unused, and customers either went without or switched brands. There are frequent discussions of trust and resilience becoming depleted, and those are beyond the scope of this book.

Denial-of-Service Properties

Denial-of-service threats can be generic, or they can be intensely specialized to a targeted system. They can rely on the capabilities of the attacker or be amplified by some property of your system. They can persist or go away on their own.

Bespoke or Generalized

Attack mechanisms like a zip bomb or a DDoS require little knowledge of the target. They are common because they work. When they don't work or when they're insufficiently disruptive, dedicated attackers will design bespoke attacks just for you. A clever attacker needs to jam only one bottleneck to gum up the whole works. That bottleneck can be in components from your suppliers or in your bespoke code.

Your bespoke code is more likely to have these bottlenecks because they tend to go undiscovered. An attacker gets a less general payoff from exploiting them, and your engineers and ops folks get a lot less help from the defender community at large. These may be simple: fixed-size buffers, compute pools, storage, or they may be more complex. Attackers may aim for cache misses or complex database joins. They may be empirical ("That seems slow, can we make it slower?") or theory-driven ("I bet if we combine three random dictionary words, no one will have done that search.").

Attackers, like Ewoks, often surprise us with the cleverness of their attacks. Their lack of technical sophistication doesn't prevent their old-fashioned rope net from capturing people or their logs from swinging and crushing advanced vehicles.

Amplification

Some attacks are relatively symmetrical: they use attacker resources at the rate they use yours. Others, like the zip bomb, use an amplifier of some form, where the problem is worse. The amplification factor is the ratio of resources consumed, and the higher the ratio, the more value to attackers. Amplification factors cluster in the range 10x–50x but range up to 51,000x (CERT, 2019).

Network protocols still have substantial amplification, and it used to be far worse. The Internet was a different place in the 80s, and many Unix systems exposed a service, chargen, that just sent a stream of characters. It's a useful debugging tool if your networks aren't highly resilient. It was fun to send a packet saying "Hey, can you send lots of characters." It's more fun if you send it with a spoofed source of the broadcast address so that every machine in a network suddenly gets a stream of characters. (Both are fun from the perspective of the attacker.) There are lots of current equivalents. Some of them are from servers, like DNS, that are designed to serve all callers. Others are systems like memcache, which are designed to return results as quickly as possible. Running on UDP to avoid setup costs and not authenticating are great properties if speed is all that matters. And if there are no controls on who can call the system, then it can be used to send data to any system whose UDP packets you can fake.

Caches, by design, want to send lots of data quickly. That's great for attackers, and caches can amplify attacks by a factor of tens of thousands. That is, the attacker sends bytes of request, and the system sends back tens of thousands of bytes.

Amplification doesn't happen only with network requests: the video transcoding request discussed earlier in the "Compute" section of this chapter amplifies both in compute and network bandwidth costs.

Authentication Targets

The attacker doesn't need to be logged in to flood your network with packets. They do need to be logged in to run a fork bomb. Authorized users can usually consume more resources than anonymous ones, and that plays into why DDoS attacks can be so irksome: anyone can join in, and chasing them all down is uneconomical. Retail store websites will expose potentially expensive search to anyone to help sell. Others may restrict more expensive queries to authenticated users.

Ephemeral or Persistent

Some interruptions are transient. When a tractor beam stops, a ship can fly away. Others are more permanent. When Han Solo shoots a communications console, someone needs to send a repair tech.

There are attacks that work until the attacker (or their computer) loses interest, and there are attacks that work until you clean them up. From the attacker's perspective, when the packets stop, the fun stops, but if your disk is full, your disk is full. So, networks will often recover fairly quickly at the network layer, and network load balancers and similar tools will recover more slowly (if they fail over, do they fail back? Should they, or is the secondary the primary until it has problems?). Similarly, compute attacks like fork bombs went away with a `kill()` or a reboot. Thus, attacks on compute or network are mostly transient, while attacks on storage, bandwidth, and battery require intervention.

Early in my career, DDoS and compute attacks were the most common form of DoS, so most attacks were transient. A little noticed impact of the rise of the cloud and IoT is a change to a property of threats: persistence is more common. This change in property is unusual. Despite the popularity of phrases like "the fast moving world of cyber," if we step back a little bit, threats remain remarkably stable. The first six chapters of this book follow "STRIDE" because even though it is a decades-old model, *it remains useful today*. Attacks such as spoofing users or login screens continue, and remote code execution via memory corruption has not been solved (although attack techniques have improved dramatically to overcome evolving defenses). This is useful to you as an engineer, because the knowledge in this book will serve you well over many years.

Direct or Emergent

Denial of service often directly threatens a resource, such as network capacity, and when the attack stops, things come back to normal. But there are also emergent denial-of-service threats.

Those who've worked on complex systems know that they display emergent and unexpected behavior under load, including cascade and bloat behaviors, and that these can pile up. If a system is sending lots of messages because it can't get through to some service, then resources, especially network and storage, can be consumed. If many systems are unable to reach that service, their logging and reconnect attempts may magnify the problem. This is not just theoretical. In December 2021, Amazon's AWS East-1 displayed exactly this behavior. And it gummed up not only AWS but a great many services that depend on it (Amazon, 2021).

Denial of Service in Specific Technologies

While the mechanisms of denial of service are broad, the ways it manifests, like many other threats, has technology-specific aspects. Budget and battery matter for cloud and IoT, respectively. Authentication services can amplify denial or service, and some standards even encourage a version of that. Some deride blockchain as a denial of service on the energy grid, and there's certainly have been instances where miners moving en masse to locations with cheap energy has stressed local capacities. There do not seem to be AI-specific elements of denial of service, although some would claim that ever-greater costs to train and operate models or neural nets themselves constitute a denial of service.

Authentication Services

Authentication services can come under denial-of-service attacks, and when they do, the availability of the rest of your system only matters to those who are logged in (and aren't automatically logged out). If your authentication service relies on text messaging, then connectivity failures, including people who are simply in a bad reception zone, can't log in.

Some security standards call for exponential backoff, and attackers can turn such systems into denial-of-service services by just attempting to log in. Consider very small exponents, such as 1.01 or 1.1. I was going to comment on the odds that your auditors would ever notice, but Han Solo asks that we never tell him the odds. (I won't, and they won't.)

Cloud

The cloud brings us an interesting defensive opportunity as we come under attack: we can make trade-offs between spending money and accepting slowdowns. (It's more flexible and useful if we make decisions before we come under attack.)

There are predictable spikes in traffic. One is a Christmas morning spike as new devices are brought online, impacting both services and bandwidth in predictable and intense waves. When power comes back on after a storm outage, there's a version of that spike, but it's smaller and less predictable.

Protocol Design

The design of protocols offers opportunities both to design for graceful degradation under load and to contribute to denial-of-service attacks against others. This applies even if you're designing a restful API on top of HTTP over TLS. If you are outside that space, consider how your design will operate under pressure, if it has the ability to say "ask again later" and how it might be used to amplify attacks.

IoT and Mobile

Battery issues will be exceptionally important to IoT devices, many of which have batteries that are not replaceable. For widely distributed devices, bringing a battery pack to the device may not be feasible. Battery recharge cycle counts may also result in denial of service.

In the Mirai attack discussed at the beginning of the chapter, IoT devices with default passwords were used to form a botnet. IoT devices, even ones that have been working, may be impacted by a "Christmas morning spike" attack on cloud services. Devices that rely heavily on the cloud can be impacted. In 2016, the Petnet pet feeder stopped working because of a server issue. (Apparently, they didn't properly dogfood the system.)

Smart devices can also contribute to TCP-amplification denial-of-service attacks. These are surprising, because of the TCP three-way handshake, but there are a set of problems that device designers should be aware of, including sending a great many RST packets, SYN-ACKs, or using PSH packets to send data before the handshake is complete. Marc Kührer of Ruhr University Bochum and his collaborators continue to find innovative ways to abuse TCP for denial-of-service attacks, and many of those attacks seem to relate to specific choices made by IoT vendors.

Many smart devices degrade poorly when their cloud disappears. These disappearances can be temporary or even permanent. The permanent ones can happen for budget reasons. For example, Logitech used to sell a remote called the Harmony. When the company discontinued its cloud service, it had the effect of "essentially bricking the otherwise functional smart remotes devices." The company relented in the face of the outcry (Palladino, 2017).

IoT, and in particular phones and wearables, may be subject to weather, droppage, and similar accidental physical denials of service. It can be hard to distinguish accidents from enemy action, especially if your device isn't well-hardened. There was a case of an IoT lock, which, after you used a suction cup to unscrew the "jar lid" back, you could open it with a screwdriver (McCarthy, 2018). Devices that are hardened and tested are more expensive. The standard for safes involves testing their ability to withstand 15 or 30 minutes of attack by a skilled attacker. A TL-15 safe is often $1,000 or more and is quite different than the $100–200 safe you'll see at an office supply store. Don't forget that devices will be used in stores, offices, and other places that get visitors. People's homes get visitors, and some people rent out their homes. Other devices are used in apartment buildings, where the building owner and the residents may disagree about the devices or who should control them.

Defenses

Defenses against denial of service include having abundant resources, graceful degradation, and systems testing. In this section, we'll explore each of these defenses.

Abundance and Quotas

Abundance is the simplest defense against many forms of denial of service. When the Internet was in competition with other networking technologies, quality of service was raised as a feature of the legacy carrier backbones. Internet folks liked to say that quantity of service beats quality of service every time. But eventually, abundance runs out, and we need to discuss economics. That includes artificial scarcity such as quotas, but also thinking about the economics of scaling or degradation.

When your system supports them, quotas for compute or storage ensure that subsystems can't run out of control. This helps even "single-purpose" servers. If you cap consumption to "most" rather than "all," your logs and systems management tools keep functioning when that business function runs amok. Similar to scarcity, network providers can help with defenses against bandwidth-flooding denial of service at the Internet layer. (Defenses against radio spectrum flooding are a complex topic.)

Designing for availability can also include pushing intelligence to the edge. Toward the end of the first prequel, *The Phantom Menace*, Anakin Skywalker saves the day by destroying a single Droid Control Ship, and all the droids shut down. The baddies learn their lesson and move intelligence to the edge, to each droid. You can learn the same lesson. For example, the Petnet pet feeder could have sent `cron` jobs to the device so that it wasn't reliant on the network or cloud service being available. Content distribution networks (such as Akamai or Cloudflare) are helpful for protecting web services from DoS. Some will also allow you to push business logic of various forms.

Regardless of your use of quotas, its crucial to consider graceful degradation and resilience testing. Even more than other security properties, availability is a systems property. A system is only as secure, or as available, as its weakest link.

Graceful Degradation

Graceful degradation is a systems property that can be engineered at many layers of the system. Like security, it's easier to design it in than to bolt it on, and the operations community has a great deal of experience trying to maximize the availability of systems whose availability was treated as a simple problem.

It's easy to fall into thinking about simple request/response models. Many systems are far more complex, and it's important to engineer both component availability and service-level resilience. At the service level, being aware of which requests are expensive, and gracefully turning them off can allow the overall system to provide gracefully degraded service. To the extent that you control the protocols in use, being able to send a "too busy, come back later" message is helpful. Your attackers will ignore it, but your friendly clients can stop contributing to the problem.

Even without such a message, "client" components should be designed to back off gracefully, rather than becoming part of the problem with rapid and insistent retries.

The components being attacked should be able to actively refuse expensive operations to let the less expensive activities continue. In the extreme, that may be a server just sending "overloaded" error messages, but doing so is far better than disappearing. Your clients can start backing off intelligently.

There are a variety of graceful backoff algorithms. Most involve exponentially slower requests, where a system will wait a random amount between 0 and 2^n seconds, sometimes starting at something a little larger than zero, and sometimes with the backoff or recounts capped. Whatever algorithm you choose should be designed to avoid hammering the servers 2^n seconds after the servers drop offline. (Naive exponential backoff can have precisely this effect.)

Similarly, you should recover gracefully from an abnormal shutdown. If your device knows it lost power, an extra little delay will help your service recover gracefully, rather than getting hammered when power comes on after a disaster.

Resilience Testing

Again, resilience is a systems property. Checking that each component is hard to tamper with should roughly compose to a system that's hard to tamper with. (Confused deputies are a primary way this composition fails.) In contrast, testing that each component of a system is available under load tells you less about the availability of the system as a whole.

Resilience testing is important. Cloud systems often have strange dependency chains that are best exposed by testing, with tools like chaos monkeys. Intentionally breaking your cloud service is a wise practice.

Resilience is easier to achieve with a business model. When Logitech remotes didn't require a subscription, there was little budget to update the cloud backend. But who wants a subscription for a remote control?

Maintaining a resilient and tested infrastructure for emergency administration and disaster response can appear expensive until you don't have it. Google reputedly maintains a separate network of IRC servers, designed to be resilient when everything else is failing.

Budget management services are a must for elastic cloud services. These can be explicit, and for smaller cloud services, it may be sensible to simply react and beg for mercy if your bill jumps 10- or 100-fold in a month.

Both graceful degradation and resilience testing are covered over many chapters of the excellent *Building Secure and Reliable Systems* (O'Reilly, 2020).

Conclusion

Building the second Death Star so it was fully functional as a battle station is an unusual response to the unusually thorough and permanent denial-of-service attack on its predecessor. But graceful accumulation of features and properties to face anticipated threats can be as important as graceful degradation. Before moving on from praise for the Empire, I would like to take a moment to say I hope you can plan for resilience without such massive loss of life and resources, and I also hope you're not working on anything planet-destroying.

All systems have constraints, and all resources are scarce. Design and testing mean that even if the attackers have analyzed your defenses and found a weakness, you can maintain availability.

6

Expansion of Authority and Isolation

"These aren't the droids you're looking for," Ben Kenobi tells the Stormtroopers who have just stopped him. On whose authority? In fact, this is the first time we see the application of Jedi mind control because, in fact, those are the droids the Stormtroopers are looking for. Kenobi shouldn't be able to convince the Stormtroopers to let them move along. He uses his power to expand his effective authority and accomplish his goal.

> In the prequels, Kenobi is a general and was removed from rank only as a result of a coup and an order to commit war crimes. Star Wars geeks may focus on the idea that Kenobi is still a general. So, at a stretch, he might be able to issue orders to troops. Regardless, he does not assert authority as a general but rather uses his Jedi powers. So...that's not the argument you're looking for.

The *E* in STRIDE stands for "expansion of authority." Historically, it has also stood for "elevation of privilege," "escalation of privilege," or "privilege escalation." The *privilege* versions are all synonymous. They're also better known than the expansion of authority definition. For most of this chapter, we'll consider authority in a broad sense and get precise about how these all relate only at the end of the chapter. If all these terms are new to you, focus on the idea of authority. If you've been exposed to the privilege frame, stay with me. At the end of the chapter, I'll explain why I'm shifting my thinking to authority.

Expansion of authority can feel different from other threats. Tampering or spoofing can feel like mechanisms or even goals. Expansion can appear (or even be) more like an effect or a stepping stone. But each is a threat: an action an attacker can take, and a threat to a property we want a system to have. Expansion of authority is a threat to the authorization system.

Authority means "the effects that a program may cause on objects it can access, either directly by permission, or indirectly by permitted interactions with other programs" (Miller, 2005). Generally, there are three ways to control the use of authority. They are permissions, attenuation, and isolation.

Permissions may be the easiest to understand. For example, Unix protects itself by setting the ownership and permissions of files in /etc, /usr/bin, and many other places on which the operating system relies. Attenuation means to reduce or limit; the login process will attenuate its own authority by changing user ID from root before spawning a shell for a regular user. Thus, that shell doesn't inherit the authority to call the setuid API or bind to low-numbered ports. Isolation means software or hardware that limits what the code can do. For example, a user can send signals or attach a debugger only to their own processes, not those of other users. That's isolation provided by the kernel.

Moving down from Unix to raw hardware, isolation is provided by the CPU's execution levels (rings). And moving off a single system to networks, isolation is provided by firewalls.

Another way to think about these defenses is that the second Death Star is a fully armed and operational battle station—it can implement permissions and use Stormtroopers to enforce them. It also has a shield, operated on a small moon, which provides isolation for it. We'll talk about all three—permissions, attenuation, and isolation—in the "Defenses" section.

Expanding authority means moving from one level of authority to a greater one: from unable to run code to able to do so; from regular user to root to kernel; from unable to set permissions to the admin of a cloud service; from "random droid trapped in a net" to god of the Ewoks. Figure 6.1 shows an example of how this works on a Unix system. Luke's processes can interfere with each other, but Luke's cannot interfere with Leia's (and vice versa). Leia might expand her authority to be able to run code as root, and as a general, she might claim that authority over rebel systems. Because she's wise, she probably would choose to use a limited account to reduce the impact of any mistakes she makes. We often talk about "lower levels" of the system, and from that point of view, Figure 6.1 is drawn inverted to align with the "higher privileges" framing.

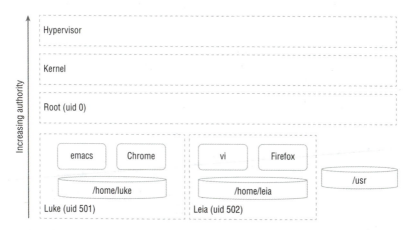

FIGURE 6.1 Authority levels

Many well-known attacks and attack types have authority expansion as their effect.

Log4shell led to logged data being executed. The "Shellshock" vulnerability in bash let environment variables be executed as commands. (As an aside, many of these have *shell* in their name because getting to unattenuated shell access is a powerful milestone for the attacker.)

Moving to families of attack, SQL injection lets web users embed SQL commands in strings passed by web parsers. The SQL interpreter treats those strings as commands. The web parser does not mean to give the web user the authority to craft commands. Cross-site scripting (XSS) exceeds the authority of the person crafting a URL to cause those who use that URL to run commands that the attacker intended. Stack smashing leads to code execution, either local or remote.

Locally, stack smashing might exploit a vulnerability in a setuid root program and let an unprivileged user run arbitrary commands with root's full authority. Remotely, a program that accepts connections over the Internet allows those Internet-connected users to run commands. You'll learn specifics about the issues that allow these expansions in Chapter 8, "Parsing and Corruption."

Authority is granted by system owners to principals, and by principals to programs. For example, as shown in Figure 6.2, George Lucas is a system owner. He creates an account "george" on his laptop. User george can set permissions on the file "Empire Strikes Back script."

He can also create accounts for his collaborators Leigh Brackett and Lawrence Kasdan to log in to his computer. They're principals, and they're represented by those accounts. As they run programs like emacs or vi (obviously) to edit the script, they implicitly grant authority to those programs to access any file that their user ID can access.

Moving from the local system to the network, the authority to communicate on various networks implies a responsibility to identify and categorize remote connections. Those connections should get only limited access to the listener's authorities. Those authorities include calling operating system APIs and acting on behalf of, as a deputy to, some principal. For example, if a program, let's call it "login," creates a shell on behalf of a user, then that shell has tremendous authority, including reading and writing files, creating and deleting them, and invoking other programs. Another program, say, "simple-httpd," might be designed with more limited authority: to read files.

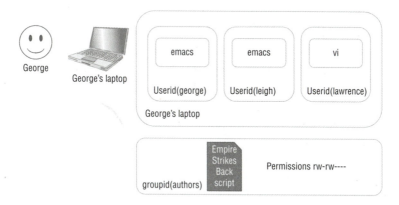

FIGURE 6.2 Authority grants

At least that would be the intent. Programs often have lots of authority and may even try to attenuate or delegate that in various controlled ways. A simple httpd might have a notion of accounts and let specific accounts see specific files. A result of that requirement is that it must have access to all those files, at least at some point in its execution. It may implement code to check that that user can access that file, or the httpd may shed that access by setting its user ID to that user and defer the checking to something else.

Many expansion of authority threats involve violating the intentionally designed controls, while others rely on unexpected behavior of those controls.

In this chapter, we'll look at those common privileges that are both targets and jumping-off points for common forms of attack. Each of these violates the goal of authorization. Authorization is much like its English meaning: to give permission, assent, or approval. Accounts like root have permission to do a great deal more to your computer than a website does.

Expansion Mechanisms and Effects

While the details are infinitely varied, the mechanisms attackers use to expand authority are all fairly similar. Jedi, Sith, and even bounty hunters sneak onto a ship, and their local access gives them complete access to the computers. In our world, vulnerabilities that allow for remote code execution by a parsing or execution error result in the attacker having more authority. These are discussed in more detail in Chapter 8, "Parsing and Corruption." To give you a brief idea, remote code execution can happen because an instruction processor is tricked into treating data (from input) as code. This happens when a CPU gets instructions at the end of a stack. They also happen when a Unix shell sees a semicolon or backticks, indicating the next command, or executes the contents of the backticks. They happen when a SQL parser gets a semicolon or forward ticks. In each case, there is code/data confusion.

An attacker can also gain authority when we intentionally run their code not knowing what it is.

Let's consider this common pattern:

```
curl $URL | bash
```

In this instance, bash doesn't know where `curl` is getting its data. The Unix design philosophy included "small programs that do one thing well" and combining them via pipes. Because they were generally running in the same user context, they assumed that input wasn't malicious. What would be the point? The bash shell tends to expect that its input is from a trusted source.

If you haven't run across the pattern, `curl` is a command-line web browser, and it will fetch the contents of a (presumably remote) URL and feed those commands directly to the bash shell, giving that site the authority of your local shell and probably installing (at least) the software you want. Some security people get apoplectic at the pattern, which is slightly worse than other installer methods. I don't like the pattern for interactive use and worry about it more when it's used in build scripts reaching out to arbitrary sites, because it bypasses code or artifact repositories and so makes your builds less reliable.

Code in the middle of such a chain will frequently, unwittingly, help attackers demonstrate that point. Sometimes these alter control flow; other times the flow of control remains in accordance with the original design, and arguments or effects are unexpected.

For example, SQL injection happens because a web server includes its input in the SQL commands it sends to the database. The web server's control flow is unaltered. The database trusts the web front end to send it well-formed code.

Running code written by someone else usually results in that code having all the authority that your account does. (This is less the case on modern phone operating systems.) This applies equally to compiled code or a shell script. Web browsers are an unusual case. They work hard to attenuate the authority they grant to HTML, JavaScript, or WASM, and even that granted to browser extensions.

Code that carefully tests its inputs for validity for carefully defined purposes may be attacked if it tests that input while the attacker can still change it. For example, if you put your validation code in JavaScript that runs in a browser, it is trivial for the browser owner to tamper with it.

Code is not the only thing you might regret taking as input. If your program takes filenames and if it can act on behalf of many users—for example a web server or a mail server—then you have to ensure that the user can act on that specific file. This problem is hard because of complexities such as canonicalization of filenames, symbolic links, union views of filesystems, or quarantines for Internet files. This is an example of the "confused deputy" problem, which we'll discuss more throughout this chapter.

Canonicalization Is Hard

To make the complexities more concrete, let's consider restricting access to the file .HTAccess, as served by the Apache web server on a Mac. Should Apache HTTPd recognize that as the file that defines access control? The Mac HFS filesystem is case insensitive, while Apache is generally written with an assumption that the underlying filesystem is case sensitive. So moving a perfect copy of a website from Linux to macOS might change its behavior. (Or perhaps Apache accounts for this—checking requires more than grepping the code.) Alternately, still on the Mac, consider the case of the humble Calculator app in /Applications. If you open /Applications in the Finder, you'll see the app. But if you open a terminal and type ls /Applications, it's not there (in macOS Monterey, anyway). Which is right? I have an opinion, but what's more important is for you to understand that these views of the filesystem can get tricky quickly.

If you don't know the answers, how well can you carefully delegate authority?

The final major cause of expansion of authority is permissions whose technical meaning is broader than a person intended. This can happen because of usability flaws in an access control system or because controls are relaxed for debugging, and once things work, they're rarely further tightened up.

There are many starting and ending points when someone expands authority, and Table 6.1 shows some common examples. (Specific brand names are shown only as examples.) I'm using "normal" to mean an account without administrator rights or privileges.

TABLE 6.1 Common Authority Expansions

Environment	Starting Authority	Ending Authority	Comment
Traditional Unix server	Remote entity	Normal user	Remote code execution
	Normal user	Root	Classic "privilege escalation"
Multiuser Unix server	Normal user Anakin	Normal user Obi-Wan	Sometimes called "horizontal" elevation
Windows desktop	Normal user	Local admin	
	Local admin	Domain admin	
Mobile device	Local app (Angry Birds)	Local apps (Angry Birds, Bank)	
	Person with device	Full authority over device	Jailbreak
Cloud	User	Enterprise administrator	See also Table 6.2
	Any less privileged	Cloud admin	

Authority in Specific Scenarios

As complex as authority is for traditional desktop computers, at least their span of control was local, and the user interfaces can be rich. Who has which authority is often incomprehensible with smart devices, sometimes by design and sometimes because of lack of design. This boiled to the surface with years of exploitation and patching for jailbreaking phones. Cloud systems quickly require complexity. Each of these will be treated in its own section. First, we'll discuss the new models of authority that blockchains are exploring.

Bitcoin popularized a new authority mechanism: proof of work. Having done the work to mine a new coin, the chain was extended in a way that all participants had to accept to make future commitments to the chain. It's unclear how important this will be over time.

AI/ML systems don't have a lot of unique expansion of authority threats, but they do suffer an interesting issue, which is that an attacker who can feed you training data has implicit capability to change your model and thus the actions of your system. This is slightly outside the strict definition of authority, because ultimately it's people who are empowered to select the training data.

Confused Deputies

Up to this point in the book, I've been using the term *confused deputy* somewhat loosely. It's time to ground it in authority and explain it more fully. First, C3-PO is not a confused deputy because he never gets tricked into using his capabilities to help the Empire.

A program we see as a deputy usually has some extra authority and tries to ensure that it uses it in constrained ways. A *confused* deputy uses its authority in a way that, with the benefit of hindsight, it shouldn't. There are distinct groups of programs that display the same sort of confusion.

- Setuid programs insufficiently reduce their authority and inadvertently provide it to others.
- Daemons—either network listening daemons, which pass authority to remote callers, or local privileged daemons, which pass it to local callers. Sometimes one daemon enthusiastically serves both populations at once! Avoiding that anti-pattern informs the design of the qmail mail transport system.

- Exposed API servers are a special case of daemon code. This includes public APIs, app APIs, and private APIs.
- Internet of Things gateways, including hubs and cloud systems.
- Normal programs, such as zip.

This may lead you to ask: is there anything that is not a deputy? Yes. Most video games are not. Classic programs like Microsoft Word are not, but it may become one as it becomes more cloud integrated, especially if the cloud can direct where it stores or caches files; where it collects, installs, or runs fonts; where it collects templates and what it calls them; or otherwise influence how it acts.

We met the zipslip issues in Chapter 5, "Denial of Service and Availability." You may remember they're what happens when the creator of a zip file specifies full paths and the unzipper writes to those paths. Doing so, it uses the authority of the person running "unzip" on behalf of the person who wrote the zip file. It made sense to bring them up since we were learning about surprising things that happen when you uncompress data. But really, the confusion is about how authority is used. We were previously talking about the impact, not the threat.

Another, older zip issue was preservation of permissions. The attacker created a zip with a setuid file in it, and unzip faithfully preserved it on decompression (Galacia, 2005). The setuid program would be setuid whatever user ran unzip. If you use the root account routinely, it would thus be setuid root; otherwise, it would allow horizontal (user to user) expansion, as shown in Table 6.1.

A web server is an example of a daemon deputy. Early web servers mirrored filesystems: making the directory `/users/obiwan/public_html/` available as `jedicouncil.galaxy/~obiwan/` made it easy to deploy a web server and have users opt-in by creating a directory. The deputy pattern's trade-offs contributed to the rapid growth of the Web, and the pattern also made it feasible to confuse those web servers.

In each case, the issue is someone can specify enough control information that the program acts on their behalf. This can be because of parsing failures with filenames, race conditions, policy specification, or interpretation problems. The canonical example of a filename parsing issue was reading `../../etc/password`, or in today's world, `/etc/shadow`. Naïve filters might remove `..` before, say, Unicode decoding, which conveniently translates %2E2E into `..` and now your string is problematic again. Race conditions happen when a temporary filename is predictable, when a link can be inserted and changed, or otherwise when a gap between the time of check and the time of use allows an attacker to redefine what the deputy is looking at.

But "deputy" is a fine description of a lot of code that attempts to attenuate, or even simply handle complex data types (such as an unzipper). We build deputies as we build abstraction layers or isolation boundary. Similarly, in the world of very small devices, deputies are a common design pattern to let those very small devices communicate more broadly.

Generally, parsing problems that lead to an attacker being able to run arbitrary code (the sort covered in "Parsing and Corruption") are not seen as confused deputy issues.

Threats vs. Impacts

If someone threatens to sue you, the threat is the lawsuit. A lawsuit can have many impacts: your time and money are spent on lawyers. The court may impose damages. If you mouth off to the judge, they may threaten you with contempt, and the penalty might be jail. Even if your behavior raises an eyebrow, very few people would be so pedantic as to argue with the sentence "The judge is threatening to throw me in jail for contempt!" This overlap between threat and impact is a part of the way we speak. Even experienced security people will conflate them, perhaps to our detriment.

Internet of Things

In Chapter 1, "Spoofing and Authenticity," we considered a set of scenarios from the perspective of spoofing, which is crucial, but we also need to consider authorization more broadly. A "valet key" doesn't allow access to the car's trunk or glovebox. Many thermostats have a "hotel mode" that constrains available temperatures. If someone sells a device at a yard sale, is it easy for the new owner to remove cloud authorization? Similarly, when a couple breaks up, can whoever ends up with a device or devices quickly and confidently set the new authorizations?

Authority on devices is often distributed in complex or even baroque ways between the device maker, owner, and authorized users. Common patterns include commands being sent from cloud services, often as a proxy for apps. Device hubs running platforms like Zigbee, Powered by Alexa, or Apple Home are also authorized to run commands, possibly with the participation of an app. So, for example, if you use Alexa to tell a third-party soundbar to play a song, Alexa (and thus AWS) has authority to control the soundbar. If you use Apple home to control the lock on your door, the hub and Apple's iCloud servers probably have the authority to unlock your door. The details are very implementation dependent. The best of them may relay signed commands and be unable to initiate the commands themselves. The very best will also have those signed commands contain both dates and nonces to prevent replay attacks.

Mobile

In mobile, apps are isolated. So you not only can elevate but expand: "move sideways" between permissions of various apps. This, too, is an elevation of privilege. If you are running as App A and take over App B, you go from permission set A, granted to your app, to A+B, which may be small but was not intended by the designer of B, or the operating system that should have constrained or managed those permissions. Calling this elevation can be confusing, and this "horizontal elevation" contributed to me preferring *expansion*.

There are also the issues of jailbreaking or sideloading. *Jailbreaking* refers to breaking the manufacturer's controls on what applications can be executed; *sideloading* refers to various ways of bypassing those controls or loosened versions thereof. This can include loading an Android package via USB or installing with an IoS developer certificate.

Depending on your point of view, jailbreaking and sideloading are people either taking control of devices they've paid for or breaking important controls designed to keep mobile systems free of the threats that plague more traditional (Windows) computers. However you feel about the moral answers to these questions, these are questions of technical authority. The phone and operating system manufacturers reserve, for themselves, the authority to decide what code is run on which device. The authority rules gets no clearer when we add corporate mobile device management tools.

Cloud

When we consider infrastructure or platforms as a service, we've all gotten used to running code in the cloud, and we accept assurance that the cloud provider won't interfere with our instances. Is that decision technically grounded? (We can consider that question separately from the contractual obligations.) Most cloud systems run on something approximating other server computers: Linux on Intel or ARM processors. They're nominally managed by software that runs underneath the virtual machines, containers, or "serverless" processes that we use as we deploy our cloud systems. That software has authority, like root. The cloud infrastructure software generally attenuates how that authority is exercised. Either no one or a very limited set of people can log in interactively. We expect that interactive shells are forbidden because they're unscalable and a source of implementation error, but we have limited tools with which to check that. (There are designs that are stronger, which allow software to process encrypted data or to perform database operations on data that's never in plaintext. There are also designs that seem to sprinkle magic cryptography dust around, without ever addressing the fact that the service operator has the authority to change the software that uses that key, to read memory from the VM host layer, or otherwise to bypass that expensive magic dust.)

When we move to software as a service, the software designer has probably implemented an authority system. It may or may not be well considered. Frequently, systems distribute authority, with hooks for events like login or message receipt that deliver great flexibility to the customer—or an attacker who's broken in. Even when the designers have not implemented such, "software robots" or other automation systems may layer them on. Reasoning about the security of these systems can get very complicated very quickly.

For example, as shown in Table 6.2, a software system could easily have three major groups of authority: that at their cloud provider, that within their cloud account, and those for their customers. The first is entirely outside their control, the second they must manage using the tools provided by their cloud provider, and the third they must define.

TABLE 6.2 Authority in a Cloud System

Authority Category	Levels of Authority
Cloud provider, say, AWS	Root @ AWS
	Administrator at AWS
	Administrator for S3
	Customer service rep for S3
Company deploying SaaS on AWS, say, Slack	Slack's AWS account administrator
	Slack's IAM administrators group
	Slack employee, AWS service user
	Slack employee, root @ instance (assuming they deploy virtual machines)

(continued)

TABLE 6.2 (Continued)

Authority Category	Levels of Authority
Slack customer: rebelalliance .slack.com	General Leia (company admin) Luke (Slack user)
Slack Application provider	Giphy can read a channel and post
	Google Apps can read a channel and change permissions on documents, create calendar invites and more in its own system

Defenses

There are two types of important defensive patterns. One group is what your code does; the other is the context in which your code executes. Defenses against expansion and elevation attacks are conceptually simple. Unfortunately, despite that simplicity, they're often practically either intricate or nuanced.

When your code takes input from untrustworthy parties, it parses that input and acts on it in various ways. When you use insufficient care, your code will give attackers their way.

So it's crucial that you don't accidentally create a parser, a deputy, or a permission system. Thoughtful design and avoidance of technical debt will repay itself quickly in both security and reliability, perhaps more than any other investment in security. The trouble is these things sneak up on you, especially parsing. If you wake up to discover you've accidentally created such a thing, the best move is to take off and nuke it from orbit. Then rebuild cleanly. However difficult that happens to be, it will probably be less difficult, over time, than maintaining it. However, management will often demure for a variety of business or psychological reasons.

Those business reasons, along with the general difficulty of getting code right even without those categories of problems, means that isolation tools and design patterns are incredibly useful. (This is also a place where "zero trust" can come in handy.) These tools include the following:

- Permissions or capabilities.
- Sandboxes.
- Containers.
- "Side-effect-free" code such as Lamba functions. (A Lambda function runs code where someone else provides the server infrastructure, and the Lambda can't alter any files on disk. Amazon took the term from computer science; Google and Microsoft call the same thing Functions, as in Azure Functions.)
- "Phoenix" systems that are regularly burnt down and rebuilt. (That takes away an attacker's current access, but if you rebuild exactly the same system, the same exploit will work when the attacker uses it again.)

The final step for each defense is to ensure its usability: by the normal humans who use it and also by the developers who develop on top of it.

Least Privilege and Separation of Privilege

"Your weapons, you will not need them," Yoda tells Luke as he enters a place that's strong with the dark side of the force. Yoda is advocating for the principle of least privilege. Without weapons, Luke is less likely to hurt himself.[1]

An attacker who exploits your code has added its privileges to theirs. They may go from unable to run arbitrary code on a machine to able to do so. Once they can run arbitrary code, they may be able to achieve their objectives, or there may be additional barriers. Those barriers are imposed by an architectural feature. If your code runs as

---

[1]If you have other justifications, I'll just say…the danger is only what you take with you.

domain admin or root, then the attacker can likely do what they want without further barriers, because it has all the privilege. This is such an anti-pattern that in recent versions of macOS, Apple has been steadily reducing the power of the root account, and by the early 2020s, root was no longer able to alter the core operating system files.

The "root can do anything" pattern is incomprehensibly danger-ous. Actually, that's not quite right. Giving all the authority to an account (root, domain admin) is *comprehensibly* dangerous. Security professionals enjoy arguing about how hard it is to become root from a normal user account, and the answer is complex to quantify. If you develop code to run as a normal user from the start, there's plenty of security and reliability benefits and very little downside.

We can contrast code that has all, or most, privileges with the opposite pattern: code that has only the privilege it needs to accom-plish specific goals. The phrases *least privilege* and *separation of privi-lege* (or duty) are common in security. Least privilege refers to minimizing a program's authority: designing it to work with as little authority as it can. Separation of privilege means giving the authority that a system needs to a set of programs, separated in meaningful ways, like running as different Unix user IDs. (You may have noticed that I've switched the words *privilege* and *authority* here; we'll return to the goal later.) Separation of duty refers to breaking responsibilities across people. For example, a bank manager has the keys to the safe deposit room, and I have a key to my safe deposit box. You can simi-larly design a system that separates the authority granted to principals and thus programs.

Limiting privileges and the "principle of least privilege" seem like excellent ideas. There's an old joke: the difference between theory and practice is that in theory there's no difference. A first step is to ensure that programs can run as "a regular user" rather than administrator. I'd like to assert that first step is obvious, but looking out at the world, that's empirically untrue.

In the early days of Windows, the default user was an administra-tor. Developers shipped programs that assumed they always ran as administrator, often for no reason except they never bothered to test if they could run without administrative authority, and so they put various files in directories that later became protected.

Microsoft spent the better part of a decade increasing the pressure on those software creators. Some were companies that were still around and that upgraded the latest versions of their software to run without such privileges. Other software, well, the company was gone, it was created by the boss's nephew during an internship and the code's gone, or there's no budget. So that difference between theory and practice has a very long tail.

Both writing your code to run as a normal user and using a normal user account day to day dramatically improves security.

In practice, deciding if you've achieved "least" can be complex. Programs that are very flexible, such as the Windows Shell, the macOS Finder, and web browsers, present a challenge for the principle of least privilege. In these instances, "privilege management" systems that temporarily grant increased authority can help implement least privilege.

In more constrained circumstances, least privilege implementations can learn from the qmail mail transport of the late 1990s, which has a small constellation of programs. Each program runs as a separate Unix user, and most of the programs have the authority to read from exactly one directory and write to one other. (This is implemented with a mix of user and group permissions.) Thus, the qmail family of programs are designed, as a whole, with the least authority that they need, and the authorities are separated between the various parts of the system. Figure 6.3 shows how this works in more detail. You don't need to understand the details to continue, but you can see that code runs as five user IDs (qmaild, qmailq, qmailr, qmails, and root). Qmaild listens on port 25, collects mail, and passes it to the queuing system. Qmails sends it either to a remote system (via qmailr) or to a local user. In the local user case, qmail-lspawn, running as root, creates a user process for local mail delivery. Because only that process runs as root, it can be subjected to greater scrutiny.

Figure 6.3 is redrawn from a paper on the security architecture of qmail (Hafiz, 2004). If you'd like to learn more, it's a worthwhile side quest. That qmail was supplanted by Postfix had little to do with security.

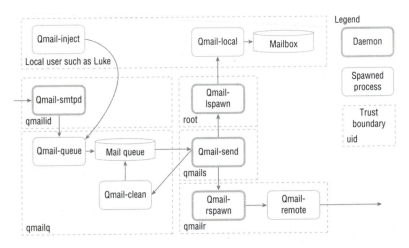

FIGURE 6.3 Major qmail processes

A similar sort of design can be implemented in modern microservice architectures. This requires that the permissions assigned to those services are considered and managed, rather than a spaghetti of calls.

Architecture as Barrier

Perhaps you can simplify your parsing, perhaps not. Parsing remains risky, and the more exposed code is, the more sensible it is to isolate that code. The earliest patterns for this leveraged accounts and permissions. Over time, Unix daemons moved from running as root to running as their own user ID, and permissions for those accounts were restricted. A modern version of this is illustrated by the previous qmail example. Running as a separate user ID is a form of isolation, which is a crucial part of any resilient defensive strategy.

Permissions

Traditional permissions can be used to protect files and other objects from other principals. However, permissions have problems of expressiveness, and as Mark Miller writes, "In practice, programmers control access partially by manipulating the access graph and partially by writing programs whose behavior attenuates the authority that flows through them." (We'll delve into Dr. Miller's work on authority later in the chapter.) Understanding the interplay of permissions was hard even when systems were simpler, and Cops (a very early system configuration checking tool) included a graph construction tool that looked at all permissions for ways to exploit them.

Capabilities

A *capability* is a specific software pattern, and a pretty nifty one. It combines two things that are often thought of separately: identity and access. If you have the *capability*, you have both. The *capability* equivalent to (read, /etc/hosts) might be 789432. You call open(789432), and you can read the hosts file. Similarly, (write, /etc/hosts) might be 723190. They're similar to file handles or secure pointers.

Of course, the numbers are much longer to make them unguessable, or, in some implementations, it includes a message authentication code to make guessing easy to catch. Thus, giving a program a *capability* explicitly grants the authority associated with that *capability*. Because the numbers are unguessable, programs can use only the capabilities they're given. This contrasts with setting permissions to a principal and results in much more strictly limited access.

The term *capability* is a nifty bit of naming, because it works both as a noun, meaning that software object, and as a verb, the ability to do something. In this subsection I've been italicizing *capability* to mean the specific software object, in the hope of not being too clever by half.

Unfortunately, we have no Emperor who can force-lightning people for overloading a term, and *capability* has another, incompatible meaning. According to the capabilities man page: "Starting with kernel 2.2, Linux divides the privileges traditionally associated with superuser into distinct units, known as capabilities, which can be independently enabled and disabled."

Isolation Tools

Isolation tools provide a property called *non-interference*. That means whatever a developer does, their code can't interfere with someone else's code. It's not optional; the isolation tools prevent it. Files can't be opened; memory can't be read or written to. Isolation also means an attacker whose code takes over the intentionally running code also can't interfere. This was an essential goal in building time-sharing functionality into early computers, and it's also tremendously helpful for security. There's a wide range of isolation tools, ranging from user accounts and sandboxes within those accounts to application identity on mobile phones to virtual private clouds.

The very best way to isolate your code from other code is to remove that other code. Code that isn't running can't be exploited; code that isn't present can't be started. Reducing extraneous code not only makes a system more secure, it's also faster because that extraneous code never uses a CPU cycle or a bit of storage or network.

Of course, the isolation tools can be buggy, hard to configure, or configured too openly. You can also reduce their power, for example, running as root by default. Creators of desktop and mobile platforms are making this impossible, but on Linux or the IoT, you're free to disable the safeties.

Sandboxes are intended to constrain what can happen within an account. A common way to break in to a Unix server was to exploit a network-listening daemon (a long-running program). Those servers had many setuid root programs. An attacker who broke in and who had an exploit for that setuid program could expand their authority. The Unix permission model doesn't make it easy to say "not executable by a member of the group daemons," never mind "not executable by (a member of the group daemons) or (a member of the group qmaild)."

This led to the creation of a sandbox, called *chroot*. It gave a program a limited filesystem with only known dependencies available. Unfortunately, it was hard to use and relatively easy to break. More modern sandboxes, including AppArmor, sandboxd, and AppContainer, add a layer of constraints that surround and protect the operating system and other accounts from a daemon. (The name *sandbox* implied it was safe to let an attacker play there, and it unfortunately stuck.)

Containers, such as Docker, are yet another set of boundaries, designed to prevent anything inside the container from reaching outside of it. Similarly, a virtual machine is intended to be isolated from the hypervisor and other code. Many times, this is frustrating, and so we use configuration to reduce the isolation. For example, not being able to copy and paste between a host operating system and a virtualized guest operating system leads to tools like VMware Tools that reduce the isolation in favor of usability.

Code as Barrier

Once you've designed your system to run with the least authority it can and you've separated the authorities it needs into various subcomponents, there are plenty of opportunities to have code act as a protective barrier. Those include attenuation and careful handoff between programs. It's also crucial to parse input carefully. It's so important that the topic gets an entire chapter to itself: Chapter 8, "Parsing and Corruption."

Attenuation

To attenuate is to reduce the force or effect of something. A program can attenuate authority by choosing to not grant it to its clients. For example, a normal Unix shell allows the user to run any executable program with the convention of `./mycode`. We could create a shell that allows the execution of programs only in the system path and not allow the user to set a path. (The bash shell can be invoked as `rbash` to do this.)

Similarly, we have different ways to design an API that takes commands. We could accept full commands from our counterparty, say, `ping 1.2.3.4`. We could also accept a list of commands, or even pointers to commands. We could do this with a table of mappings, such as `command1:netstat`, `command2:ping`, and others we anticipate. The remote caller would send `command2 1.2.3.4`. This last design minimizes the likelihood of errors, but many parsing risks remain and will be covered in Chapter 8.

Many interpreters will take an argument of a script, such as `python mycode.py`. We could create a version of Python that does less and requires all code to be in an approved directory, like `/usr/local/python/site/`. Each of these *attenuates* the authority granted to their caller in different ways, tuned to the functionality they offer.

The sudo program is designed to allow its callers to run code with root privileges. Sudo itself could run anything, but the design goal is to attenuate that authority so that only specified users can run specified commands. This turns out to be tricky, in part because sudo must parse not only the input command but also a policy file that declares who can do what. That policy language is written in a moderately complex language to let administrators specify a wide variety of allowable commands.

Defenses for Deputies

It's easy to say "Don't create a deputy that can be confused!" It's harder to do, and even harder when your code is already in production.

So, it's not easy to create a deputy that can't be confused. In fact, sudo, a program that exists almost entirely to do this, has had a long string of security issues (not all of which were confused deputy problems). Confusion, at the programmer, system, or user level is hardest to prevent when the abstractions seem like thin layers that we can peer through.

The first step is be aware that your code is a deputy. This is easy with daemons, setuid code, and code that processes complex file structures. It is less obvious with some of the emergent cloud patterns, and especially as we borrow expensive technical debt by integrating libraries we don't fully understand. When you know your code is a deputy, build that functionality into a small, isolation-friendly subset that's easy to reason about.

The second step is to be careful about configuration. If you take configuration from a user-controllable file, you must scope either that configuration to that user or the entire execution to that user. If your code makes API calls that use your authority and those APIs don't specify the user as a parameter, that will likely lead to confusion.

Third, be careful with input and output, such as where you take input or especially if your code has extra authority.

Fourth, don't attenuate. Do I have your attention? Good. It's true, I've been talking about attenuating, but rather than attenuating, build up precisely the set of authorities you want to pass to each client. (For example, when your code is on a traditional Windows or Unix system, it may be reasonable to pass file descriptors rather than filenames.)

Fifth, deputy access control should be either *precisely* the same as the next layer or obviously different. Almost the same is a prescription for misunderstanding. Subtly different is a nice label for "shockingly easy to misuse."

Handoff

A common modern handoff is via application protocols, such as "mailto:" These protocols seem simple and safe, in that they are one-way, and the data associated with them is limited to anything that can be encoded into a URL. But the application to which data is handed may well have been coded with the assumption that it would be invoked by a user, and that user won't be attacking themselves, as they already have the ability to run code. Violating this assumption often has hilarious results, assuming you're the attacker (Lawrence19).

Mailto takes as arguments an email address, as well as subject, cc, bcc, and body content. I'm sure my mail program is ready for bizarre content in the bcc field, but I'm not sure yours is. More prosaically, if you implement such a handoff system, it's important to realize that the clients may not expect random content from the Internet.

The defenses you build in code and the architectural patterns that you deploy will serve to constrain attackers and, we hope, prevent them from reaching their goals. With that, we turn our full attention to concepts of authority and privilege.

Authority and Privilege

To this point, I've treated authority and privilege as interchangeable terms, on the assumption that you might have heard of privilege but haven't really thought about what it means. If that's the case, you can transfer those loose understandings over. It turns out that the concept of privilege in computer security is a mess, and it makes your job much harder than it should be. For example, on Unix systems, "bind to a low-numbered port" was a privilege reserved to root; on Windows, it was not. (It wasn't even reserved to the Administrators group.)

If you're forced to work in privilege and permission systems, understanding why they can go wrong can help you think about constructing solid defenses. If you can replace them, it's like moving from a language with implicit casting to one that's typesafe. It's a little harder at first, but entire classes of bugs may disappear, and you can code faster and more confidently.

Access Control (Background)

The fundamental task of an operating system is to manage access to resources, including processors, storage, and peripherals. It defines accounts and uses them to define and check authorization via various system calls. Operating systems also mediate how often these resources (especially processor) can be accessed, or how much, via quotas.

Access Control Implementation

These calls often involve a tuple like (userid, action, object). Here's an example: (adam, read, /home/adam/.bashrc).

To be explicit, the code that implements access control generally looks something like this:

```
fd = open(uid, file, flags) {
  // flags are read, write, execute, etc
  if (uid == root) return (kernel_open(file, flags))
  if (check_permissions (uid, file, flags) return
(kernel_open(file, flags )
  // uid should be handled at a different layer, but
it's illustrative to call it out here.
  // Also, this design means any caller can open a file
as any UID, which is probably not what the
designer wants
```

The uid is a subject, the finest-grained unit that may be granted access rights. The file is an object, the finest-grained unit on which access rights can be defined.

Flags can be simple, like read, write, execute, create, or delete, or more nuanced like append. This pattern exists across a great many systems including desktop or mobile operating systems and cloud providers such as Dropbox. The pattern shows in databases or other applications, with file being replaced by some other descriptor, such as a row or column or stored procedure.

These tuples are often expressed as permissions or access control. An example permission might be (adam, execute, a.out). There are limits to how expressive one can be in the Unix model of permissions for user, group, and everyone, so some systems define access control lists (ACLs), which are lists of access control statements and rules about how to handle conflict, such as "any deny rule wins" or "the most specific rule wins." To be precise, those are access control entries (ACEs), stored in ACLs. In practice, "ACL" is sometimes used to refer to either an entry, the list of entries, or the sound that a confused engineer makes trying to make sense of it all.

Expansion of authority can allow an attacker to bypass these types of checks or to do things beyond the intent of the human being responsible.

Permissions and Policy in Access Control

Expressions like `(adam, ~/.bashrc, read)`, `(group:staff, a.out, execute)`, or `(adam@example.org, flickr.com/photos, modify)` are statements of *policy*. They are structured expressions of the intent of the system owner or users about who may do what.

Ideally, they are comprehensible and match the intent of the user who sets the policy; both turn out to be hard. Users may not know who's in a group; cascades of ACL inheritance may work differently than expected. Data may be accessible to unexpected parties, and it may be hard to grant access to exactly the right group. You might want to allow "system designers who know the location of the second Death Star" but exclude members of the groups "Bothans" and "bounty hunters."[2]

The `(user, object, action)` tuples have several serious downsides, including name resolution, but more importantly, we give each program very broad authority to act on objects on our behalf because predicting the authority that program will need is very difficult.

Predictions Are Hard, Especially About Policy

If I need to express policy against future needs, I will likely do so in a way that's expansive, because I don't know what the future will hold.

---

[2] If you're paying close attention rather than getting distracted by my Star Wars jokes, you may notice that it's unclear if I mean to exclude only Bothan bounty hunters, or anyone who's either. In fact, I meant to exclude anyone who's either, and in reading my own text noticed that I had been accidentally unclear, accidentally proving my own point about how hard it is to get it exactly right.

But in the moment, I might be able to describe very specific policies. For example, an expansive policy might be "Microsoft Word can read and write in `~/Documents` and subfolders." That's what I usually want, until Word is corrupted and the attacker uses that delegated authority to ransomware all my files. Today, I only want Word to write to `~/Documents/threatsbook/expansion.docx`.

If you're going to introduce a sandbox, one of the challenges is how to get a person to say, "This program may access this file, but no other file I have access to," and to do so in a way that's fluid, not annoying, and protects against future threats.

When Windows 8 was introduced, it took away the ability of sandboxed apps to call the traditional `open()`. Rather, apps call `FileOpenPicker` and `FileSavePicker`. As shown in Figure 6.4, those APIs and the associated user interfaces (file pickers) run at a higher level of authority than the app, and the person behind the computer uses them to say where the app may read or write. Most people are not even aware that there's a security difference between the file picker dialog and the app. As perhaps an entertaining side note, I knew about this because of conversations with the people who designed it, and it was challenging to find the documentation that verifies the claims. The Microsoft documentation "Open files and folders with a picker" doesn't mention security or capabilities. The file picker is not listed as a boundary in the "Security Boundaries" page, (which, to be fair, is a COM page, highly ranked by search engines for its title), but access to Documents is listed as a restricted capability in "App capability declarations" (Microsoft, 2018-a, c, and d).

Problems with Privileges and Permissions

Related to permissions is the idea of privilege. For a moment, let's define privilege as the ability to alter security functions, properties, or rules within a system. I tend to think of permissions as tied to objects, and privileges as tied to accounts, but we reach the limits of that model quickly.

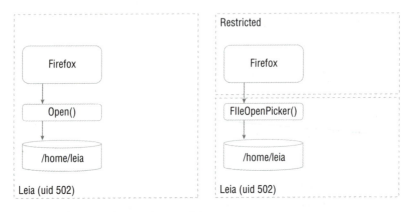

FIGURE 6.4 A file picker architecture

Privileges can be implicit or explicit. On a Windows or Mac even a "normal" account has an incredibly rare and implicit privilege: to run code on that machine. Most of the people in the world are not authorized to do so. "Execute code" is a privilege, often granted implicitly to any authorized user of a traditional operating system, but on mobile phones, it's gated via app stores, and on kiosks it's denied. Similarly, "send network packets" is a privilege, as is "listen for packets" and "listed on ports below 1024" is a separate privilege. As you've seen, Linux now tries to break these privileges up into what it calls capabilities.

Mobile applications must accept that network privileges can be arbitrarily removed when cellular bandwidth is a concern. They can also be removed by airplane mode, but that's turning off the radio, a separate privilege. There's a subtle and important difference. An application that elevates privilege might send its data via another app when the first apps's "send packets" privilege is removed, or turn airplane mode off entirely, a privilege that should not be accessible to any normal application. (I can make the same statements with the concept of authority—an app with authority to send or receive with the radio may not have the authority to power the radio on or off.) As an aside, this is a reliability feature for the cellular network, not the airplane.

If airplanes crashed when phones were in normal mode, some terrorist would be boarding with a backpack of phones.

Privileges can be direct or transitive. Web browsers grant a subset of the execute code privilege to every website we visit, along with every website to whom it passes the favor and every proxy that can tamper with HTTP connections. The intent is that the browser grants that privilege only within the browser, but browsers also have complex behaviors about downloading files, and the permissions associated with a file already on your computer are different than the permissions with a file loaded via the Web.

Permissions are useful in part because they're familiar. We've learned to understand them. Designing permissions to grant additional capabilities that are not equivalent to Administrator is hard. For example, the Windows Backup Operator was always equivalent to Administrator, and the various Windows privileges have been quietly deprecated. Droids were given access to entire facilities through access ports, until a certain R2 unit ruined it for everyone.

In fact, system designers can define both permissions and privileges and can use either to deliver the same effects. For example, on Unix, an account is created by modifying `/etc/passwd`. Thus, permission to write to the file `/etc/passwd` grants the ability to create accounts. This write permission can be granted by calling chmod on the file, by adding a user to the wheel group, by using sudo, or perhaps in other ways. On Windows, an account is created by calling `NetUserAdd()` or other APIs each of which checks the caller for membership in the group Administrators or Account Operators. Therefore, on Unix account creation is a matter of permissions, while on Windows account creation is a privilege.

Stepping back, trying to understand privilege via an object/account definition doesn't even work well. On Windows, users are objects, objects are turtles, and madness lies down this path. It's not even the Dark Side—my anger has not made me powerful. We need to walk this path for a short while so you can see why we need alternative ways to make progress.

This squishy base makes it hard to reason about privileges and permissions. My goal for this book is to enable every engineer to reason crisply about security. And so this chapter has been a struggle. I'd been using the concepts of permissions and privilege for more than 25 years. I've reconfigured daemons that had no concept of sandboxes to run in sandboxes. I believed I understood these concepts. I discovered that I'd never really disentangled them. Figuring out what a permission was and what a privilege was to explain the old frame of "elevation of privilege" nearly and unexpectedly scuttled this project. It was only in rereading Mark Miller's 2005 PhD thesis that I gained an appreciation for his approach of considering authority.

Most of today's desktop systems use permissions rather than authority, and it's to their detriment and ours. Systems that delegate via authority, which implement the principle of least authority, can be far more secure. I now refer to the E in STRIDE as "expansion of authority."

Newer Approaches to Policy

Again, *authority* means the effects that a program may cause on objects it can access, either directly by permission or indirectly by permitted interactions with other programs. This allows us to reason at a policy level and design mechanisms to support those policies. (You may think we're in esoterica here, but it's important for giving your designs a solid basis.) But if you're designing modern technology for something like an IoT device or a microservice cloud architecture, it's helpful to ask what authority each process should have. That question informs the answers to "What permissions should be set?" and also prompts you to think about "Where and how do we set policy for the system?"

Authority as Design Pattern
The old solution is that each program runs with the full authority of the user who invokes it. Newer solutions use capabilities and authority models.

A simple example, quoting Dr. Mark Miller, is the difference between these:

```
$ cp foo.txt bar.txt
```

Your shell passes to the cp program the two strings "foo.txt" and "bar.txt". The cp program uses these strings to determine which files it should copy.

By contrast consider how cat performs its task:

```
$ cat < foo.txt > bar.txt
```

Your shell uses these strings to determine which files you mean to designate. Once these names are resolved, your shell passes direct access to the files to cat, as open file descriptors. The cat program uses these descriptors to perform the copy. Now consider the least authority that each one needs to perform its task. With cp, you tell it which files to copy by passing it strings. By these strings, you mean particular files in your file system, to be resolved using your namespace of files. In order for cp to open the files you name, it must already have the authority to use your namespace, and it must already have the authority to read and write any file you might name. Given this way of using names, cp's least authority still includes all of your authority to the file system. The least authority it needs is so broad as to make achieving either security or reliability hopeless.

With cat, you tell it which files to copy by passing it the desired (read or write) access to those two specific files. Like the cp example, you still use names in your namespace to say which files you wish to have cat copy, but these names get evaluated in your namespace prior to being passed to cat. By passing cat file descriptors rather than strings to convert to descriptors, we reduce the authority it needs to do its job. Its least authority is what you'd expect—the right to foo.txt and the right to write your bar.txt. It needs no further access to your file system.

In other words, if cp is running as anakin, his shell gives cp the authority to read any file anakin can read; it is given all of his authority, and we know how that works out. In contrast, cat is given the authority to read exactly one file and write another.

In the policies expressed in the previous section, there are no program identities. Any program running as uid adam may read .bashrc. For many, this seems like a natural state of affairs. In an authority-centered system, we need to be able to reason about the set of access that a program has.

Changing a system from the permission and privileges approach to an authority or capabilities approach is hard work. That hard work is worth it because few programs running as user george have the full authority of his account. Each has the authority, and only the authority, it needs to do the job it's given in the moment.

For example, emacs is very powerful. It can run Lisp code that can do anything that the user who invokes it can do. Let's assume that we modify it so that all calls to read() are replaced by a file picker UI, of the sort discussed in "Predictions Are Hard, Especially About Policy." (We'll ignore some complications like reading startup files.)

Now our modified emacs can't read the script for *Revenge of the Jedi* unless Larry or Becky or George click it. It can't run ransomware that encrypts the script for the Phantom *Menace*. (OK, maybe that would have been nice, but whatever you think of the idea, we don't want to grant that authority to every program we run.)

It turns out this can be easy if you control the operating system. You "just" make fopen() a call that requires special permission to use and add a file picker API that requires human input. (There are again, gotchas. If you change fopen() then anything that calls it has to be re-tested.)

Apple has made a change like this to macOS, requiring apps that want to edit arbitrary files to have a permission called Full Disk Access. In contrast, Microsoft has only imposed this on "modern apps." The approaches represent different philosophies and priorities: Microsoft values application compatibility more than Apple. Apple was willing to impose an extra step on backup software and other tools that require this greater level of authority.

Capabilities in Access Control

Sadly, almost all of today's systems use permissions and privileges, rather than authority and capabilities, so it's worth understanding them both so you can work with them and so you can design better.

But! Technology is being built and rebuilt at remarkable speed, and new systems can work in new ways. Key-centric references can be built into new systems with relative ease, and they make implementation and reasoning about implementation much easier.

For example, if you're building microservices in the cloud, you're probably building them to call service discovery APIs. Those service discovery APIs can choose when to return access and when not to. If your final API endpoints are changed with the permissions, you have something similar to a capability system. That is, if I have RESTful API endpoints of `/1234567/` to read Darth Vader's calendar and `/8ddf8e78/` to write them, then my service discovery can choose who reads and who writes. If I call `/calendar/darthvader/read` or `/calendar/write/darthvader`, then each has to ensure that they implement a proper access control chokepoint.

Framing our understanding in authority makes it easier to reason about the security of what we're building or deploying. Constraining the authority of each component and using isolation and attenuation as we delegate or invoke further functionality makes our systems more reliable and secure.

Conclusion

Why is it possible for the Empire to install a tracking device on the Millennium Falcon? The panels have no locks, and the connections to power are accessible throughout. Perhaps it's better for anyone on the ship to be able to quickly make repairs? (Especially on that ship...)

And why does no one find that tracking device? Perhaps it's the complexity of finding it among the "special modifications" that Han Solo has made. Perhaps it's the urgency of getting to the Rebel Base on Yavin before the Death Star arrives.

Like the Falcon, modern systems accumulate complexity and fail to implement isolation or defense in depth, and attackers take advantage of that.

A few modern programs, running on desktops, need broad and flexible authority to act on behalf of their users. Most of what we create needs far less authority, and even less if we're thoughtful about its design. This means we can code defensively, pass on our authority carefully, and backstop both by planning for accidents with isolation techniques. Each of these means that we alone can exercise our authority.

7 Predictability and Randomness

ngineers like predictability. It would be hard to build a Death Star if halfway through setting up the superstructure, gravity kicked in like a tractor beam. Attackers also like predictability. If your main program runs commands it stores in `/tmp/setup.sh`, then an attacker who can create that file gets to run their commands and is in the money. If your Sabbac game sets its card order based on the date each night at midnight, then an attacker who discovers that is really in the money.

It's important for you to understand when unpredictability or randomness matter, and it's important to understand that they are (predictably) different. You can have numbers that are difficult to predict from a few examples, or you can have ones that are random. For now, let's define random to mean even perfect knowledge of the system won't help you anticipate the next output. For example, well-shaken new dice are effectively random, and when those are used with carefully designed rules and operations, they can give the house a predictable advantage and pay for nice casinos like the ones in Las Vegas or Canto Bight.

Computers, however, are predictable. That predictability leads to threats from informed or brute-force guessing (and testing those guesses) and some surprising truths about the odds of those guesses succeeding. We'll also look at threats to time itself, or at least how technical systems track it. From there, we'll cover predictability in specific scenarios, defenses including permissions and authority, large search spaces, and the importance of assuming transparency.

Predictability Threats

Attackers love to imitate the Emperor and cackle that "Everything is proceeding as I have foreseen!" They might be predicting a filename so they can write it before you, a sequence number on a network protocol so they can spoof packets, or how you'll change your password by incrementing a trailing digit so it passes the password update requirements.

Think back to the discussion of capabilities in Chapter 6, "Expansion of Authority and Isolation." Remember that a capability is a long number that's hard to guess, such as 67890123 being the capability to write to `Documents/threatsbook/predictability.docx`. We can be more specific about the threats to such a system: they include both finding a specific capability and finding any valid capability. In that chapter, I mentioned "unguessably long," and in this chapter we'll get specific about how to think about that phrase.

If you want to ransomware my files, any valid capability is useful to you; if you want to read this book before it's ready, then only a few of my documents will satisfy.

Guessing and Testing

Some things are predictable: what's the next number in the sequence 1, 4, 9, 16...? (It's 25.) Other things are guessable: I'm thinking of a number between 1 and 5. (I'm thinking of π .) What's that? Choosing π is cheating? It's a real number between 1 and 5. Get used to your assumptions being invalidated. Now I'm thinking of an integer in the range 1 through 1 million, inclusive. No silly tricks, but I'm giving you only a single guess. I can personally enforce the single-guess rule, but having a computer do so can be tricky.

Each guess takes some time, as does testing it, which means that clever attackers seek to optimize the order of their guessing, and smart defenders make optimization impossible.

Dictionaries and Guessing

Which of these is more likely to be someone's password: RememberAlderaan or dg1298L;dsaf4lt? While we might hope that they're equally likely, or even that people will shy away from predictable passwords, RememberAlderaan seems more likely than the other, equally long string. And perhaps RememberAlderaan1 or even RememberAlderaan1! are still more likely as people are pushed by password rules. Smart attackers will build "dictionaries," lists of possible answers; organize them by their best understanding of likelihood; use them to structure their guessing—and even publish them on the Internet.

Dictionaries are enabled by three things: a small search space, a lack of randomness, and human limits. The search space is the number of total possibilities. So, a lock with three spinning dials, each settable to a number between 0 and 9, has 1,000 possible combinations. The padlock on a school locker, with three numbers between 1 and 36, might have 36^3 (46,656) possible combinations, which seems like a lot. If you have to test them all one after the next and can test one a second, it could take almost 13 hours, which would be pretty boring. (We'll assume that the lock is both silent, so a stethoscope won't help, and physically high tolerance, so there's no chance that it will accept a 32 in place of a 33.)

More specifically, by lack of randomness, I mean that the distribution of answers is not uniform. Some answers are more likely than others. Human limits include memory and willingness or ability to type or tap long random strings reliably.

Uninformed Guessing (Brute Force) Computers excel at boring, repetitive work, and 13 hours isn't a very big search space. Cryptographic keys tend to be 128 bits or more to create a very large search problem. (On average an attacker will test half of perfectly random keys before finding the right one for a specific message. In this case, that would be 2^127, which is give or take "a trillion trillion trillions"—it's roughly 170 followed by 37 zeros. Even for computers that are good at repetitive work repetition, that's infeasible, and I'll get more specific about what that means when we reach "large search spaces" in the "Defenses" section.) This form of guessing, where each answer is equally likely, is called "brute force."

The difference between brute force and The Force is that brute force requires neither magic powers nor extensive training. In fact, brute force is usually performed by software that'll do that boring, repetitive work.

By design, a guess in a cryptosystem applies to only one tuple of plaintext, key, and ciphertext. If you have to test whether a particular password gets you into my account at my mail server, you're checking a username/password combination. If you have a list of hashed passwords, you may be able to run an algorithm like the following one (we'll come to why I'm using the term "hashed" in just a minute):

```
List dictionary[words] // a set of candidate passwords
List passwords[hashes] // a set of hashed passwords
For word in dictionary {
  Candidate = hash(word);
  If 'Candidate' in passwords: print 'Candidate'
```

From the attacker's perspective, this is nice because the output of each hash operation gets compared to each entry in the passwords list. If the list is 50 hashed passwords, they do the hash once and get to compare it to 50 stored passwords.

We use a hash algorithm because if we encrypted the list of passwords, then anyone who steals the encryption key can simply decrypt the list. And in fact, we use what's called a *salted hash*. The "salt" is a small random value that changes per password, and we hash (`salt`, `password`) and store `salt, hash`. (To be concrete, "small" here means enough to have a unique salt per item in a list—usually 32 bits or more—and there are few arguments against 128 or 256 bits.)

So, as shown in Table 7.1, even if we have the same password, our stored password values are different. (For readability, I'm using short salts and truncated hashes.)

TABLE 7.1 Passwords and Salts

Password	Salt	Stored Value
RememberAlderaan	abc	abc,d2224c78779
RememberAlderaan	cde	cde,eea78a17ab5f

The end result is that the attacker's work to hash one salt potential password combination reveals at most one password, rather than one hash leading to revealing every user whose password is RememberAlderaan. (The galaxy is teeming with Rebel sympathizers.) If we assume that table lookups are faster than hashes, then that's a good thing for the defender. In fact, we design hash algorithms so they can't be sped up.

A brute-force attack will always work, given enough time, which is why cryptosystems have very large search spaces (key lengths).

Informed Guessing Now, if RememberAlderaan is a common password, maybe attackers will order their dictionaries so it comes before other 17 character candidates. The attacker can put their dictionary in any order they want, and today, the order is informed by the large password breaches that exposed tens of millions of passwords. Attackers are generally guessing at a biased search space. As they target a specific person, knowing the other passwords that person has used, or their hobbies, family names, and important dates like birthdays and anniversaries, can dramatically change the odds.

Memorable strings are much easier to remember and even to type, and that contributes to the effectiveness of dictionaries. (As an aside, if you're still typing in your passwords like a pre-industrial Ewok, get a password manager.)

Time/Memory Trade-Offs Including Rainbow Tables If you have an expensive operation, caching results can be helpful. If that operation is hashing passwords, attackers might store hashes of the most common billion or trillion possible passwords, or password-salt combinations. If a salt is only 12 bits (as was the case for Unix password storage), that's only a 4,096-fold expansion in storage needs. Yes, only. It seems like a lot, and it is, but if you have a billion 8 byte sequences and a billion 16 byte hashes, that's 24 billion bytes, which is 24 GB. Expanding that by 4,096 times would require roughly 100 TB. But that's to store a billion passwords—roughly three for every person in the United States.

As we think about what to store, we come to time-memory trade-offs. If salts are missing or small, you can precompute values for popular passwords (say the top few million.) Rather than re-computing, you store the results. That trades off the storage against later compute time.

There are much more clever optimizations available, including "rainbow tables." These allow for a flexible trade-off of storage space and the cost of a lookup.

The Birthday Problem

There are attacks where the attacker needs to get a very specific hit; other times any match will be fine. Forgetting about the second case is easy and will lead to trouble.

For example, let's say you have a web server and you want to require the right big number to access photos, so you create URLs of the form `/pictures/19800521/photo1`, `/pictures/19800521/photo2`, etc. Now, I might not guess the right big number to see the pictures that George Lucas has uploaded. If `/pictures/19800522/` are photos from *Empire Strikes Back* director Lawrence Kasdan, I might be excited anyway. Of course, that's a trivial increment by one, which is worse than small random numbers, which are worse than big random numbers.

If you're trying to guess my password, you have to match a single line in the list of stored passwords. But if any password will serve, your work factor goes way down.

There is an important insight from statistics, called the *birthday problem*. It's a simple problem: how many people have to be in a room before there's a 50 percent chance that two of them share a birthday? Now, I'm hopeful that by this point you'll sense a trap. If you didn't sense a trap, that's okay; consider yourself warned. With that warning, write down the number. Some people will have written down 182, because that's an intuitively obvious number, and it's very wrong. The first person has a perfect shot at not sharing a birthday. The second person has a 364/365 chance of not matching the one person already there. The next person has a 363/365 chance of not matching, and the overall odds are $1 \times 364/365 \times 363/365$. As we add people, the odds of not matching anyone in the room drop to just under 1 in 2 at a mere 23 people. Now, what are the odds that with 23 people in the room, someone will share your birthday? This goes back to 1 in 365—again the difference between needing to guess any valid value and the need to guess a specific one.

The birthday attack is relevant because an attacker sometimes needs to match a particular birthday, sometimes they need to match any birthday, and the odds of doing that climb surprisingly rapidly. For example, maybe they need a file that hashes to a particular SHA-2 value, or maybe they need a file that hashes to any SHA-2 value that's been signed by your key? (SHA-2 is a cryptographic hash standard.)

Cryptographic Threats

Sometimes those new to security want to design their own cryptosystems, which is awesome. It can be a lovely learning experience, like seeing your Battle Station destroyed by some farm boy flying a fighter he's sitting in for the first time. The chances that your system will survive are way, way worse than the odds of successfully navigating an asteroid field. So feel free to design something, but please don't field it.

There are also threats from timing—if your cryptography works faster in some circumstances than others, attackers will use that to siphon information. That brings us to: time.

Time and Timing Threats

That "time is an illusion" doesn't prevent systems from relying on it for security purposes. There are attacks that rely on changing the time, attacks that rely on timing, and this is as good a time as any to talk about sequence issues, if we don't run out of time.

Many network protocols rely on clocks being in rough alignment. They expect remote systems to respect expiration times. Threats include messages that appear too early, too late, or where time is used in place of sequence numbers or nonces.

Information Disclosure and Time

Either knowing what time a remote system thinks it is or how long an action took can be useful to attackers.

As we saw in Chapter 4, "Information Disclosure and Confidentiality," measuring how long an encryption or decryption takes can tell you how many bits are in a key. Similarly, attacks like Spectre use timing to see what data is in a cache and if a given operation results in a cache hit or miss.

It turns out that when you let an attacker run code, even constrained code, they can determine local time accurately enough for all sorts of mischief. In fact, in a document about Spectre, Google engineers write both "Merely enumerating all the clocks is difficult" and "Surprisingly coarse clocks are still useful for exploitation" (awhalley, 2018).

Remote systems helpfully serve up the time in a great many ways, ranging from the time protocol (port 37) through banners, headers, message content, logs, and other details exposed by mail servers, web servers, and other protocols.

Tampering with Time

Attackers can reset the clocks on their own computers, moving them backward to avoid expiry of various secrets or software licenses, to send messages in the past ("Oh, yes, I sent the cancelation email before the trial expired!"). They can move them forward to unlock time-release items or challenges. If they can't manipulate the clock directly, they may be able to move time zones (McKenna, 2019). Both are often exploited against mobile games. It's also easy to speed up or slow down the apparent clock speed on a computer.

Somewhat more surprisingly, you can change the time of a remote computer, spoofing a DHCP or NTP server. (NTP has defenses against making large adjustments all at once.)

Predictability in Specific Scenarios

Either a cloud or IoT system may have a lack of high-quality randomness, read your specs carefully for cryptographic-quality randomness. There are also threats to network traffic, local systems, and even business processes.

Network Traffic

Many of the core IP network protocols, including TCP and DNS, have very predictable message formats and do not support cryptographic authentication or integrity. Many TCP/IP stacks originally used predictable initial sequence numbers. Some of these were predictable without any interaction. In other cases, they were related to other initial sequence numbers, so anyone who initiated a connection with a host could make better guesses about other TCP sequence number in use. "Better" here includes a range from "you can't miss" to "it'll take many guesses." In the 90s, sequence numbers were incremented by a predictable counter, so if you knew one, you could predict the ones being used in either existing or new connections (Bellovin, 1996). Such prediction allowed nearly perfect network traffic spoofing, splicing, and other tricks.

Similar problems existed in the many higher-level protocols, where they are sometimes protected by lower-level cryptography. These problems are best known in Internet-style networks, whose designs are transparent. But the core problems of performance and bootstrapping trust are not specific to Internet protocols.

Local System Threats

When an attacker can run code on a local machine, there are many places where a lack of randomness makes an attack easier. These include the filesystem, memory layout, and a host of operating system details like process IDs.

Filesystem Threats

There's a family of threats where attackers and defenders race to control a shared resource. These attacks have a few names, including *race condition*, because it's a race to see who writes the file and "time of check, time of use." That's a description of the issue: something is checked and then used while the thing being checked is subject to manipulation after checking. (The phrase is commonly abbreviated TOCTOU and pronounced "tock-too.")

Historically, files in /tmp/, such as install.sh, were a favorite target for attackers, and defenders evolved from /tmp/install.sh to appending a process ID or even a random number (/tmp/install.pid, /tmp/install.ABCD). Attackers could often predict the next process ID (pid) because most operating systems assign process IDs sequentially. So if your process is PID 421, then creating /tmp/file.422, file.423, and file.424 is likely to create a file that another process will rely upon, especially if you're in a position to invoke the process that will look for /tmp/file.422. Similarly, if the name has a random four-digit number, the attacker just needs to make 10,000 files (or links, if they're considerate of your disk space, or apprehensive about an accidental denial-of-service attack interfering with their expansion of authority).

Writing content to a file that someone else's code relies on is a common race attack. There are also variants where an attacker will create a symbolic link to a file that you own and then change the link to point to a file they own. If you've checked the link and the target of the link, can the link still change?

There are other important temporal logic issues with code, especially in large distributed systems. (For example, if two processes on opposite sides of the planet write to the same address in a filesystem, whose data does the consistency algorithm pick?) These are security issues in the sense that they can hurt the integrity of a system, attackers can certainly invoke them, and they are also called race conditions. They're harder for an attacker to leverage to get an advantage than the local system versions.

Memory Layout Threats

For the first 50 or so years of computing, the layout of code in memory was highly predictable. That made it easy to write attacks that overwrote memory on the stack or heap or to assemble chains of instructions from existing code. The first tools to make memory unpredictable simply inserted a canary on the end of the stack, and if the canary wasn't present, then leaving the stack was handled differently. The value of the canary was unpredictable, so an attacker had to take care to not overwrite it. More recently, libraries are loaded at different addresses via address space layout randomization (ASLR), and other randomization tactics are used to reduce predictability.

Many software exploits include a stage where they write executable code into memory and then execute that memory by causing control flow to jump there. Randomizing memory layout in various ways makes these attacks harder but not impossible. These defenses are now generally enabled by default but can be turned off. (If you're on a low-end platform, it's worth ensuring address randomization and other memory-safety tools are enabled.) If your process discloses arbitrary memory, it makes it easy to bypass these defenses. We'll touch on these defenses again in Chapter 8, "Parsing and Corruption."

Business Processes

Race conditions can impact any system where there are unique resources, such as droids in inventory or dollars in a bank account. If you allow calls such as "check balance" and "send money" to happen without explicit locking, then an attacker will find a way to overdraw an account.

Defenses

Defenses against prediction attacks are generally simple and reliable. Many race conditions took advantage of design patterns that are disappearing. Defenses against guessing and prediction attacks require design work and sometimes nuanced trade-offs, but they're pleasantly mathematical. The hardest defense for many to wrap their heads around is transparency, so we'll close the "Defenses" section with that.

Preventing Races

To avoid races in database systems, apply locks to crucial sections, and patterns like ACID in design. (ACID stands for atomicity, consistency, isolation, and durability.)

The pattern of writing crucial files into shared temporary space made a certain amount of sense when disk space was expensive and scarce. Avoiding filling up a crucial filesystem might have been worth the risk, but those days are behind us.

To avoid shared storage races, the best pattern is simply to use private storage for crucial resources. Set up a new storage space for the purpose, rather than using /tmp. If you need to share, set the permissions to share with a very small set of principals, like a single user or group, and then check that the permissions are what you expect them to be.

The jargony label of "time of check/time of use" is helpful insofar as it suggests a fix: ensure that the thing you're working with cannot change between the time you check it and the time you use it. For example, if you open the file and then check the file handle, you at least know that no one has swapped the file out from under you. (An attacker might still have an open handle to the file.)

Formal mathematical methods can be used to reason about state and are showing increasing use in industry. One of these tools, TLA+, helps deal with large distributed system temporal logic, and Amazon has talked about how it has found important edge conditions with it (Lamport, 2021, Newcombe, 2015).

Defenses Against Guessing and Searching

Han Solo may want to never hear the odds, and that makes him a bad role model. Understanding and even manipulating the odds is a crucial part of defending our systems.

Large Search Spaces

Large search spaces make both prediction and guessing harder. The smallest meaning of large is "relative to fleets of modern computers working for days or months." At the larger end, completely random 256-bit keys can take so long to search for the key that if every atom in the universe was a supercomputer, they still wouldn't have a chance until the real Death Star destroys the Earth, or even until the sun explodes.

For cryptographic keys, large is at least 128 bits. (Asymmetric keys need to have specific mathematical properties. So not every number makes a good key, and keys need to be larger.) If you can try a few billion keys a second (say, 2^{32}), it will still take you 2^{95} seconds to try half the possible keys. A year, as you'll recall, is a bit under 2^{25} seconds, so someone will write "a long time ago" in about 1,000,000,000,000,000,000 years.

Up to here, I've tried to expand the powers of two, and I'll encourage you to start thinking in terms of doubling each time the power goes up by one. So 2^2 is 4, 2^3 is 8, 2^10 is 1024. The growth has literally given us the commonplace "exponential."

Salts expand the search space for an attacker who's gotten a copy of something they can attack offline. Salts multiply the search space and should be unique per item. For example, if you have 2^32 salts (roughly 4 billion) and your database is "people alive on Earth," on average every salt will map to two people.

Slow Guessing

With older password storage algorithms, we can measure attacks in hundreds of gigahashes per second (a gig is 2^32). Cloud costs for those speeds are on the order of tens of dollars an hour. When attackers can test guesses at those speeds, it changes the effectiveness of defenses, especially when there are dictionaries of common passwords.

There are two types of techniques to slow them down: online and offline. Online defenses are when your software can notice and respond to attacks. Either these can be constant rate slowdowns or they can grow with repeated test failures, possibly even exponentially, or block clients. This is why it's OK to have four-character PINs on ATMs. After a few bad guesses, the ATM will eat the card.

Offline defenses work even if your attacker can bypass your software and directly access the database of values. The offline ones store the output of functions that are intentionally slow to compute, like iterated cryptographic hashes.

Newer algorithms such as Argon2 or Balloon are designed to be tunable and generally allow you to increase iteration counts to adjust the safety margins for stored passwords.

What parameters to use is an interesting conundrum. Some security people recommend times into the seconds per hash, while acknowledging that can create a denial of service on your application (Burman, 2019). It's certainly tempting to make very conservative recommendations, but even moving from 2^{36} hashes per second to 2^{10} is a dramatic improvement. I suggest a good bound is "as slow as you can make it without frustrating users." Doing specific calculations with your parameters—the number of users, the length of the salts, the password rules—may result in different answers for your application.

Key Derivation

It turns out that people are bad at remembering random 128-bit or 2048-bit numbers, however nicely we encode them. *Key derivation* is a term for taking a human-memorable secret and turning it into something that resists dictionary attacks. (It's also called *key stretching* or *password stretching*.) For example, let's say you want to encrypt a spreadsheet with a list of Bothan spies. If we naively use "remember-Alderaan" as the password, then an Imperial cryptographer can simply run the sort of dictionary attack already discussed. So, we use an approach that's very much like protecting a password that's going to be stored in a database: we hash it repeatedly, with a salt. (There's a little more to it, and there are standards for key derivation, like the cleverly named password-based key derivation function, PBKDF-2. I guess calling it R2-D2 would have made searching harder.)

The derivation usually involves a "key-stretching" approach, which is designed to defend against dictionary attacks against the password. For example, Microsoft Office uses 10,000 iterations of PBKDF-2 with the password to produce a document key. This stretching is important anywhere human-controlled data is used for security; the key stretching is nearly identical to the way passwords are stored on a Unix system, with the differences being how the stored values are used and possibly the algorithm used for stretching.

A common pattern is to use a user-memorable password to protect a fully random cryptographic key. In other words, derive key1 from a password. Then use key1 to encrypt a strongly random key2, and use key2 to encrypt the data you want to protect. There are variants on this, such as random keys per document (or other data elements such as a database row or cell), with the master key stored in a system keychain. Most important, the key is derived from the password, rather than the password being used directly.

Rotation

"It's an older code, sir, but it checks out." Those words allowed Rebels to land on a moon of Endor, leading to the destruction of the second Death Star. And they incidentally show us just how good Star Wars world building can be. Rotating keys so that an attacker who steals one has a limited time to exploit it is excellent security practice. It risks breaking things. But rotation is a powerful tool for limiting exposure.

And as the quote from *Return of the Jedi* illuminates, there are circumstances where not shooting your own shuttle craft requires managing your codes (or keys) so that more than one is valid at a given point in time. That's not trivial work. It requires discipline and careful consideration about what to do with each key and when to do it. Password expiry also shows the downside to rotation. If people have to be involved in each rotation, that can be a lot of frustrating work, and it turns out people will cleverly manage by appending things like Feb22 to their password; attackers will also try such things, especially when they're engaged in a focused attack and may have several samples of Han Solo's password.

Randomness

A lack of randomness makes searching much easier, and even a subtle pattern can be tremendously helpful to an attacker.

As much as some bugs feel like they randomly appear, computers as algorithmic systems are predictable, not random. Systems can produce something that appears random, but it's really just "pseudorandom." (NIST defines random as "A value in a set that has an equal probability of being selected from the total population of possibilities and, hence, is unpredictable." They define pseudorandom as "a deterministic process (or data produced by such a process) whose output values are effectively indistinguishable from those of a random process as long as the internal states…are unknown" (NIST, 2018). The difference is computers have state, dice don't.

These functions would take a seed and iterate over it in ways that are designed to make it hard to predict the next or previous output. (Earlier, I talked about predicting next values—being able to determine earlier states is also a flaw. For example, if we're guessing TCP sequence numbers, if we can get the latest value, and we can backtrack, that lets us spoof an ongoing connection.)

For many years, this was the practical limit. Systems that really needed randomness would ask the user to type randomly or otherwise use microsecond timing of physical input and use that as the seed (or fold it in with other data to be the seed). Obviously, that works better for a desktop computer than a cloud server. As the cloud grew in importance, chip makers added special hardware that (essentially) derives very high quality randomness by measuring thermal noise (Hamburg, 2012).

Today's operating systems tend to have fairly high-quality randomness available, and experts pay very close attention to making sure those functions work. However, you may have to ask for the cryptographic quality randomness. Many systems will default to giving you bad randomness because it's faster. There's advice—which often predates the inclusion of true randomness in chips—that you shouldn't trust the random number code in the operating system, and you should run your own. There may be circumstances where this is true or where mixing in additional randomness may be helpful to you. But you'll probably make your system less secure if you go down this road.

By way of example, people will often look for randomness in changing aspects of the environment, looking to things like process IDs and uptime.

Process IDs are one of many predictable elements of an operating system. User ID numbers are predictable on Unix. Uptimes tend to cluster around the smaller numbers, and various populations of machines have characteristic bell-like curves. Xboxes might cluster around a few hours; phones and desktops at days to weeks. Computers treated like crops might cluster around half a week.

Counterintuitively, if we take 8 bits of randomness from uptime and combine it with 8 bits of randomness from hardware, we have increased the predictability of the data we're using, and that's bad. It is, of course, possible to do this in a way that defends your system against a biased hardware random number generator and a bug, design flaw, or backdoor in the system cryptography. This is so exceptionally specialized that I myself would look to get expert help.

The last aspect of randomness to be aware of is that it's impossible to statistically test if a stream is security-quality randomness. A test can find (some) flaws, but not the absence of flaws. In other words, a stream of data can pass a statistical test while still being highly predictable to someone who knows how it's being produced.

Usability

Engineering systems that are both usable and lack predictability is hard. The better answer usually involves either avoiding the trade-off or hiding the randomness from people with abstraction layers. Pretending that people can handle a barrage of randomness quickly and accurately is bad engineering; demanding that they spend their precious attention on it is a poor use of their energy.

The tension between what people can remember and the effectiveness of password cracking is one of the reasons that multifactor authentication is so important. There's little overlap between the conflicting requirements of usable and protectable in passwords.

More generally, people are generalizing machines. We seek patterns and causation as part of how we make sense of the world. When security seems arbitrary, incomprehensible, or ineffective, many rebel against it. Explaining your security so that people can work with it helps both you and them and brings us to the question of transparency versus secrecy in security systems.

Assume Transparency

Some attackers are dedicated and focused and will spend time to learn how your specific defenses work so they can bypass them. If you discover they've succeeded, you'll have to change your defenses. So, it's better to design for that eventuality.

Some of the oldest principles we have in computer security predate computers but come to us from cryptography. In 1883, Dutch linguist Auguste Kerckhoffs published articles on military cryptography. The principles he espoused include "The system must not require secrecy and can be stolen by the enemy without causing trouble" (Translation from Petitcolas, 1997). That is, the security of the system should depend on keys that can be changed without requiring the whole system be replaced. Despite putting forward six principles, "Kerckhoffs Principle" today is broadly used as shorthand for "Don't rely on obscurity."

A classic example of obscurity would be to store a house key under a potted plant. Anyone who knows which plant can access the key. If you put the key in a lockbox with a combination, the defenses are the physical strength of the lockbox and a combination. So, we can place the lockbox right next to the lock.

Cryptographic systems today are designed with this principle in mind. AES-256 is better than anything you or I would design. It has undergone years of careful analysis. Its security is only dependent on the key being kept secret.

Moving from cryptography to software more broadly, locally installed software such as Microsoft Outlook is carefully reverse engineered by attackers in labs. Microsoft both fixes specific memory corruption issues and, to make exploitation trickier, randomizes memory layouts every time an Office app runs. In contrast, Visual Basic for Application (VBA) macros have been a well-known source of security problems. Changing the behavior of VBA causes substantial trouble, because many organizations have made extensive investments in document macros for business automation (Gatlan, 2022).

Software as a service can't easily be put into a lab, so it's natural to ask, should we use obscurity to protect it? After all, we know how hard it is to deploy the darn thing—an attacker won't be able to stand up a copy! As hard as that may be, getting it to work perfectly is not a prerequisite for analysis. But much more importantly, if (or when) an analyst discovers a flaw, it's better if the system isn't relying on security through obscurity.

Software as a service can also have an advantage of observability. Sending logs to the Empire seems intrusive, if you sell classic packaged software or give away open source.[1] When the software runs in your cloud, you may be able to detect attacks as they are being developed and address them. From the attacker's perspective, they're no longer in a lab, and their economics or even personal criminal risk may change somewhat. (By "economics," I mean the work to find an attack may be higher, or defenders can respond sooner, or both, in each case affecting return on investment.)

---

[1]And possibly in other situations. Expanding respect for privacy may lead to conflict over what can be sent from mobile apps, or even cloud-enabled systems.

This brings us to the interesting question of secrecy for machine learning models in the cloud. Machine learning can be a helpful category of tools for defenders. Such tools are used heavily for detecting spam and other abusive content, and they're expensive to create and tune. So how do we best apply Kerckhoffs principle? At one level, we can consider the model as a whole as a key: we expect to regularly tune and update it, and so our reliance on the secrecy of the model is bounded. Attempts to quantify the attacker's work effort are attractive on the surface, but they're easy to get wrong, and the results are often fragile. That is, a clever new attack can dramatically reduce the attacker's work effort.

However, there is a class of attack, or "model theft," against such models. There is a debate about how practical such attacks are against fielded implementations, but first, recall that attacks only get better. Second, recall that we're in a section about assuming transparency. Engineering always involves trade-offs, and in this case, the models may be less aligned with Kerkhoffs principle but still worthwhile in the cloud. (I hope it's now obvious that a downloaded machine learning model is pretty easy to steal and analyze, and so your security should not depend on attackers not doing that.)

It is very tempting to get nuanced about this. It's a trap. There are good reasons that these principles have been in use for a century and a half.

If describing your defenses provides a "roadmap for attackers to bypass them," your defenses are weak. Your designs should be strong even if an attacker knows what they are, and you should absolutely analyze what your own staff can do with questions like "How would you attack this?" I'm frequently surprised by the answers from people outside the security organization.

That brings us to the Death Star plans. First, the Star Wars answers. The Death Star is indeed weak. We know from *Rogue One* that Galen Erso has secretly built a vulnerability into the Death Star. More to the point, the design flaw is obvious. There are no dampers or blow-out panels around the reactor. The Rebellion needs only a very short time to find the flaw, plan an attack, and brief pilots before the Death Star shows up. Lastly, if you'll accompany for a few more moments of even deeper Star Wars theorizing, Vader knows. He's not just hopping in his TIE Fighter to go hunt Rebel scum, he's making sure that he's not in the Death Star if it blows up. (Also, as mentioned in the introduction, that brilliant little short from Dorkly, *The Death Star Architect Speaks Out*, has the architect explain that no one asked him to account for space wizards who can make that shot and a torpedo that can go miles down a narrow shaft.)

Moving from the Star Wars answers, the trouble was that the Empire has a habit of punishing people who question its plans, so no one felt free to question or criticize the Death Star system. As a result, it blew up with countless lives on board. Make sure your security remains strong even if rebels steal the tape backup containing your system architecture. Now it may sound like I'm still in Star Wars, but these lessons translate well to our world.

Obscurity Hurts Defenders

A set of attacks that we now call *stack smashing* have been known since at least the early 1970s. It wasn't until after they were widely publicized in the 1990s that they were addressed (Shostack, 2008).

The proximate cause of many was the C library `str` functions had no information about the length strings. When you copied data from one to another, you could "smash the stack" when the target of the copy was at the end of the stack. This resulted in the contents of the source string overwriting the memory. As long as the details remained obscure, system designers didn't understand the scope of the problem.

Conclusion

Fear leads to hate. Hate leads to anger. Anger leads…to the dark side. It's predictable, and it's why Jedi learn to search their feelings. If Jedi just guessed at what they were feeling ("I feel bad!"), then their ability to resist the Dark Side would be much lower.

Prediction and guessing attacks are powerful. It's easy to forget the amazing speed of modern computers. We can build quite strong security against them, requiring large search spaces, slowing our responses, and using quality randomness to influence how long the search will take.

And time can be an important part of defenses as well. Keeping our clocks synced allows us to better expire and rotate keys so searchers don't have sufficient time to exhaust our randomness.

Parsing and Corruption

Like the corruption of a Jedi, the corruption of memory proceeds in stages. A seed is planted, it grows, and eventually, a Sith tries to harvest it. The seed may be as small as a single bit, and the reward harvested is often the ability to run code of the attacker's choosing.

Input corrupts, and unconstrained input corrupts deviously. Input corrupts because it is the source, the carrier, the medium whose message is LULZ. Almost all attacks are inputs. But useful programs must process input, and interesting programs, those that surprise, delight, or even merely serve us, take complex input. That input is sometimes deviously and cunningly designed to have specific and detrimental effects. To be clear, the surprise is to the programmer who wrote the code, not the one who crafts the input.

This chapter will look at memory corruption, which happens frequently when parsing input; it is a step on the way to exploitation but is not synonymous with it. Memory can become corrupt accidentally. Usually these bugs (or cosmic rays) will lead to a crash or uselessly weird behaviors.

After we look at corruption and the threats to parsers, we'll consider defenses, including input validation in its many flavors, memory safety tools that seek to limit and constrain corruption, and then robust defensive patterns, including Recognizer, Single Parser, and safer language design. The Recognizer pattern concentrates all parsing in a Recognizer, which hands it off to the rest of your code. It's helpful to have the idea in the back of your mind as you go through the chapter. The quick version is, when parsing is concentrated, it's easier to evaluate. When it's distributed, it becomes easy to interleave with business logic or even forget that the input hasn't been checked.

What Is Parsing?

Parsing is the act of taking input, separating it into tokens, and putting those tokens into a structure of one or more objects in memory. (A token is the smallest unit that has a distinct meaning.) It sounds so simple! Anyone who's ever stared at a regular expression and wondered why it matched—or didn't—has the start of an intuition for why parsing is hard. Tokens can be as small as a single bit and are frequently more than one character: numbers, operators like ++ or +=, and variable names are all tokens.

Parsers work over a wide range of input complexity, from handling simple text input like a phone number in a form to parsing the human or machine-readable code of a program or a PDF or a web page. Parser output is used directly by our programs—sometimes with a validation step, sometimes combined with other information, and sometimes passed on to other code. A validation step ensures that the data meets business rules. Validation is sometimes performed on raw input or intermingled with parsing in what's been described as a "shotgun" approach, as opposed to a targeted one.

How Parsers Work

We often imagine that parsers read and validate input and produce a sane object for us to work with. Parsing a phone number, we might read exactly 10 digits, which works OK if you're in the United States and the person entering the number hasn't included parentheses, dashes, or spaces. So, you might read 15 or 20 characters and use a regular expression like `[-()0123456789]+` to check it. Of course that allows 86-75(309), but maybe that's an acceptable input to your dialer code.

If you need to parse phone numbers that go to more than one country, you have to account for a leading plus and a length that varies based on the country code. And as you go down this apparently simple path, you end up with regular expressions like this:

```
^(?:(?:[\+]?(?<Country>[\d]{1,3}(?:[ ]+|[\-.])))?
[(]?(?<Area>[\d]{3})[\-/)]?(?:[ ]+)?)?(?<Num>[a-z2-9]
[a-z0-9 \-.]{6,})?$
```

That's a cut-down version of a recommendation (Reick, 2008). Don't miss the inclusion of "a-z" in the number part! The apparently simple problem turns out to be complex enough that there are libraries to manage it. Google's `libphonenumber` documents the complexities in an FAQ and a "myths programmers believe about phone numbers."

And so we see how even nominally simple data can get complex quickly. One of the challenges in parsing a phone number is that the format varies based on the data. That is, a phone number starting with +1 (North America) will most likely have 10 digits, while in parts of Europe, landlines have 7 digits and mobile numbers have 8, so the content of the data influences the control flow of the parser, a problem that quickly leads to surprising behavior. Similarly, common date formats, like 4/1/04 are impossible to parse without context. Most obviously, is it an American date that could be more specifically written April 1, 1904, or a British date, like 4 January, 2004?[1]

---

[1]For the online sources in the bibliography, I gave up and just copied in dates as they're presented on the sites I saw. Probably some lovely person has now had a heart attack and fixed my formatting; I hope they also made sure to figure out what the source format was.

More generally, parsers recognize input and produce an object to be handled. We'll return to that after a discussion of how we think about that input.

A "Bit" of Context

It's common to say that "our input is a JPG" or "our input is JSON." But that's not really true. Your input is a stream of bits. That stream may be coming over a network or from the local disk. You may well hope that it's a JPG or JSON or even some format that doesn't start with a J, but really, in memory, there's a set of bits to be organized into something useful.

All Input Is Bits

All input is bits.

Or, as we say in hex:

```
41 6c 6c 20 69 6e 70 75 74 20 69 73 20 62 69 74 73 0a
```

Perhaps you prefer binary? As C3-PO knows, that's the language of moisture vaporators (and everything else?):

```
01000011 0011000 10010000 …
```

These are the phrase "All input is bits" as displayed by hexdump. Each representation carries the same meaning, once decoded in a specific way. We can look at each in more than one way. There's the on-the-page representation, starting with "All" or "41 6c." We might shift our thinking and think of them as a hexadecimal representation of the string. But they're also a set of ASCII characters, and I could sneakily replace a zero with the letter O. As long as they're on a page, you might not notice. If I swap the font for a programming one, then the zeros are displayed quite differently (∅ or θ), even though the data hasn't changed. Similarly, Unicode contains a RLO (right-left ordering) indicator that changes display order without the underlying data changing.

The key point is that there is more than one correct way to interpret the data. They are simultaneously true. (In the future, those bits will be translated into curves in a PDF, and we'll express those curves with ink on paper, or raster images to show on your screen. And there will be even more true interpretations.)

All Code Is Bits, Too

A little understanding of how computers execute instructions may give you more visceral wariness for input. When most books show low-level code, they show assembler instructions, like MOV, ADD, or JMP. These are mnemonics.

All code is bits. Those assembler instructions are transformed into machine instructions and stored in memory as bits. And that means that if you can write into a location where the processor expects an instruction…well, it's all bits.

As Ben Kenobi explains it, binary is what gives a computer its instructions. It's an energy field used by all digital things. It surrounds them and penetrates them, and it binds the Internet together. Oh wait, I think he was talking about the Force.

Understanding that all code is bits, you may be able to start to imagine what happens when "data" bits show up in a place where something expects code bits. The binary language of moisture vaporators does something when fed to a dehydrator. In fact, it probably crashes the dryer because the processors are a little different. But if the series of bits is crafted by someone fluent in over 6 million forms of communication, then perhaps they can craft a series of bits that does something unexpected, and that brings us to the threats in parsing. It's easy to say that the CPU should just track what bits are what. But generally, the CPU will execute whatever the execution pointer points to.[2]

---

[2]This is largely true for mainstream systems. There are designs that seek to change this, such as memory that is not executable and cool historical and experimental technologies that track the code/data distinction for reliability or security.

So what does the instruction pointer point to? Bits. Instructions are just sequences of bits. For example, 0x88 might be MOV, while 0x80 might be ADD. Easy, right? You just move from byte to byte and it's code. Or maybe it's the data that the code operates on. So after an 0x88, there's a byte of source and a byte of destination. Hah! No. There are variants for handling 8-, 16-, and 32-bit words in x86. There are 18 or so variants that are described as "MOV," and more for specialized forms of move (Mazegen, 2017). So, it's not trivial to decide "This sequence of bits is code," or even "This sequence of bits has these boundaries or will do this if executed."

When I say all code is bits when executed, I'm illustrating this with code we often assume is executed by the CPU, but in reality, even that code requires a runtime such as `crt0`. The same is true of Java bytecode and even higher-level languages like PostScript.

All Data Is Tainted

Just like you can never quite get the smell of Tauntaun out of your clothes, you can never quite get data to be perfectly clean. You can check it, sanitize it (more on that later), and as you pass it around from function to function, it always has some potential to surprise you.

Security experts call data "tainted." As it goes from layer to layer, we can reduce that taint, by checking it against various expectations that we have and becoming more confident that it meets our goals. But new functions or methods might not run the same input checks and so tracking what it's been checked for is a helpful practice. You can document that with types, with comments, and with unit tests.

Threats to Parsers

Attackers don't want to run code, but running code is often a fine route to their actual objectives. Two common building blocks are writing bits to locations where they'll be treated as code or writing bits that cause your code to behave unexpectedly.

Threats to parsers include getting them confused about order issues, how tokens are delimited (where one ends and another starts), code versus data, and ingenious ways to pass attacks as arguments. There are also problems that stem from complex formats, formats with external dependencies, and shotgun parsing, that is, scattered parsing code, the opposite of Recognizers.[3]

All of these problems are magnified when combined, and they are frequently combined in elaborate, compounded formats. To the extent that we can control the formats we parse, simplification is a powerful lever for reducing security flaws.

Most of the security bugs that get fixed each day are problems with parsers, which are often described as "memory safety" issues. As I write this, the sarcastically named "Fish in A Barrel" group stated that "70 of 78 vulnerabilities disclosed [via an open source fuzzing platform] in the past week are memory unsafety," and "13 of 21 (7 of 9 high/critical) vulnerabilities fixed in Google Chrome 105.0.5195.52 are memory unsafety." Similarly, Microsoft reports that "70% of security vulnerabilities that Microsoft fixes" are memory safety (Fish, 2022; Levick, 2019).

It's important for us to keep our eyes on a broader set of threats, while understanding that parser issues are tremendously frequent sources of problems.

SQL Injection Example

Let's take a relatively simple to understand example, with an attack form you may have heard of: SQL injection. The way SQL injection works is pretty straightforward: a program constructs SQL statements

---

[3]This section and the "Defenses" section are strongly influenced by an analysis called LangSec. Papers I'm drawing on heavily include Bratus, 2014 and 2017; Momot, 2016; Poll, 2018; and Sassaman, 2012.

from input and sends them to a database. The code to create a list of products based on customer input looks something like this:

```
sprintf(*Query, "SELECT * FROM products WHERE name = ",
"%s", input);
```

If the input is "`OR 1=1;'`, then `Query` will be as follows:

```
SELECT * FROM products WHERE name =" OR 1=1;'
```

Well, `1=1` is always true, and so the code will always match, and we'll get back a list of everything in the `products` table. What's happened is that input was parsed and then used in a way that led the database to treat it as an instruction. The fix for SQL injection is to use parameterized statements. A parameterized query tells the SQL parser what structure to expect, and then everything in the data is… parameters. This works way better than trying to add checks that sanitize the input. Parameterized statements are an example of the controlled input grammars that we'll discuss in defenses.

SQL injection is sometimes understood as "the attacker can read your database." This is true but incomplete. The attacker can send *arbitrary* SQL code to the database. They borrow the authority of the database user, and their code can do anything the attacker imagines—a category that certainly includes many things we didn't expect. That includes reading more data than expected, writing data, and possibly even invoking a shell and passing it arbitrary commands.

Surprising Output

Shortly after he chortles that "Everything is proceeding as I have foreseen," the Emperor discovers that things are not going precisely as he's foreseen, and it's only a few more minutes before his protégé throws him over the safety railing into the reactor.[4] Attackers are surprising like that. One little slip can ruin your whole day.

---

[4]At least there's a safety railing there, because we can predict that without one, people will fall in.

What we really want is to know that input will not make our programs surprise us.

A parser takes some input and produces an object in memory. That object will be handled by other code that expects it to be well-formed (whatever that means). The goal of a parser is to put only bits that will be safely handled into only the expected objects.

This is shockingly hard.

This section could well be titled "surprising input," but what we're worried about is not the input, but the effects that input has on our code. We want those effects, including the object the parser produces, to be unsurprising to any other part of our code, even if the input was surprising. That is, the parser should protect the rest of the system. That includes avoiding memory corruption as it runs. It also means prioritizing safety over taking every bit of input. You may have to truncate long strings, not include message parts that fail sanity tests, or otherwise discard input to ensure the result is safe.

If you choose the quick and easy path—as Vader did—your code will become an agent of evil, terrorizing generations of developers.

Tokenization Problems

As data is parsed, the issue of what constitutes a token is crucial. If you're parsing C code and you reach a +, is that a token? It's undecidable until we see the next character. If it's an =, then that's part of the += operator; if it's a 1, then that's the start of the next token. And so our parsing is context dependent. Each character is not independent.

In an ideal world, encodings would be simple, and parsing would be easy. In our world, there are overloaded meanings and encoding flaws, each of which makes tokenization harder. (There are other problems, such as the complexity of the language. The previous mention of regular expressions is a forerunner of complexity that we'll get to, and this sentence is intentionally complexified as an example of how jumping backward and forward makes your brain hurt. Parsers struggle in related ways.)

Overloaded meanings are where a single input can have two effects on the parser. For example, if you have a token that's bounded by spaces, say a filename, what if you have a filename with a space in it? Frequently, we use escape characters, and now the parser is more complex.

Similarly, if you're parsing HTML and you encounter a fragment that is missing a closing quote or two, how should you handle it? Consider code like this:

```
<a href="https://threatsbook.com rel=" noopener>
```

Is the `href` target `https://threatsbook.com rel=` or `https://threatsbook.com`? If it's the longer string, what do you do with the characters `noopener`? Does the `>` close the `a` tag, or is it part of the value of the `rel` key?

Your code might choose to try to help, speculatively attempting to find an insertion that reduces parsing errors and perhaps treating a space as if it were preceded by a quote. Of course, that doesn't work with the `img alt` tag, which is a natural language description of an image, usually a phrase or even sentences.

It's unclear if what's missing is really *closing* quotes. We've barely scratched the surface of two tags, and complexities are multiplying. Imagine what the code would look like.

If you can't tokenize reliably, how can you build objects reliably? You might hope to end up with a parser that's fully predictable. And while rebellions are built on hope, parsers should be built to enforce order.

Repeated Input

There are also threats from repeated input, that is, the same key repeated with different values. If you receive an email with the following headers, how will your mail client display it?

```
From Darth Sideous <darthsideous@sith.org>
From: Darth Sideous <sideous@sith.org>
```

```
From: Senator Palpatane <Palpatane@senate.republic
.galaxy>
```

Obviously, this is a trick question. We all know that the Sith are too contentious to share `sith.org`. But that's not the real trick. The real trick is that there is no correct answer in the sense that even if there is an answer in a standard, your email client may not be compliant.

Some parsers will look for a From address and proceed when they find one. Others will parse the headers all the way through and simply overwrite early values with late ones. A modern library might have a method like `parseheaders()` that returns a dictionary of `(name, value)` pairs. Inside that method, the dictionary is likely constructed by taking each line and breaking it into a name and a value and inserting it into the dictionary, possibly with overwrite checks (which results in the first value being kept) or without (which will result in either an overwrite or the value being a set of values).

Yet other parsers may match on `'^From'` or `'From:'` (Yes, with and without trailing colons. One is the SMTP envelope, which older mail servers would include; the other is the SMTP header.)

Ambiguous Types

Programs take input in many ways, including standard input or from files they explicitly open. Many of these are either accidentally or maliciously ambiguous or overloaded. For example, when a filename starts with a dash, how do you provide it as an argument to a command-line tool? ("How do you remove a file named `"-f"`?"). Ambiguous semantics means programs must have a way to disambiguate them. When we want to help the program, we can use a path like "`./-f`", and when an attacker wants to confuse it, they can use overloading.

A similar issue can arise with files with semicolons in their names, or other characters that the shell treats as special. (For a good laugh, create a file with a slash in its name on Windows, and share that file system with a Unix client you don't mind rebooting.) The issue of determining type from input plagues Excel, with genes being officially renamed to avoid Excel treating them as dates. Membrane Associated Ring-CH-Type 1 is no longer March1, but now MarchF1 (Whitwam, 2020).

If the special characters are command separators like a semicolon or backtick, then the shell may treat the remainder of the name as a command to run. This can happen with filenames, with environment variables, or with other input.

Length and Counting

A failure to check lengths was a key security flaw in the C string functions. Older code that assumes that a char is a byte that is a character can get confused when it encounters Unicode.

There are many problems with integer math: underflows, overflows, and type conversions that happen when you accept numbers from clients.

It won't be long before you encounter systems with nested length information, and you'll have to decide what to do when the sum of the subparts is not the same as the container length. For example, do you stop parsing at the HTTP content length or keep going until you reach a `</html>` tag?

If the two disagree and there's further content to be parsed, you have to choose where to put the read pointer. If your code does one thing and someone else's code does the other, your parsing of the same input will differ.

The "HTTP request smuggling" family of attacks uses precisely these sorts of inconsistencies between content lengths and transfer encoding headers to send extra headers past HTTP proxies.

Shotgun Parsing

A "shotgun parser" is one that's scattered all over the place, in derisive contrast to one that's concentrated. When the parser is scattered all over the place, Worf has to run back and forth. Wait, what's Worf doing here? Isn't this a Star Wars book? This illustrates when the parser is scattered all over the place, it's harder to understand what it does.

Shotgun parsing also tends to mix transformation logic and business logic in. Many codebases develop shotgun parsing over time. As you'll see in defenses, refactoring (and isolating) such code is a tremendously powerful response to repeated attacks against the same surface.

Nested Formats

It's fine for marriage to be "that dream within a dream," but a dream within a dream is a parsing nightmare (Reiner, 1987). It's not just that dreams are unstructured and ephemeral, it's the nesting. For example XML has no limit on how deeply elements can go.

Each layer of nesting adds complexity to parsing code. Unlimited nesting means the parser must depend on the data being parsed in order to terminate. (If nesting is limited, you can use a countdown loop and know how many iterations you'll have.)

External Dependencies

When Darth Vader says, "Join me, and together, we can rule the galaxy as father and son," he's imaging how Luke will respond. It's either Vader's undoing or his salvation, but when you join external documents with your own, you have a galaxy of new parsing challenges.

Structures whose parsing relies on external information create a set of problems. For example, let's look at XML's external Data Type Definitions (DTDs). First, we have to retrieve the entity, which creates denial-of-service issues if the server is unavailable, and we have to figure out what to do. Second, retrieval may disclose who's processing a document. Third, we have to retrieve it so authentically and without integrity issues. Fourth, we have to believe that the server won't send us a special version based on properties of the client, such as IP address or geolocation. Most important, we have to pause our parsing, get the external dependency, parse it, and then resume parsing the initial data. The whole parser has to hang out and wait while those other methods run.

Also, if the external entity can contain another external entity without limits, you may end up with an endless loop of dependency fetching.

Code/Data Confusion

Even if your parser doesn't intentionally run code, there are frequent accidents where code and data get confused. How does that happen?

That can happen because something overwrites the stack or because input isn't tokenized the way each parser expects. In a Unix shell command, a semicolon (;) generally separates commands and allows you to enter more than one on a command line.

In a very real way, all of these problems are parsing problems. A stream of bits gets put somewhere the attacker wants them to be and interpreted in the way they hope.

Overly Powerful Input

There are a few ways in which parsers give control of their parsing or execution to their input, including giving environment variables control over execution through a less-careful input parser.

There are a few environment variables, such as LD_LIBRARY_PATH and IFS, which dramatically change execution. LOCALE changes how numbers are parsed. (Is 1,33 "one and a third" or "one comma thirty three"? The first is a common European presentation; the second is common in North America.) It's tempting to clear out such known dangerous variables; see the "Allowlists and Denylists" section of this chapter to see why it's better to select the input you know how to parse.

Intentionally Running Code

Some parsers are designed to execute code as they run. There's something nice about a format that explicitly runs code. That nice thing is: no one can claim to be surprised when a malicious program does malicious things; after all, it's by design. Formats that intentionally run code include Microsoft Office documents (macros), PDFs (the entire format is essentially a program to be run), HTML with JavaScript, and even TrueType fonts. At least, we can hope no one is surprised. But people frequently are. There is an important question of who it was that intended the code runs.

There are other formats that are Turing complete, which is to say we can't even determine if they'll stop, never mind what effects they'll have. There are things that are surprisingly Turing-complete, including the card game, Magic The Gathering, and PowerPoint—even with macros turned off (Wildenhain, 2020)!

Sometimes, of course, an application benefits from or even requires programmability. Clearly, Magic The Gathering does not, and one could debate if PowerPoint does. Such a debate may be intellectually interesting, but more to the point, we can ask, could we achieve those goals with less authority?

An interesting edge case of this is package installers, where some packages will run arbitrary code during setup and others pause to ask permission. PyPi unavoidably runs a `setup.py` function when you install code, while the Mac package installer asks, "This package will run a program to determine if the software can be installed." Here, the usual expected result is that new code will run, and the package manager knows that it will end up with all the authority of your account. The dialog is about ensuring the person knows that, too, as it continues, "To keep your computer secure, you should only run programs or install software from a trusted source. If you're not sure about this software's source, click Cancel to stop the program and the installation" (Lakshmanan, 2022).

Denial-of-Service Threats to Parsers

Parsers are also subject to denial-of-service attacks. When the first step in processing a format is to decompress it, the expansion can lead to either memory or a CPU denial of service before we even get to the other threats discussed earlier. Generally, see Chapter 5, "Denial of Service and Availability."

Bad Advice

The last threat to individual parsers is bad advice. There is a lot of bad advice out there; I'm sure I've given some of it. I don't mean to cast stones from a glass house but to prepare you so when you face these threats from the Dark Side, ready you will be, young Jedi.

The bad advice includes "parse carefully," "canonicalize," and "use a type-safe language." These are actually reasonable starting points but insufficient. Parse carefully isn't clear. Canonicalization is good, but we need to check that the use of the data matches the rules by which it was made canonical: data normalized as a URL may still be an unexpected file path. And type-safe languages are great, but not all threats are type confusion. Each of these commonplaces is bad because they tempt us into complacency. They are good, but not good enough.

The really bad advice is to sanitize, and "it's just deserialization." Sanitization is covered in the "Input Validation" section. Deserialization is parsing and carries all the complexities of any other parsing.

Chained Parsers

Systems are often built from smaller systems, and each of those systems may have a parser. In fact, SQL injection is a good example of this. The web server has an HTTP parser, and the database has a SQL parser. These are chained, and the chaining may have a formally defined grammar or contract. (If it doesn't, someone is almost certain to be surprised by data that's passed; that's one of the reasons that fuzzing, discussed later in this chapter, is so effective.)

Each successive parser must be explicit about what it recognizes and passes on. For example, if we have a phone number in an HTTP post, then perhaps the HTTP parser checks that it's no more than 20 characters and passes it on but makes no attempt to do sanity checking that the phone number and the address are in the same country.

It's not enough to say, "The HTTP parser passed it," and it's certainly dangerous to continue with "Therefore, it's safe." Safety comes from a precise understanding of what an object variable, field, or element will be used for and not making unwarranted assumptions about what it will be. For example, the XML parser might pass on a file with as yet unfetched remote files hosted at `sith.org`. Perhaps those have been fetched and integrated and no more remote includes are possible. The object might contain a set of exploits as CDATA that have not been further analyzed. In consuming the object the XML parser produces, there must be a clear contract about what's emitted and what's consumable.

Use of those bits can include calling another API. When you do so, being conservative in what you send it is a baseline of reliability. Including elements of your input may be unavoidable, and you may lack the context to check or validate it. To the extent that you can communicate what you did, it will put a limit on the tendency to blindly trust.

Layering

In much the way that all input is bits and the interpretation of those bits is layered, attacks are usually carried in many layers of encoding. Lower layers probably cannot perfectly parse data intended for higher layers. They cannot at the network layer because of packet reconstruction and other complexities (Ptacek, 1998) and should not because of speed and the Single Parser pattern: they are likely to get it wrong. (The pattern is described in the "Defenses" section.)

For a concrete example, consider a phishing email. It is sent from the phishing sender to your mail server, and in that sending, it is an SMTP message in an SMTP envelope, sent over STARTTLS, which is SMTP over TLS. That TLS message is in a set of TCP frames, broken into IP packets, and further fragmented into Ethernet frames. Should the Ethernet switch attempt to validate the IP packets? Should the router validate the TCP stream? Should the Ethernet switch check the email message for URLs on some list of phishing sites?

Many security devices, such as firewalls or intrusion detection systems, attempt to violate layering with the very best of intentions. And, to the extent that they catch some naive attackers, that's fine. But the history of that subfield is one of bypass attacks. Almost all these attacks have, at their core, the difficulty of perfectly understanding and reproducing the ways in which the receiving parser will operate.

Specific Parsing Scenario Threats

At the very low end of IoT devices, there may be a bootloader that hands control to something, often integrated by a compiler into a single image. These systems are less likely to have memory defenses (described in the "Defenses" section) and so parsing code that is viewed as safer on modern operating systems may be riskier in IoT.

Parsing Protocols + Document Formats

Broadly speaking, network protocols, APIs, and document formats are all agreements on how different programs can communicate. Agreement on message formats and content allows parties to communicate. When defining a new protocol, careful specification is expensive and slows us down. So, we tend to be informal and agile, potentially taking on enormous technical debt as we do.

When we have more than one codebase handling an API or a file format, we end up with interoperability issues. Those magnify the debt. Each time a counterparty implements something slightly different, we have a choice: the apparent bugginess of strictness or interoperability with its attendant riskiness and code complexity.

As examples of that document challenge, both Microsoft and Adobe went through a process of improving their document parsers to address abundant security issues (in Office and PDF, respectively). Each faced an uproar over "anti-competitive" behavior when they stopped reading "malformed" documents. Each process was initiated for security and had the effect that competitors had to spend money to rewrite what they thought was perfectly good code.

Replacing the early C library's string handling APIs created a similar compatibility problem. It was infeasible to break every program that called `strcpy`, so new functions were added to the libraries. Each programmer had to rewrite their code to use those new functions.

A final example of the security/compatibility trade-off is that the Web has 30 years of accumulated badly written HTML. A browser that strictly parsed HTML and rendered only what's standards-compliant would render a very small fraction of that. Many of the authors of the code...well, their fire has gone out of the universe. No one will rewrite that enormous pile of documents, and so we're stuck.

C Code + Memory Safety

When parsers are not sufficiently cautious with their input, memory corruption can be a result.

The myriad ways attackers make use of that corruption are fascinating. This chapter is not a guide to exploitation, writing exploits, or weaponizing exploits, which is to say making them work reliably under a variety of circumstances. Even though I don't want to overwhelm you with the details, it is worth taking a quick tour. My goal is to reinforce your understanding that an attacker gaining control of even a single bit is exceptionally dangerous.

For some, this may be a gateway into a new world. If you want to really understand what a computer is doing, these techniques expose deep innards of systems. Classic books like *The Shellcoder's Handbook* (Anley, 2011) and *Exploiting Software* (Hoglund, 2004) teach the details well.

- *Stack smashing* attacks involve writing to executable memory. The first public demonstrations overwrote the execution stack, specifically the pointer to the next function. The term *stack smashing* is used both as shorthand for memory overwriting and specifically for the problems where the stack is overwritten.
- *Return to libc* attacks change control flow to jumps to attacker-selected but existing memory. The standard C library is a popular target because it has calls like `system()` and `exec()` that allow for arbitrary command execution.
- *Return-oriented programming* is a set of techniques that takes advantage of code already in (executable) memory space, stringing it together to achieve an attacker's goal. The code in memory is treated as "gadgets," and the gadgets are given unexpected input. Because gadgets are in executable memory, this bypasses many of the memory safety techniques listed in the "Defenses" section. This can be clever. Not only can you jump from gadget to gadget to execute commands of your choice, but you can build branching code! (This is useful if you need to adjust parameters to evade memory defenses.) In fact, it's been shown that the small gadgets that return-oriented programming uses are a Turing-complete language.
- *Use after free* happens when there are two pointers to the same section of memory. One of the pointers is deleted when the object is released but the code forgets to clean out the other one. Depending on the attacker's control of the forgotten pointer, it could be used to read or write or execute. One typical flow is as follows:
  1. The attacker gets the OS to free the original object.
  2. The attacker gets the OS to fill the space of the original object with data that they control.

3. The attacker gets the code to de-reference the dangling pointer, which now points to the attacker's memory.

(There are use after free issues without multiple pointers, which I'm leaving out for space reasons.)

- *Type conversion* and *promotion*. If you have C code like this:

```
char char1, char2, char3;
char3 = char1 + char2;
```

then the value `char3` may be greater than a char. Therefore, `char3` may be promoted to be a larger type, and it may drag `char1` and `char2` with it! Exploitation of these issues is more subtle, but the easiest problem to understand is that these values are used in tests that control execution flow.

If you do decide to learn more about these techniques, be warned: the road to the dark side brings much suffering on the way to power.

Discovering these techniques required deep technical insight and mad skills. Today you need neither—tools and sample code make them easy. You need to know that input is like plutonium. A small amount can be dangerous for a very long time. You need to be careful where you take it in, you need to be careful in how you store it, and you need to be cognizant of where it goes. You do not need an understanding of the mechanisms by which it will kill you.

Memory Structures

I've referenced "the stack," and it's time to be more explicit about what that is. The local variables of an executing program are stored on a stack, subject to push and pop, and handling a mix of code and data. (Think of a stack of plates, perhaps on a cafeteria spring. You can push plates onto the stack, or pop one off, but only at the top of the stack.)

You're expecting hex dumps here, aren't you? The sort of thing that looks like this and makes your eyes glaze over?

```
Dump of assembler code for function main:
0x8000490 <main>:       pushl  %ebp
0x8000491 <main+1>:     movl   %esp,%ebp
0x8000493 <main+3>:     subl   $0x4,%esp
0x8000496 <main+6>:     movl   $0x0,0xfffffffc(%ebp)
   . . .
```

(From Aleph1, 1996) Well, don't worry. While it's interesting knowledge, and you need to know it to write some attacks, I don't think you need to see stack listings, learn to read them, or understand them to understand the key message. That key message is in a few parts:

- Strings and other variables containing user-supplied data often end up on the stack.
- If you copy more data than expected, you can smash the stack with that user-supplied data.
- Some users are attackers.
- The instruction pointer points to the smashable end of the stack.
- Code is bits. Data is bits. They are stored identically in memory, and there's no way for the CPU to distinguish.
- The CPU does what the instruction pointer tells it.

So, the fix is to stop putting unbounded data onto the stack. Most modern languages will manage memory for you in a forgiving way. C will handle memory exactly the way you tell it to. Exactly. EXACTLY. You need to understand what you're telling C, C++, and other languages that allow manual memory management.

Complementing the stack, the other major type of memory is the heap. The heap is where persistent variables and data structures live, and the memory has to be managed with the `alloc` family of calls. (You also can't write unbounded data to the heap.) Modern languages will manage memory for you. They track the memory they've allocated so that a garbage collector can come through, pause your code at the least convenient time possible, have a cup of java, and sweep up your unused memory, leaving little bits here and there so that new allocations are fragmented. I kid! Java is not the only language with annoying garbage collection. More importantly for our purposes, the heap is a convenient place for an attacker to drop code or other resources that they'd like to have available as they run an exploit. This is often accomplished via "heap spraying." The memory is then accessed by attacker code.

Defenses

It's both crucial and insufficient to say the defense against parsing problems is extreme care. It's crucial because so many security problems happen in parsing, and it's insufficient because it's not actionable. The LangSec community is an academic movement. They see "the Internet insecurity epidemic as a consequence of *ad hoc* programming of input handling at all layers…" They make a convincing case that the total cost of formal specification is frequently worthwhile. But they don't have to pay the cost of changing your software or the software of your competitors or ecosystem.

This section is focused on a set of defenses including how to think about robustness, defensive parsing, and validation techniques. From there we'll look at stronger patterns from LangSec, and then we'll close with a discussion of memory safety because so frequently the corrupting effect of bad input is memory corruption leading to code execution.

The Robustness Principle

An early expression of Postel's Robustness Principle was "Be liberal in what you accept and conservative in what you send." In 2012, a set of researchers focused on language security "patched" the principle to read as follows:

- Be *definite* about what you accept.
- Treat valid or expected inputs as formal languages, accept them with a matching computational power, and generate their Recognizer from their grammar.
- Reduce the computational complexity of your parsing. (This last one is paraphrased; all from Sassaman, 2012.)

As Sassaman and his collaborators point out, even Postel's formulation doesn't require being naïve. It doesn't require you to accept bizarre input. You can be robust, recognize the message is bad, and discard it.

Even if you have no control over the formats you must accept, you can be conservative in what you send. Don't make it hard to parse your output. Emitting relative path names, escape sequences that could be simplified, or expressions destined for eval where you could avoid that means that parsers are locked into needing to parse such constructs. Being conservative in what you send remains solid advice and can help us avoid creeping complexity.

Input Validation

Validating input means ensuring that it matches your expectation and that you can predict its effect on your code and the objects your code emits.

Because all data is bits and can be used in an endless variety of ways, validation can't be "complete" without specifying the format or contract against which validation was performed. In the SQL injection example, prepared statements put code and data into carefully separated variables.

Validation is best accomplished before writing to a strictly typed variable, such as `Signed32bitInt`, `email_address`, `URL`, and the like. The string type, which could be used for any of those, makes it hard to form a specific contract (Poll, 2018, Arce, 2014). You might make more specific types, such as `unsafe_path` or `filesystem_path_canonicalized_from_user`. Notice the naming: "unsafe" implies we've done no checking, and `filesystem_path_canonicalized` makes it easy to track that those are performed before assigning any data to it, without implying anything else. Calling a variable safe would make it easy to be dangerously optimistic.

There's a crucial question of where security validation happens. Security validation must happen when the data can no longer be altered by untrusted parties. In the web context, that means the server checks what's sent to it. Even if you have a list of dates in a drop-down menu, if someone alters the HTML with the browser's source editor, or the HTTP call with a proxy, they can insert an arbitrary or even malformed input. Similarly, calls to the kernel need to copy data into kernel-only memory before validating it.

That doesn't mean you can't put a "courtesy validation" in the browser, something that checks the input is likely going to be parsed correctly on the server. It's nice for usability reasons, and you may worry that that will either violate the single parser principle or disclose your validation routine. Don't worry about disclosing your validation routine; if your security depends on its secrecy, you're in trouble. Recall the section on transparency in Chapter 7, "Predictability and Randomness."

Validation Challenges

Validating input is crazy hard. We aspire to check both the format and the semantics. Let me tell you the story of Joda the Conservative Librarian of Time. Some software, which recorded only birthdays, set the time to 00:00, a nice, conservative choice. On April 13, 1941, the clocks in Saskatchewan, Canada, "sprung forward" at midnight as part of a daylight saving transition. And so, patients who were born on that day could not be born at midnight. And so the validation functions of a widely used library, Joda-Time, were unable to accept a patient's date of birth when lab tests were ordered (Lyon, 2020).

What should you do with a partially invalid input like that? If your answer starts with "obviously," please take a deep breath and consider how that might go wrong. One common pattern is to attempt to repair the data, or sanitize it, which we cover in the next section. Another would be to use the date without the time, which makes sense when the patient is an adult but perhaps exact age is crucial in natal intensive care.

Another problem with validation happens when your validation tables lag behind reality. Here's an example:

```
Planets = [Mercury Venus Earth Mars Jupiter Saturn
Uranus Neptune Pluto]
```

When Pluto was demoted, previously correct code became wrong.[5] A more down-to-Earth version of the problem is when a new

---

[5] Planetary scientists dispute the authority of the International Astronomical Union to decide what's a planet and question the process by which the vote passed only on the last day of the conference, after many attendees had left (Stern, 2018). And as Han Solo pointed out, Pluto's too big to be a space station.

subdivision is built; it takes time for the names and geographical coordinates of the new streets to propagate, and some companies can't handle providing services until their databases are updated. To make matters worse, when you update your validation tables, input that was acceptable before may break.

Careful documentation of precisely what's being checked helps us write code that manages these challenges to reliable functioning. Careful definition of contracts and unit tests helps ensure our code is unsurprising.

Sanitization

On seeing spoiled produce at a grocery store, most of us would point it out to an employee for removal. You don't pick it up, ask for a discount, and try to make use of it. Bad input is like spoiled produce. You should not attempt to sanitize it. You should reject it, explain your rejection, and move on to the next request. Otherwise, you risk transforming the input into something dangerous.

Examples of failed sanitization are easy to find. Perhaps the most famous was PHP's Magic Quotes feature. The failures were complex and require some understanding of the feature, so let's go with a slightly contrived example. Say that you reject any input with the string "script" and then uppercase it all. (You might not even think of uppercasing as sanitization.) But if the input contains `script`, you'll end up with SCRIPT, as you can see in Table 8.1.

TABLE 8.1 Sanitization Rule Results

Input	Rule	Output
script	Remove script	script
script	uppercase	SCRIPT

Surprise! If you up case ı (U+0131, a lowercase, dot-less i), you get an I (U+0049, the common English uppercase i.) Having sanitized the input, you broke your own validation.

The goal of sanitization is often to deal with data that fails an explicit validation check. If you must parse data that fails validation, throwing some of it away may be feasible, and it may also be possible to invoke a more sandboxed parser to try to make sense of it.

Canonicalization

There are a wide variety of valid, usable interpretations of any set of bits. It's common to aspire to a "canonical" representation and to believe that will solve your parsing problems. And while canonicalization is useful because it simplifies checking, it's no panacea.

A typical example of canonicalizing is a Unix path. We resolve symbolic links, replace a leading ~ with a user's home directory, and on seeing a .., we remove it and the preceding directory name. Ideally, this looks like the output of `realpath()`, and we can check it and pass it to `open()`. That checking might ensure, for example, that it starts with `/usr/local/include`, which is nice for open, but if we pass it to another program, especially one that is setuid, then that other program may need to do different checks.

As formats become more complex, the definition of canonical can become complex. Dates are (ahem) a canonical example. But let's look at URLs. The URL encoding of % is %25. If I do a Google search on "%25," that will be encoded as %2525 (Nadel, 2021). When I canonicalize that string, do I return a % or a %25? That is, should I ensure that the output of the canonical function, passed to itself, returns an identical string? We expect both that it returns something unambiguous and that ambiguity does not overly restrict use. You might assert that this is ambiguity over the encoding we're using, and we can solve the problem by being specific. And while that's a key point of this chapter, the various encodings continue to trip up real system designers.

When a format has layers of encoding, it gets complex quickly. You want to translate anything starting with a percent marker (%) into their ASCII equivalents before doing your UTF-8 decoding.

Or perhaps it's the other way around? I am not being glib or evasive here, I honestly don't know, and the references I checked do not give me a simple answer (OWASP, 2013; Zalewski, 2011).

Allowlists and Denylists

Allowlists and denylists are ways of constraining input. They're also called whitelists and blacklists, but the technology world has been steadily moving toward clearer and more inclusive language. For example, is a blacklist like a business that's "in the black," or is it a negative thing (NIST, 2021)? Denylists can be a "garden path." Perhaps because we think of an attack and say, "We should disallow that!" The denylist grows until we can't think of another bit of evil, and we hope our attackers stop at the same point. So, allowlists are far more effective for security, because they fail relatively safely.

To explain, let's say we have a list of characters we won't accept in input destined for HTML output (that is, an HTML denylist):

```
evil = ["';`&<>]
while (c = input[i]) {
    if { c ~= /evil/ then i++ ; }
    else { output += c ; i++ ; } }
```

Take a moment to think about the way this goes wrong. (Hint 1: What's missing from the list? Hint 2: How does that generalize?) In contrast, an allowlist looks like this:

```
acceptable = [A-Za-z0-9]
while (c = input[i]) {
    if { c ~= /acceptable/ then output += c }
    i++ ; }
```

You can use an allowlist pattern within a Validator. Ideally, your allowlist is a courtesy, for reliability, because your Recognizer has already ensured compliance with a grammar. Good selection of what's allowed must be both constrained and sensitive. Don't be naïve about it. Early attempts to prevent SQL injection led to people named O'Connor being unable to log in or to email addresses with + signs being rejected. Especially if the text contains names, it may extend beyond a basic A–Z/a–z character set.[6]

Memory Safety

The challenges in safely parsing arbitrary protocols with handcrafted code can feel like raising an X-Wing Fighter out of a swamp. Fortunately, help is available. It takes the form of using safer code, analyzing your less-safe code with static analysis, and compiling it with defenses that make exploitation harder. Lastly, you can use testing techniques, including fuzzing, to detect issues in your compiled code.

More generally, if you're writing in C or C++, there are many security specific pitfalls and gotchas. Defensive books such as *Effective C* (Seacord, 2019) are broader than *Secure Coding in C and C++* (Seacord, 2005), which remains an excellent deep reference.

Safer Languages and Libraries

Many modern languages, including Python and Go, have been designed to protect developers from some of the flaws that pervaded C, C++, and even Java. Popular improvements include type safety and safer string handling. Not all modern languages have made the same choices, and note that I'm using the term "safer," rather than "safe." You can write bad code in any language.

Selecting a safer language for new projects can pay off handsomely. The initial work to learn a new language results in fewer bugs in the future. Of course, it's hard to rewrite entire projects, but it's possible to rewrite parts of a system, such as the parsers.

---

[6]Microsoft Word will replace the English word *naive* with *naïve* with a dieresis, a pair of dots. However, it will not mark the *n* in Señor, which it considers a separate letter.

There are libraries designed to make parsing safer. For example, Microsoft's Everparse project takes C-like definitions, produces F* code, formally proves its security, and then compiles it into C without losing provability. (F* is a programming language designed for provability.) Everparse has been used to produce verified versions of protocols like TLS and the Signal messaging protocol.

Static Analysis

Static analysis is a family of techniques to analyze code "statically," that is, without running it. It can find vulnerable code constructs and be integrated into build pipelines, and there is a wide range of tooling available.

Static analysis tools are justifiably criticized for sometimes incomprehensible output, false positives, and sometimes for speed—they can be slow to run on large codebases. They can also be challenging to deploy, producing copious warnings. Despite these challenges, static analysis is a powerful tool for your toolbox. Many organizations deploy them slowly, using settings to ensure that new code is clean, and gradually deploying rules to older code.

Defenses in Depth

Major platform vendors have dedicated teams that design defenses to make memory safety issues harder to exploit. These defenses, with names like "address space layout randomization" or "nonexecutable" memory regions (ASLR, NX), are outside the scope of this book. Variation in those defenses means that the same issue of memory corruptibility in the same code may compile into something exploitable on one platform but not on another.

It's crucial to emphasize it is extremely dangerous for an attacker to be able to read or write memory in ways that are not precisely and carefully constrained. If memory can be corrupted, good programming practice is to fix the corruption rather than arguing over exploitability. Memory can be corrupted in ways that are exploitable on one platform but not another. It can be corrupted in ways whose exploitability is not yet understood, because the art of turning corruption into an exploit is advancing, as are the defenses that make that transformation difficult. Your correct belief that an issue is not exploitable may depend on a parser detail that changes later, making you vulnerable.

In the best case, you spend scarce skilled resources to prove that you should do what I just told you, which is to address the corruption. In the worst, you mistakenly assess that an exploitable vulnerability is not, and leave your code subject to attack. (If fixing corruption issues is an overwhelming or seemingly Sisyphean task, perhaps your code needs refactoring.)

Dynamic Analysis Including Fuzzing

Dynamic analyses are those that run your code to see how it behaves when fed input that's malicious, malformed, or even just random.

Recall that processor instructions are just bits, like those that run a moisture vaporator. Fuzzing, sending random input and seeing what happens, is remarkably effective at finding bugs. This is especially true for code written in low-level languages like C but not limited to such code. Because parsing is hard, when fuzzing was invented, between a quarter and a third of programs failed to what we now call *dumb fuzzing* (Miller, 1990). And to be clear, fuzzing can be exceptionally simple, on the order of `cat /dev/random | target`.

Of course, the parser failures that simple fuzzing exposes tend to express as crashes. It would be remarkable to see those random bits do something interesting. Fuzzers also tend to produce many crashes around the same line of code.

Fuzzing is most dramatic when targeting C-like languages, but that doesn't mean it only works against them. As you apply it to programs in languages with type safety and modern parsing libraries, basic fuzzing discovers fewer problems, but context-aware fuzzers are now common.

Earlier in this chapter I cited some statistics ("70 of 78 vulnerabilities disclosed via OSS-Fuzz in the past week are memory unsafety"). This shows that fuzzers are much better at finding memory safety issues than other issues, and the issues they find tend to be inarguably high severity.

LangSec

LangSec, or language-theoretic security, is an academic movement. They point out that parsing failures are intertwined with security pain, and that as the languages and code parsing them grow in complexity, the opportunities to make them do shocking things also grows. This chapter draws heavily on their work, while acknowledging that every engineer may not have the budget, skills, or scope of control to act on all of their suggestions.

Simple design, like formats that can be parsed with regular expressions, makes parsing far less risky. Conversely, powerful languages with complex grammars (say, PDF or Office) are more dangerous. Compound length declarations, where both outer and inner objects have lengths that may disagree, are more dangerous than simpler declarations. Other flawed patterns include self-modifying formats, formats that require multiple passes, and eval-style commands. And please, don't write another Turing-complete language by accident.

Many developers never get to define a named language or file format, so the recommendations of LangSec may seem like they're in a galaxy far, far away. But many of us get to define little languages, little state machines, or little protocols. The contract between an API caller and a callee is a language, and simplicity and predictability contribute to not only security but predictability, testability, and resilience.

If the problems here are ones you focus on, learn more at `LangSec.org`.

Recognizer Pattern

A Recognizer takes input and produces output that is limited to what the rest of your code expects. When you unify parsing code into a single place, it becomes easier to reason about. A Recognizer accepts valid input and discards invalid input. (This may lead to rejecting an entire message or rejecting part of it, passing on a data structure that differs from the input.) In the Recognizer pattern, valid input is defined by a grammar, and parsing is completed before an object is passed to validation or application logic. What your code expects is ideally defined by explicit grammars, or sometimes by contracts, supported by unit tests or the random behavior of clients.

It may be helpful to run the Recognizer isolated from the rest of the application. As discussed in Chapter 6, qmail took this to the level of running as a separate user ID and passed messages through files. Of course, that requires you to deserialize those files, which is yet another parser to secure.

It may also be helpful to consider Recognizer and Validator as connected patterns. The Recognizer simply parses (tokenizes and constructs an object), while a Validator checks the meaningfulness of those objects, beyond what's in the grammar. For example, ensuring that a URL is currently "valid" (perhaps the server returns an HTTP OK message and an HTML document) or that an email doesn't get rejected at a delivery attempt.

Single Parser Pattern

For any format you handle, select and use one parser. Of course, for most of the formats we parse, we didn't write the parser. Why write your own JPG parser or renderer when there's a dozen open-source versions? The selection of an unsafe parser will lead to a never-ending parade of bounty hunters at your door. And while people earning money in bug bounties aren't scum or villainy, selecting a better parser will let you focus on other work. A few things to look for include an Open Source Security Foundation Badge and use of memory-safe languages. Having at least a few security issues acknowledged can be an indication of maturity; having a parade is probably a good predictor of the future.

If you have two parsers that take the same input, use the same schema, and produce two different outputs, then at least one of them has to be wrong. At the least, their wrongness will produce inconsistency. Depending on the nature of the inconsistency, clever attackers may be able to take advantage of it. (Of course, this also means that changing a legacy system to use a single parser will cause behavior changes, which makes it an expensive change.)

Therefore, one organization having two parsers for a format is an expensive way to cause errors and a great way to incentivize finger-pointing and blaming. On the error front, Apple created two parsers for its `plist` format, and differences in the way they handled comments led to one (in place to perform security checks) passing a file to another, which ran commands the first ignored as parts of comments. The Saskatchewan/Joda birthday story is another instance of multiple parsers with incompatible Validators.

As we shift from a single organization to an ecosystem of software handling the same network protocol or file format, having more than one parser is a great way to check a specification. Such parsers, running on different systems, don't need to produce the same object in memory, but they do need to act in unsurprising ways when communicating. For a long time the IETF claimed[7] to require two parsers for any standard network protocol.

A variant of the two-parser problem shows in network intrusion detection. A classic paper by researchers Tom Ptacek and Tim Newsham shows what attacks they label insertion and evasion are inevitable with a network observer (Ptacek, 1998). This also applies to web application firewalls: if they have a different parser than your endpoint, they may not interpret connections the same way. For example, if the firewall gets a packet with time to live set to 2 and thus

---

[7]For several years in the late 1990s, I delighted in pointing out that BIND was the only DNS implementation.

the packet will transit only two more hops, should it expect the endpoint will see the packet or not? And the point applies to more than firewalls. If an application proxy terminates a TCP connection, it parses the protocol and crafts messages to send on. As a separate parser, it may construct an object and then use that object to construct messages. (It may also either blindly copy or apply a zero-copy philosophy, in either case giving less protection.)

Designing Protocols and File Formats

In discussing parsing in specific situations, I assume the format has been defined. If it has not, the effort you spend to specifically, concretely, and formally define the protocol will pay off. Additionally, there are some design principles. These include simple design, limiting recursion or nesting, and ensuring that the full document is present (avoiding includes, especially remotely). Sometimes there are good engineering reasons to include other input. Doing so in a clearly delineated "includes" section at the start of a document will at least constrain parsing complexity, and the pattern of "include anywhere" has enabled an awful lot of remote file inclusion issues.

Language Complexity

Computer scientists have a way of discussing the complexity of languages. They divide languages into several categories, including regular languages, context-free languages, and context-sensitive and recursively enumerable languages. C3-P0 understands this entire hierarchy of language complexity and would be excited to explain it to someone! If C3-P0 is not available and you'd like to learn more, a good place to start is with a paper by Sergey Bratus and collaborators, Beyond Planted Bugs in 'Trusting Trust' (2014).

Conclusion

Like a Jedi is tempted by the power of the Dark Side, attackers are tempted by the power of unconstrained parsers.

Yoda warns Luke Skywalker that only a fully trained Jedi Knight with the Force as his ally will conquer Vader and his Emperor. Similarly, only a fully trained parser will conquer all the inputs its fed. Unfortunately, we don't have Yoda, or even dramatic music, to warn us of the dangers of parsing. It's easy to lose track of where input came from or what validation has been done. It's easy to lose track of the many threats as we parse.

But finding a careless parser is the fastest route to SQL injection, cross-site scripting, stack smashing, buffer overflows, remote code execution, and other forms of expansion of authority.

Eternal vigilance is the price of liberty, and it's also the price of maintaining a parser. There are fewer heart-stopping moments if you build on solid foundations.

9 Kill Chains

Up to this point, we've talked about individual threats. But in the real world, individual threats are less interesting than the chains that bring them together into an attack on a system.

Rebels analyze the stolen Death Star plans and find a weakness. The Death Star conveniently shows up (rather than a fleet of Star Destroyers), and the Rebels are able to use their X-Wing fighters and Jedi-in-training to deliver a torpedo to precisely the right spot, where it destroys the Death Star.

Other than X-Wings and Death Stars, threats don't show up in a vacuum. Technology has a context, and that context defines the attacker's journey. For every attack, an attacker will engage in some reconnaissance or experimentation. That may be as limited as "Send attack packets to sequential IP addresses" or as sophisticated as "We'll set up a collection of fake businesses, and then recruit people to 'work from home,' reshipping packages and laundering money for us." Even the folks who scan sequential IP addresses need to hear the responses, put those into a database, and then use the results.

To this point, we've looked at individual threats: the building blocks that attackers will combine into something useful to them. Let me present an example of a chain:

1. Analyze the plans for the Death Star. (Reconnaissance.)
2. Discover that a small fighter might deliver a torpedo. (Weaponization.)
3. Fly to the Death Star, fly down a trench. (Delivery.)
4. Make the shot. It's like shooting womp rats back home. (Exploitation.)
5. The torpedo makes it to the reactor system. (Installation.)
6. The torpedo blows up at precisely the right place because of self-contained control logic. (Command and Control.)
7. Actions on Objective: There's a Death-Star-shattering kaboom.

The parenthetical step names are explained later in the chapter. Different chains can have different steps, even different numbers of steps. This chapter dives into many widely applicable kill chains.

We'll consider chains of threats to software that listens for connections (servers), software that connect out (clients), and the hybrid messaging systems where a server is listening for, queuing, and delivering messages to a client. Both the client and messaging will be grouped into "desktops," where they traditionally run. All of these chains—client, server, messaging—end with an attacker gaining the authority to run code. Other chains lead to attackers gaining authority by obtaining real credentials.

Those two strategies (exploiting a program or using credentials) for gaining authority are followed by chains in specific scenarios, such as cloud, AI, and mobile. After that, you'll learn about the history of chains and see how the chains can be brought together. (I'll mangle the metaphors, twist the chains together, and develop a braid! Sadly, it won't be as iconic as Leia's braids, but then again, who is?) The chapter closes with a section on defenses.

Threats: Kill Chains

The kill chain of Reconnaissance, Weaponization, Delivery, Exploitation, Installation, Command and Control, and Actions on Objectives is a modern classic (Hutchins, 2010). It has a good blend of specificity and generality that made it powerful, and we'll talk about its history later in the chapter. But while its creators have trademarked it as "Cyber Kill Chain®," there are many kill chains in cybersecurity, developed to model other attacks. Because of its explanatory power, I'll use those steps as appropriate in this chapter and also vary them as needed. Also, I'll generally use the term *step* for a discrete task, and when multiple, similar steps might be needed, I'll call that a *stage*. Thus, the Delivery stage of the Death Star kill chain involves steps of flying to the Death Star and delivering the torpedo. Of course, it was crucial to stay on target as those steps were executed.

The idea of looking at attacks in steps is not new. Security experts frequently represent them as either chains or trees. We use chains to look back at what attackers did, and trees to represent unfolding possibilities. We call the chains *kill chains* and the trees *attack trees*. Of course, a chain is a very simple form of tree, and the distinction is largely focused on "did this happen" versus "could this happen," rather than the different representations having inherent comparative value. The terms kill and attack are roughly synonymous.

As you read through this chapter, you might notice that some of the chains aren't really chains or even trees, but more braids. Software security expert Gary McGraw has called them fractal, and it's a great description. By fractal, he means self-similar. At any point, the attacker can fork off an entire side kill chain to obtain some needed stepping-stone. That chain is a step in a larger chain, much like the triangles in a fractal (Sierpiński) triangle are made up of smaller triangles.

You may have noticed that the chain in the introduction skips over at least two related chains: "Steal the plans for the Death Star" and "Rescue the Princess." For modeling purposes, we omit these details.

Some of the larger, more complex operations, say, those run by intelligence agencies, have included the step "Break into software provider and insert malware into their software." That's both a complete chain in itself and a link in a longer chain. Part of the reason that this chapter is positioned late in the book is because you're now better able to handle that fractal nature. Additionally, the chains or graphs that relate to how computers are compromised (as opposed to network attacks) have some points of concentration: the ability to run code as a given user and the ability to log in as that user. They're closely related: if you can log in to a Unix server as shostack, you can run code as me. But if you can log in to my bank as shostack, you can do things as me, but my bank doesn't allow me to upload code and run it. (These are places where the attacker has defeated either authentication or authorization and can thus spoof or expand their authority.)

Server Kill Chain

When I say server, I mean a system that's primarily running daemons or network listeners and has limited interactive use. The hardware doesn't matter—it might be a Raspberry Pi, an expensive rack-mounted system, or abstracted in someone else's data center. If used like a local desktop computer, all the attacks I cover in desktop chains are relevant.

Network Listeners Chain

The attacker finds a server, a system that is listening and waiting for clients to connect to it, and attacks the code that's parsing what that listener receives. Attacks you may have heard of like SQL injection or remote file inclusion all work against a server. Network worms work this way, attacking common listeners like SQL servers, RPC endpoints, or file services.

This can be very broad, attacking vulnerabilities in widespread software, often parser vulnerabilities. Worms will often send their exploit code completely indiscriminately, preferring a hope that it succeeds to the effort of selectivity. It can also be very narrow, targeting your unique software. Penetration testers might spend weeks analyzing a web application and understanding its composition and then craft custom attack code. The links of the kill chain are the same; the specific work the attacker performs differs somewhat.

Some of these attacks work directly, using a buffer overflow in the code that actually listens on the socket. Some, like SQLi, are passed through layers of service code: the web server, all its frameworks, your business logic, and then eventually to the database.

The Network Listener kill chain does the following:

1. Recon: Find a server that's listening and information it discloses about the software it's running.
2. Weaponize: Find a vulnerability in that server. (In practice, this step may happen first. An attacker whose recon is focused on finding software vulnerabilities may then do recon to see where it can be used.)
3. Deliver: Send the exploit.
4. Exploit: If the exploit succeeds, it gains authority, often through a parser issue.
5. Install: Software is installed to help the attacker.
6. Command and control: The software gets commands, like "search for credit card numbers" or "find the cryptographic keys."
7. Actions on Objectives: The attacker uses their newly stolen authority to achieve goals.

Figure 9.1 shows steps 1–4 of the Network Listener kill chain. Steps 5–7 are common to other chains and so are not shown in this diagram. (Later in the chapter, you'll see how the diagrams fit together, with those common pieces shown with the many ways attackers reach them.)

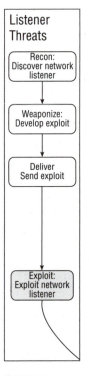

FIGURE 9.1 Network listening daemon (server) kill chain

SQL Injection Kill Chain (Example) A SQL injection attack has a slightly different kill chain from the general server model, skipping the installation and command-and-control steps.

The Reconnaissance stage can be discreet. Find a website that's probably backed by a database, and probe it by sending queries that are likely to reveal things about SQL injection. Because it always evaluates to true, inserting `' OR '1'='1` to web forms has become a classic form of recon. It doesn't get the attacker what they want, but it shows that further investigation will probably be fruitful.

The Weaponization stage involves taking a vulnerability found in recon and turning it into something that will reliably execute and obtain the data you want. You might be thinking SQL injection either works or it doesn't, but if you're going to extract gigabytes of data, you might need to select subsets of the data, rather than ask for it all at once. You might need to performance optimize your queries to avoid being noticed. You might spin up a cloud instance to hold the loot.

The Exploitation step is to use the weapon against the real target. The act on objectives might be using or selling the data you've extracted, or whatever else the attacker wants to do.

Desktop Kill Chains

This section will look at many common attacks against traditional, interactive desktop computers. It starts with attacks on complex client software that acts on the instructions of a person behind the computer. From there, we touch briefly on desktops that run server software (listening for connections) and then to messages. Those messages are similarly initiated by others and can carry out attacks much like those against servers but attack the client or through it, leaving the server untouched. The extended discussion of message-borne attacks includes various forms of phishing and scams via messages.

These five kill chains result in a compromised desktop. At that point, the attacker has access to your authority. They can run code as you and focus on their objective. Those chains are as follows:

1. Through a client like a web browser
2. Through a listening daemon
3. Through locally installed code, already present
4. Install new code
5. Attacks via messages

The first four (clients, servers, and already installed or new code) are relatively straightforward. The last, attacks carried by messages, is a bridge to attacks on clients or credential theft.

Browsers and Other Clients Chain

A client is software that initiates a connection to a server. Again, *server* means software listening for a connection, as opposed to initiating one.

Some clients will connect to a few specified servers, like an email or IM client, while others, like a web browser, will connect indiscriminately. Some of these weapons are delivered by the client to another piece of software.

The chain is as follows:

1. Recon: Find a server that you think your target might connect to. (Reconnaissance is often shortened to recon, because who can spell French words?)
2. Weaponize:
   (a) Compromise the server. (See "Server Kill Chain.")
   (b) Create a weapon to be delivered to your actual targets.
3. Deliver: Use the server to deliver the weapons.
4. Exploit:
   (a) For browsers, the weapon might directly target the client software, target a plugin, invoke a whole additional program and its parser (such as Word or PDF), or attempt to get a file downloaded and then invoked.
   (b) For message clients in addition to all the attacks against browsers, there are links (URLs) pointing to either attack sites or credential-stealing stealing ones. Attack sites loop back to step 3, which is another layer of delivery, while credential-stealing ones jump to that chain.
5. Attacking through a downloaded file. (See separate chain)

The underlying reality of the client chain includes multiple steps in weaponization and variants in how the exploit step is carried out. It starts to resemble a tree.

Figure 9.2 shows the key links in this chain.

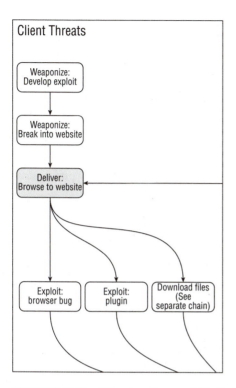

FIGURE 9.2 Client software kill chain (excerpt)

From the server's perspective, the delivery phase of a kill chain involves waiting for clients to arrive. Information disclosure by the client may help the server tailor attacks. For example, my browser enthusiastically tells every server it talks to its version and my operating system.

Some clients connect to a very few servers: messaging services like iMessage or Facebook messenger connect only to Apple or Facebook servers (respectively). A mail client connects to a few servers, each selected by the user in a configuration step. As it does so, the client is exposed to risk, if one of those servers chooses to attack it. And then there are web browsers.

We generally think of web browsers as following the instructions of the human behind them to visit websites. Many protocols have layers of re-direction at the client layer, and these expose the client to additional attacks. For example, when I direct my browser to `https://nytimes.com`, in addition to the *New York Times* content, there are links to `nyt.qualtrics.com`, `www.nytco.com`, `www.tbrandstudio.com`, and `www.googletagmanager.com`, and probably others. Browsers happily follow such links for usability reasons. And so a browser is subject to attack from servers that you may not be aware of.

The attacker has three options once a client has been brought to their server: they can target the client with an exploit, they can target a plugin or invoked document parser, or they can attempt to get a file downloaded. The same options are available once their message has been delivered.

The client likely has several layers of parser: there's a parser that handles the channel and probably a set of different ones that handle messages carried in that channel. Each is subject to attack.

Messaging Systems

Messaging clients get messages from one or a few servers, but those servers collect messages from anyone. A delivered message can attack the client or present a credential stealing attack. Those classic phishing messages are covered in the "Acquire or use credentials" kill chain. The message can also carry a client attack, including URLs or malicious attachments, jumping to that tree.

The term *phishing* has morphed from "an email designed to steal your credentials" to "a malicious message of any type." Many of these terms have been created by marketing departments and focus on small changes to delivery mechanisms, such as vishing for a voice call or smishing, via text messages.

Control of those messaging servers varies. Some, like corporate mail servers, are under your control; others, like Gmail, are operated by a third party. Some support open protocols like email; others use proprietary formats. But in all of these cases, they accept messages broadly for delivery. When they're acting as servers, they're vulnerable as servers, but here, we focus on how the messages they relay to clients threaten those clients.

Figure 9.3 shows a messaging kill chain. It starts with Recon, collecting addresses, and then Weaponization. The first contact from the attacker is when they send the message. That step can lead to an attack on a client, such as a web browser, or initiate credential theft, each of which has its own kill chains. Messaging can also continue in a kill chain against the messaging client with an exploit or a file (see the "Downloaded File Chain" or the "'Please Install Code' Chain" section).

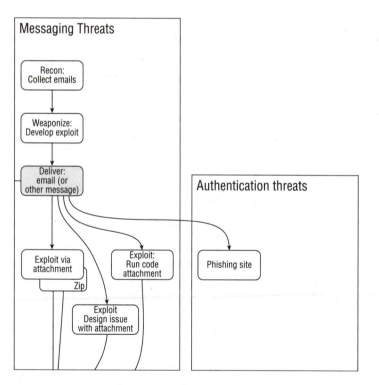

FIGURE 9.3 Messaging kill chain

Network Listeners on Desktops

Your desktop computer probably has a set of network listeners on it. The computer I'm typing this on has roughly 15 listeners for printing, SSH, bonjour, and a virtual camera plugin. Even though the system is a desktop, those listeners are vulnerable. (As it turns out, roughly half restrict their listening to loopback connections, those from the local system.)

The server kill chain applies to any of those 15 listeners, or whatever listeners a given desktop computer has. The half that are restricting their connections to loopback only require another chain. Perhaps that's "break into a low-authority account on the target" or to find server-side request forgery or a remote file inclusion attack, which will turn it into a proxy.

Local Software Package Chain

A long time ago, many local software packages contained no networking code. Think of the traditional versions of Microsoft Office or a game. If they handled files, they were local or via network file service protocols (SMB, NFS). Many of these programs did not expect to be attacked, so they are helpfully vulnerable links in either client or message kill chains.

1. Recon: Find a vulnerability in a local software package.
2. Weaponize: Craft a reliable exploit.
   (a) Attacks on parsers
   (b) Attacks that misuse features (macros, etc.)
   (c) Attacks that use features as designed (shell scripts)
3. Deliver: Send the exploit in a way that reaches the target.

From here, exploitation, installation, command and control, and actions on objectives proceed similarly to chains that you've seen.

The step "use features as designed" means using existing programs that are designed to run other code like shells, interpreters, or build systems. Because this local software chain is shorter, I'm not including a visual representation.

Downloaded File Chain

The danger from a file is realized when the file is invoked in some way. There are a few chains. Each starts with "deliver the file." We'll look at a chain for executable files, covering both scripts and compiled binaries, and then, after discussion, a chain for libraries.

When a file is an executable:

1. Exploit: Convince the user to open it.
2. Evade defenses (optional):
   (a) Pretend the file is a document via icon and names, possibly leveraging extension hiding.
   (b) Compress the file.
3. Command and control: The file may have its complete instructions locally, or it may reach out to a server for instructions.
4. Act on Objectives, with the authority given to the program.

For performance reasons, many antivirus programs used to skip compressed files. Today, to inhibit defenses, compressed files are also encrypted and sent with a password. When the file is a linkable library, issues of link ordering become relevant. (These were discussed in Chapter 2, "Tampering and Integrity.")

The Defense Evasion step is a deviation from the seven-step chain that we saw in the introduction. That chain (Reconnaissance, Weaponization, Delivery, Exploit, Installation, Command and Control, Actions on Objectives) is a useful model, and like all models, it's imperfect. Adding steps like Defense Evasion is as much a normal part of an analyst's job as removing steps (like we did for SQL injection).

Adding *abstracted* steps, like Defense Evasion, allows us to ask, "Is there another way the attacker could do that?" Frequently, engineers who know their systems well can use that knowledge to find such variants in ways that are unavailable to security experts with less specific system knowledge.

"Please Install" Code Chain

In a sense, the technically easiest way to get code installed is to entice an authorized user to do it for you, by telling them that the code has some useful function. The code can advertise one function but do something else, or it can really fulfil that purpose and surreptitiously do more. These are sometimes called *Trojan horses*.

Attackers have broken into software companies to install malicious code that will be delivered to those company's customers. Examples include M.E Doc tax software, used in the infamous NotPetya attack, and SolarWinds, each of whom delivered altered code to their customers (GAO, 2021, Goodin, 2017). Attackers have also taken over open-source repositories. Project developers have even decided they were tired of companies using their work uncompensated and inserted attack code (Sharma, 2022).

There are many chains that include the step "The attacker delivers software to the victim." The steps that lead to delivery vary widely, as discussed in the preceding paragraphs. The result is that the attacker's software now has the authority of the account that invoked it. This is the case on traditional desktops and servers, and mobile devices to a lesser extent.

Attackers may not need to entice you to install code. The code and authority you have may be enough for them, and they may simply ask you to use it on their behalf. This is frequently called *social engineering* and usually involves some pretext as to why it's OK for you to take these steps. Building systems that defend against social engineering is complex. My *Threat Modeling* has a chapter on usable security, and I served as a technical editor on *You Can Stop Stupid* (Winkler, 2020), which is about processes to achieve that goal. (Most books on the subject are focused on how to manipulate people, not how to defend against the threat.)

Acting on Objectives by Running Code

Many kill chains converge at the point where an attacker has access to the authority of a person to run arbitrary code. The routes to get there vary, as do the ways that commands are sent. Perhaps the attacker logs in via SSH or RDP and runs commands interactively. Perhaps their code reaches out to a command-and-control server. Sometimes that code is widely deployed malware; sometimes it's been developed for a particular attack.

Many of the chains we have seen to this point converge on traditional desktop computers. They have clients that receive messages and do other work and pass messages to parsers of tremendous complexity and variety, including playing video, displaying and editing rich document formats, and more. They often have listening daemons, and their code is often poorly isolated and high in authority. They're often managed by overworked amateurs. It is sorely tempting to claim that if we were to design a weak link, it would look a lot like desktop Windows or Linux of the late 1990s. The vulnerabilities of such systems remain important to both attackers and defenders.

These chains are brought together in Figure 9.4. You've seen the components separately, and you can now see how they come together (with the addition of "install code" off to the side; downloaded files and using local code are not shown.)

Incidentally, attack trees are typically shown with the attacker goal at the top. In this case, I've put it at the bottom to align with how stories tend to flow down the page, not up. (The traditional representation is because trees are created as a record of analysis.)

But these are not the only major chains. I've alluded to phishing, and now to bring it all together, Figure 9.5 shows a simplified version of Figure 9.4 and adds credential theft and use on the right. I call it a *sandcrawler* because that's how it ended up. In the next section, we'll expand out the credential-focused chains on the right.

Before we do, let me comment on an aspect of the sandcrawler model. The "login" box at the bottom, which leads directly to Act on Objectives, is technically wrong but very useful anyway. It's wrong because every login causes code to run. Logging into a bank and transferring money causes code to run. The bank's careful attenuation of authority does mean less code is running. So, what makes it useful?

It aligns with intuitive models that "That's not the same as running code!" If that's your model, then the final line of the structure aligns with that.

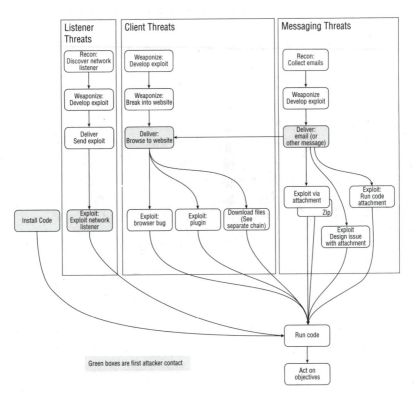

FIGURE 9.4 Chains assembled into a tree

Incidentally, not every use of a password causes code to run. Passwords go back to when soldiers needed a way to identify themselves to sentries (thus the line in the musical Hamilton, "The code word is 'Rochambeau,' dig me?/Rochambeau!" They're repeating it back to commit to memory.) It's not well known, but the older code, which checks out for sneaking past a blockade to Endor, was also Rochambeau.

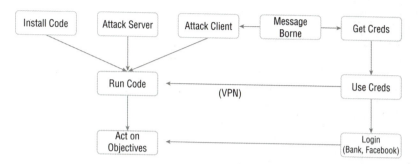

FIGURE 9.5 Adam's "sandcrawler" model

Acquire or Use Credentials

Acquiring credentials is a frequent detour in other kill chains. We've covered many of the mechanisms in the Chapters 1, 4, and 7, which deal with spoofing, information disclosure, and predictability.

Despite its immense place in our psyches, phishing is not the only way to steal credentials. Using leaked credentials is an incredibly common link in a chain. It's important to store passwords well (as you learned about in Chapter 7, "Predictability and Randomness"). This is also why a good password manager is a great way to protect yourself: you can use a unique password per site, limiting the impact of a failure either by the site or by you or your password managing deputy. Once a site has leaked a password, you should really stop using it. Here's one of mine: NXcsx2IZ. That's a real password that I used to use on a somewhat high-value site, which leaked it. I'm okay with sharing it here, because I've stopped using it.

As shown in Figure 9.6, credentials are primarily leaked or phished and are used to take over accounts. That can be a personal or corporate account, and the attacker's ability to act as you is a powerful route to acting on their actual objectives.

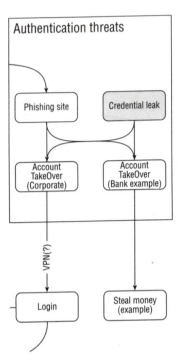

FIGURE 9.6 Account takeover chain

Phishing

Classic phishing tricks a person into entering their credentials in a fake website. This is a new set of kill chain steps, which we'll focus on to the exclusion of steps we've covered that can be delivered in messages: links to malicious websites (attacks on clients) or attachments (attacks on local packages).

A Phishing Kill Chain This kill chain is for the steps an attacker needs to follow to steal money from your bank account:

1. Select one or more targets. (Recon)
2. Craft an email which spoofs some target bank. (Weaponization)
3. Deliver the weapon by sending emails. (Delivery)

4. Someone clicks the weapon part. (Exploitation)
5. They visit a website and enter their credentials. (Exploitation, again)
6. The attacker uses those credentials to log in to their bank and steal money. (Actions on Objectives).

The phisher performs *Reconnaissance*. They select one or more targets, by collecting or filtering email addresses. This step will often include the output of information disclosure attacks, including the bulk theft of email addresses in a break-in, or email servers that respond differently when there's no such user, such as bouncing the message. It can also happen via collection of published mail list archives or marketing services such as `data.com` or Spokeo. Those attacks can be done for this chain or at another time.

Weaponization is when an attacker develops a weapon by crafting an email that spoofs a person or organization you hope the target trusts. In classic phishing, the weapon is a message that's designed to convince someone to click on a link. The weapon often involves spoofing: URLs like `Paypa1.com` (with a one, not a lowercase L) or display text that says "`Paypal.com`" but the underlying HTML `href` value points somewhere else. It's often created by tampering with a real email from that bank. These messages are usually designed to create a sense of urgency, because phishing infrastructure ends up in denylists, messages are retroactively filtered, etc.

Weaponization may be complex. For example, spammers need a mail server that lets them send lots of mail. (Modern systems like Gmail have substantial defenses against outbound spam.) This can be their own mail server, or one they've broken into (expanded authority onto). The term *server* may be misleading here: It doesn't need to be a big, rack-mounted system in a data center. Many email worms used to include their own SMTP engines, optimized for fast sending. The attacker needs a platform that meets the needs of their campaign.

Weaponization may also include creating a domain that plausibly appears to belong to the bank, like `bank-email-server.com`, at least when a busy person glances at it. That domain might be used for both email and a website. The site will involve copyright infringement for images and probably also the HTML that displays the bank's website. That HTML might be tampered with to reduce calls back to the real web servers, or left intact, to reduce hosting costs.

Deliver the weapon by sending emails, probably spoofing a sender in some way, including domains and display names.

The *Exploitation* step happens when someone clicks the weapon part (URL) of the email, and then their browser displays a website designed to spoof that of a bank. The victim enters their credentials. The browser sends the victim's credentials to the site. Those credentials enable the attacker to spoof the victim in the future. Sometimes the credentials are sent on from the phishing server to somewhere else in case the phishing site is taken down. (Password managers use different identifiers for sites, and so are less likely to send your credentials to the spoofed site.)

The final stage of *Acting on Objectives* happens as the attacker uses those credentials to log in to a bank and steal money. They laugh all the way to their bank. More seriously, logging in and really sending money is complex: your bank probably makes it tricky to add new places to send money, alerts you when one is added, limits the amount that can be sent to a new recipient, and delays the delivery of that money. It's all a real pain when you really do want to send money to Aunt Beru back home on Tatooine. These defenses may align to a "move money" kill chain, but that chain isn't specified here.

As it turns out, no one does all these steps by themselves anymore. There are efficient markets for each step. But there are two other properties that are far more important from our perspective. First, many of the steps leverage types of attack that we've been talking about in isolation. Second, those attacks have been chained together. Attackers chaining threats you've discovered into something bigger means that all of the problems you discover while threat modeling and choose not to fix are like Legos, scattered across the floor. You'll step on some, and attackers will snap others together into a profitable attack.

An Alternative Phishing Kill Chain It's reasonable for different analysts to break up a chain in different ways. To illustrate that, let me briefly share a different phishing kill chain, developed by Chris Meidinger of email security company Agari in 2014. Their breakdown was as follows:

1. Targeting
2. Delivery
3. Deception ("The criminal needs to deceive the user into following their call to action to the next step")
4. Click
5. Surrender ("The user needs to input their data to the phishing site, surrendering it to the criminals")
6. Extraction ("The phishing site needs to transmit the stolen credential or other information to the criminal")

This variant is included to illustrate George Box's aphorism that "All models are wrong, and some models are useful." The addition of the "surrender" and "extraction" steps serves to anchor defenses such as security awareness training or phishing site takedowns.

The addition of the surrender step also raises an interesting conundrum. Many security awareness programs have focused on email, rather than messages. And so many people are more wary of email and less of other forms of messaging.

Business Email Compromise and Other Cons There is another type of attack via messages, and those are traditional cons or scams. Perhaps the best known is the "Nigerian Prince" scam, but the Internet is…a hive of scams and villainy. Popular variants today include romance scams and business email compromise. (This is often abbreviated BEC, and the term *compromise* has a different meaning than the one we usually use in technical conversations.) This chain is presented to help you get a sense for how the Kill Chain technique can generalize.

In BEC, a message comes from your boss saying "We need to pay this vendor. I'm traveling; can you handle it?" There's no attachment, breaking many of the defensive scanning techniques in use. There's also either no link or no malicious links in the message, causing the messages to go through a scanner darkly.

BEC is an interesting attack because at a technical level, it doesn't really exploit or compromise much technology. (This is discussed in Chapter 8, "Parsing and Corruption," which discusses threats from correctly parsed data.) The attack involves convincing staff that an executive at their company needs a payment made urgently and that they should violate processes or treat the payment as an exception.

The kill chain is as follows:

1. Recon: Find a target, their contact details, and possibly details about an executive who will be hard to contact.
2. Weaponization: Craft a story about someone who needs to be paid ASAP.
3. Deliver the message, either via spoofing or account takeover.
4. If account takeover, install, potentially writing email rules to prevent a taken-over account from noticing.
5. Exploit: Sell the con.
6. Act on objectives.

The Recon stage involves selecting a target, often in finance, because they're the ones who can move money. The level of recon needed is higher than for a mass phishing campaign and needs to include the discovery of a relationship or hierarchy between individuals. This doesn't need to be ironclad, and a few names on LinkedIn can be sufficient. Extra details from Twitter or Facebook posts (or even press releases) about the CEO traveling can help.

Weaponization is relatively simple. Craft a story about how someone needs to be paid ASAP. These are highly templated, because the stories that work have elements of urgency, technical failures, and people we need to placate, immediately.

There are two common approaches to delivery. One is to spoof. If your CEO is named Darth Vader, the attacker will set up darthvader18@gmail and send you an email explaining that this is their personal account. Alternately, if the attacker has expanded their effective authority and can log in to Lord Vader's account, then they'll send you a real email from his real account. This will have various trickery to ensure that the real Darth Vader doesn't see the email. That might be a reply-to header; it might be rules in the email program that forward emails with the subject "Urgent: Pay Sienar Fleet Systems today!" to the attacker's account.

The attacks are unusual in that there's no expansion of the attacker's authority. Once you catch on, the attacker is powerless, except perhaps for blackmail, but generally, they're working a playbook that doesn't go there. Yet. The failure to expand authority is also a property of many social engineering attacks. (Social engineering someone's password is a common goal, and the slightly awkward phrase is commonplace. Once an attacker has succeeded at that, they can, of course, make use of it in the relevant kill chains.)

Once the attacker has sent BEC messages, they'll exploit the victim's belief that the conversation is real to provide details of where to send the money. This will happen in conversation; once the victim is drawn into the story, the mechanisms that con artists have used for centuries will all kick in. It's reasonable to think of BEC as an instance of social engineering.

Achieve your objective—aka take the money and run. Once the victim has approved the funds transfer, odds are good that the money will cascade through several other banks in rapid succession, eventually moving beyond easy reversal. Either it's left a bank as cash or it's moved to another country.

As we move into the next section, we'll move away from email-borne attacks, because as interesting as phishing is, we don't want to get hooked.

Account Takeover

An attacker with a set of credentials, say "leia/RememberAlderaan," can attempt to use them to log in as Leia. A recon step would be to find sites Leia uses. The attacker might skip over weaponization and delivery to exploitation and attempt to log in and then act on objectives using the authority of the account. (The question of "Is using the credentials exploitation or delivery?" is a trap. As statistician George Box teaches us, "All models are wrong, and some are useful.")

Stealing credentials isn't the only way into an account and may not be a way into only one account. Hijacking some trusted bit of infrastructure (like your Gmail account, your phone, or your desktop computer) will help an attacker into each and every account that you use that ties back to that account for backup authentication.

Acting on Objectives with Acquired Credentials

Once an attacker has a full set of credentials, they can act broadly as the user. That may include an interactive login, where they are enabled to run arbitrary commands, send emails, or browse arbitrary sites within what's nostalgically called an *intranet*, and more. It may include any of the actions that account can take, and many sites will carefully attenuate that authority. For example, a bank will not let me run arbitrary commands on its mainframe but offers me a few constrained commands like *deposit*, *withdraw*, and *send*.

These kill chains for traditionally defined client and server systems have been the training ground for generations of attackers, and they shape much attacker thinking (because they work) and thus much defender thinking. Many of them apply to newer technologies with minimal adaptation, but some steps will fail, and others are enabled by newer technologies, which we'll see in the next section.

Kill Chains for Specific Scenarios

The kill chain structures can be applied to computers with keyboards and monitors or to computers that look like cars and fridges. The unique ways those steps manifest are largely captured in Part I, but many of the scenarios that we've covered in these sections have unique kill chain steps. For blockchain, the transfer of authority involved in stealing keys is an unusually powerful instance, enabling later actions on objectives.

Cloud

There are a few cloud-specific kill chain steps that focus on the DevOps and automation steps that are frequently adopted as part of cloud deployments. These include pre-infected machine images. An attacker helpfully creates a copy of, say, Ubuntu, with their system admin keys and other software pre-installed and makes it available for others to use. How helpful!

Attackers will also attack the build system, or dependencies. Most cloud deployments automate building both binaries and systems. These build systems are often complex and sometimes not as well secured as "operational" systems. Many build systems will automatically fetch the latest versions of various dependencies, test those in a build, and integrate them into the main development branch if the tests pass. This is based on the expectation that the latest is also the greatest. But if the latest is both greatest and contains code put there by an attacker, then the attacker code gets integrated with everything else.

Cloud often involves the creation of microservices, and in that world, server-side request forgery (SSRF) becomes a crucial step in many chains. SSRF is an attack where the server makes a request that's influenced by the client. That influence can be on the target (address) of the request, on the content of the request, or even on the frequency and size of the request. If you're thinking these sound like confused deputies again, you would not be wrong.

In 2020, leading cloud security practitioners Rich Mogull and Shawn Harris presented a set of kill chains for the cloud (Mogul, 2020).

- Static API Credential Exposure to Account Hijack
- Compromised Server via Exposed SSH/RDP/Remote Access
- Compromised Database via Inadvertent Exposure

- Object Storage Public Data Exposure (S3, Azure Blob)
- Server-Side Request Forgery > Credential Abuse
- Cryptomining
- Network attack
- Compromised Secrets (instance/VM)
- Novel Cloud Data Exposure and Exfiltration
- Subdomain Takeover

IoT

Unique steps in IoT kill chains include "rooting the device" and "physically tampering with device." This can be impactful if you treat your customers as threats, because your device controls what content can play or if your customers expose your device to their guests or customers. The specific ways these threats manifest, such as attaching to JTAG ports or information disclosure from or tampering with software on a detached flash drive, have been discussed in prior chapters.

Mobile (IoS, Android)

In addition to the "traditional" attacks against desktops and the IoT steps of rooting or tampering, there are stages of a kill chain that involve app stores. These include spoofing or suborning a developer to upload a fake app to your real account or uploading an app that looks like yours or appears to be associated with your brand. There are denial of service via complaints to the app store owner getting your app de-listed.

The steps involved in *"Persistence"* are tricky on mobile devices, because defenses against rooting tend to block them. (Persistence is a broader concept than *Installation*, and comes from MITRE's ATT&CK, which is pronounced "attack," and which you'll meet in the "History" section.)

Weaponization as a Subchain

Weaponization is often a subchain of its own and frequently very loosely coupled with others. This book has taken the perspective that you don't need to know how to write exploits, but understanding how the weaponization step happens can help you understand security researchers. That understanding may lead to avoiding needless conflict if they contact you to get a bug fixed. It may also mislead you into thinking weaponization is always difficult and slow.

We can apply kill chain thinking to the practice of vulnerability discovery. Vulnerabilities (the sort that get CVEs) and patches don't just appear in a vacuum any more than X-Wing fighters. Both have backstories. A researcher performs Recon by choosing some targets to investigate. That investigation might happen in an artisanal way, loading code in a reverse engineering tool and looking for problematic code patterns. It might happen at scale, fuzzing many possible target executables. It might happen at scale, scanning websites or IP space. The targeting might be loose, looking at either popular programs or less popular ones that might be easier targets. It might be focused on an obscure program used by your intended target.

The specific work to Weaponize can be very different, driven by the researcher's goal. Often a proof of concept (PoC) will meet their goals. A PoC is all you may need to get a bug bounty, convince the manufacturer to fix it, get fame via a conference talk, or get a CVE for your résumé. The hard work of making the code reliable may not be needed. But if the analyst wants to go further along the kill chain, then the output of weaponization will likely require higher-quality code. That's one of two qualities that separates a weaponized exploit from proof of concept. The other is a weaponized exploit is usually embedded in either a convincing framework to get an unwitting recipient to open it or a targeted or mass scanning exploitation tool.

(Mass scanning tools may also look for evidence that a target is vulnerable, such as banners or behavioral edge cases, before trying to exploit the vulnerability.)

All that work can lead to conflict when a researcher wants to see their vulnerability fixed. They may well believe they are engaged in a good-natured outreach. Researcher expectations about bug bounties can be misinterpreted by a technology creator as blackmail. The conflicts are often amplified because many companies haven't dealt with a vulnerability report and many reporters are young or immature.

Lastly, weaponization is a place where the law of perversity in security shines. When you want to develop a PoC to show that a vuln should be fixed, it's hard work. But you can't rely on it being hard when someone else tries it.

"No One Would Ever Do That"

"No one would ever do that" is a phrase that most people in the security community love to hate. The claim is frequently made when someone doesn't want to fix something or doesn't know how. As you apply a kill chain, you may be unable to find an end result that seems worthwhile. And perhaps there is no there there, and the chain is not worth the end point. Or perhaps you're failing to consider attackers working for fame, for the respect of their peers, for the lulz, or because you once failed to meet some bizarre request of theirs and now they're strangely obsessed with you?

Perhaps the chain you see as complete is a side quest for an attacker, who wants to use your site as a jumping off-point for mining cryptocurrency, sending phishing emails, pushing their site's rank in search engines, or helping them with a scheme to entrap rebel scum?

Ransomware

Once an attacker has all your authority, they can use it to read and write to all your files. The business of ransomware expanded dramatically in the second decade of the century, with startups developing specialized and scalable models. Some provide initial access, some provide negotiation services, and some payments management. Of course, it's all criminal but profitable enough that local police can be bought off or international police won't bother.

Ransomware, like other new technology, took a while to become established. It was first described in a 1996 academic paper by Adam Young and Moti Young, which goes to show, threats can emerge slowly.

Elements of Network Kill Chains

Many of the links of a network kill chain are similar to other kill chains, but there are differences. In contrast to host kill chains, network protocols are more standardized and less under the control of general software engineers. So while you might write code that manages messages or acts as a server and will need to do so correctly, you may also need to understand a bit of behavior of networks.

Recon on Networks

Networks require initialization steps. Things like "Who uses what address?" and "How do I find that other computer?" require protocols with minimal authentication, and those protocols will often offer up valuable information like the address of a router, a domain name, or other identifiers.

Many networks use various techniques that are labeled broadcasting. Obviously, radio protocols such as Bluetooth, Wi-Fi, and cell phones literally broadcast, while Ethernet does so figuratively. Antennas and amplifiers are better than you expect, especially when they're only eavesdropping. They can pick up signals at ranges that far exceed normal operation. Again, the rule of perversity in computer security applies. Getting the Wi-Fi to work in your house is hard when you want it to work, and an attacker with a Pringles can might pick up your signal from a mile away.

Information Disclosure as a Network Threat

On an Ethernet network, any computer connected to the Ethernet can read every packet that goes by. By convention, they don't, and

Ethernet chips will discard packets destined for elsewhere for performance. However, Ethernet chips have a "promiscuous" mode where they'll pass each packet up the networking stack (using the older meaning of promiscuous as "indiscriminate" or "not selective"). Ethernet switches have replaced hubs, and the only packets sent to a machine are those addressed to it, or so we expect. There are attacks that convince a switch to do otherwise, outside the scope of this book.

At the lowest levels of the network, addresses are often fixed. For example, Ethernet addresses are configured at the factory for each chip to be unique, and these unique addresses can be used to track devices across various network access points. Again, the law of perversity applies: if a defender is tracking addresses, attackers can change them, so the defense doesn't work well, but our privacy is nevertheless invaded in the hopes the attacker will forget.

Spoofing Addresses

Network protocols generally have a source and destination address, used to tell various levels of the protocol stack to "look at this." In internet networks of networks, they're also used for routing. And at each layer of the stack, the addresses are written into packets by software. There are many checks to get them right, all of which can be overridden for various reasons. Some of those reasons are good, and some are nefarious. Spoofing source addresses allows you to send denial-of-service attacks, while spoofing destination addresses allows you to eavesdrop.

Local networks differ from local computers in that they are unmediated. There is no kernel deciding what can talk to what. As such, spoofing is easier. As networks interconnect, the routers are more and more likely to do source address filtering and only accept packets with appropriate source addresses on most of their interfaces, which makes packet spoofing at the Internet level complicated, but by no means inconceivable.

History

We can think of STRIDE and kill chains like jazz and rock and roll. They're stable genres, and they're full of new and exciting instances. New details of each threat regularly emerge, like bands releasing new songs. Only rarely does a new category really emerge, like punk rock or fusion jazz. And even less common are new schools of music like hip-hop. It may help to think of STRIDE and kill chains as those schools of music. The songs, the vulns, the attacks have fundamental similarities, and STRIDE and kill chains help us see and work with those similarities.

STRIDE has been relatively stable since 1999. In this book I've taken the liberty of redefining E to expansion of authority, and there are nuanced changes like the rise of deepfakes to implement spoofing. In contrast, kill chains are newer and developing more rapidly.

History of Kill Chains

A team at American military supplier Lockheed Martin formalized their use of a kill chain for cyber in 2010. The idea comes from military doctrine, where if you want to kill a target, you need to go through a chain of steps, from identification to selecting weapons to delivering them to achieve your objective. For defensive use, the Air Force has a set of ways to stop each step from succeeding. These are detect, deny, disrupt, degrade, deceive, or destroy. The Lockheed team also noted that if you detect an attacker at the installation step, you know that controls have not prevented the attacker from getting to install, and thus they have gone through recon, weaponization, delivery, and exploitation. (For most organizations, recon and weaponization are hard to defend against.) If you didn't detect delivery or exploitation, there may be evidence that you can go back and gather. These *indicators of compromise* can be used to search for other installations that you haven't yet seen or to tune tools to prevent additional use of the same attack vectors.

The idea of a kill chain quickly provided value to defenders, and many kill chain variants have been created. By variants I mean variants of the steps in the chain, not variation of the details within those steps. I do not mean "this attacker uses weaponized PowerPoints, and that one uses weaponized PDFs." A variant means that the *steps* of the chain are different, being used to characterize either different attacks or the same attack with different nuance or focus. For example, MITRE's ATT&CK adds a step "lateral movement" to talk about how an attacker hops from one machine to the next. Lateral is a reference back to privilege levels: the attacker doesn't gain administrative authority but uses single sign-on techniques (classically those built into Windows via Active Directory) to use the authority of the same user on system after system.

Structure and Metastructures

Creating models with the right level of abstraction to help solve a problem is an art. Balancing specificity, clarity, and generality is hard. Since the Lockheed team published their paper, there's been a small explosion of interesting new work.

The US Director of National Intelligence has created a Cyber Threat Framework. They describe it using all caps to distinguish the names of the stages:

"The framework captures the adversary life cycle from PREPARATION of capabilities and targeting to initial ENGAGEMENT with the targets or temporary nonintrusive disruptions by the adversary, to establishing and expanding the PRESENCE on target networks, to the creation of EFFECTS and CONSEQUENCES from theft, manipulation, or disruption."

Researcher Paul Pols has analyzed a set of kill chains and created a metastructure he calls the Unified Kill Chain: Initial Foothold*, Pivoting, Network propagation*, Access, Action on objectives.*

Each of the starred elements has additional detail. Both the Cyber Threat Framework and the Unified Kill Chain metamodels may be fine alternatives to the Lockheed seven-stage chain for either prospective or retrospective analyses. Both are presented to help you see there are many ways to analyze or model a system.

MITRE ATT&CK   MITRE is a US government contractor and research organization. It has a set of kill chains that are collectively labeled ATT&CK. There are currently three main sets (Enterprise, Mobile, and Industrial Control Systems). Each is usually presented as a matrix of tactics, techniques, and procedures. Tactics are similar to the stages of chains discussed in this chapter, techniques are implementations of threats, and techniques are broken out into procedures.

For example, persistence techniques include boot or logon scripts, account creation, and scheduled jobs, and specific examples are provided of real-world instances observed by defenders. Part of its usefulness comes from moderated community contributions.

The Enterprise matrix covers 14 tactics, many of which are similar to the "traditional" Lockheed chain, while others are either added or subdivided views of the Lockheed chain. I'll denote those with a +. They are Recon, Resource Development, Initial Access, Execution, Persistence, Privilege Escalation+, Defense Evasion+, Credential Access+, Discovery+, Lateral Movement+, Collection+, Command and Control, Exfiltration and Impact. The mobile and ICS matrices are similar at a high level and differ substantially in the techniques and procedures.

The Sandcrawler Model   The Sandcrawler model, presented in Figure 9.5, reminds me a little of the Jawa sandcrawler, and since I created it for this book, I'll give it that name. In contrast to the models just presented, each of which seeks to help analyze a single chain, Sandcrawler brings many different models together.

History and Structure of Attack Trees

One of the early precursors to the concepts in this chapter were attack trees. Attack trees were defined by Ed Amaroso in 1994 and popularized by Bruce Schneier in 1999.

An attack tree generally starts with an attacker's objective, such as "Read the script to *The Empire Strikes Back*." The objective is the root of the tree (in contrast to a chain whose goal is at the end). Steps to achieve the goal are children under a parent. The three ways I imagine to do that would be break into a client or a server or get a copy by email. Child nodes in the "break into the desktop" tree might be "exploit a vulnerability" and "leverage a misconfiguration." "Exploitation" might have children of "exploit a zero-day vulnerability" and "exploit an unpatched vulnerability." And so drawn graphically, this looks much more like a tree than a chain. And sometimes it has a lot of fanout from a single node. "Exploit a zero day" might have many children: Word, Excel, Adobe Reader, Chrome, Firefox, Quickbooks, Slack, Jira, Atom, gcc, and so on. The addition of named stages as part of the shift to chains seems to have been an important improvement. That was accompanied by work to organize indicators of compromise and their interchange.

Figure 9.7 shows a sample attack tree. As I've said, there is a great deal of similarity between trees and chains.

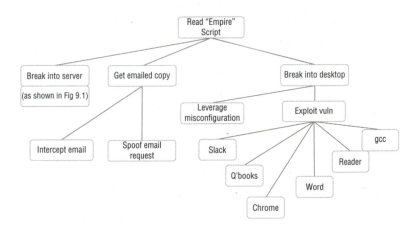

FIGURE 9.7 An attack tree

Crafting a tree or trees for a specific scenario can help you think through variations: Is there another way to achieve this goal (reach this node)? Are these nodes equivalent? Do we have controls that address each of these problems? And crafting that tree, with relatively concrete nodes, is relatively easy. Crafting trees that can usefully be reused over and over is incredibly hard, which is why most of the samples on the Internet are for goals like "get through a door."

Trees of a few to a dozen nodes are most common, with very few being much bigger than two dozen. The largest trees I've seen are on the order of a few hundred nodes, which I reviewed privately for a client. At that scale, using and comprehending the trees was fairly difficult.

Other Jargon

There's a small amount of kill chain jargon that may be helpful to you. Be aware that the terminology is changing quickly. For example, as this book went to press, Rich Mogull, whose work is referenced in the "Cloud" section, announced that he was relabeling his work from "kill chains" to "attack sequences."

APT stands for "advanced persistent threat." The term *threat* is used differently in this phrase than I've been using it in this book. Here threat is short for "threat actor," rather than the promise of future violence: "Darth Vader is a threat." Second, the term APT was a bit of a Jedi mind trick, allowing people to imply but not say "nation-state attacker," that is, a spy agency or a military that's going after another nation. These attackers bring discipline, organization, and separation of work to persistently go after objectives. Early in this chapter, I mentioned breaking into a company and compromising its products as a step in a chain—allegedly, the Chinese broke into RSA to compromise the RSA token used in multifactor authentication as part of breaking into Lockheed (Greenberg, 2021). That's persistence. Around the same time, the Stuxnet malware included four zero-day exploits and command-and-control software that jumped over air-gaps by passing software and messages on USB drives. That's some pretty advanced weaponization and command and control. The United States and Israel are believed to have created Stuxnet. (Sanger, 2012).

TTPs are tactics, techniques, and procedures that attackers use, and attacker TTPs are those that a given attacker has been caught using by defenders willing to share that information. Frankly, the term is usually thrown around without specificity as to which are tactics and which are techniques or procedures. I used step and stage to describe sets of tactics. If you care, ATT&CK is a good guide to what's a tactic, technique, or procedure.

"Boom!" is the moment at which a bomb explodes. In a computer context, does that equate to when an exploit runs? When it manages persistence? When it gets a command from its controller? What is boom in a phishing attack? Is it when a user enters their credentials in a fake website, when the attacker returns to use them, or when they transfer money from the bank? I don't know, and generally, those saying "boom!" don't either. You should avoid using it.

Blast radius means the things impacted by an attack. An attack on a single computer has that computer as its blast radius; an attack on a directory service or build system has a blast radius of an entire operational domain. Design to isolate systems reduces the blast radius of an attack, while administrative and operational needs tend to expose more systems to possible damage.

Defenses

There's a saying: "An attacker needs to get lucky only once, while a defender needs to be lucky all the time." The need for iterative movement along a chain is a strong counterargument to that idea.

That movement along a chain inspired the Lockheed team. One of their core insights was that if you find installed malware, it got there somehow. If you missed the steps that got it there, you can go back and look for them, and you can look for actions taken since installation. The techniques and procedures that an advanced attacker uses tend to be pretty similar from attack to attack, so if you find one part of a chain and compare it to a database of TTPs, you can find other things to look for.

Using a kill chain to proactively inform defenses is an excellent way to organize your thinking. The goal of a defense is to counter a threat. Defenses that are reliable and address many threats are better than the alternatives. Defenses that address chokepoints are more effective than those that address rare or obscure threats.

Using a kill chain to inform defenses is also surprisingly nuanced. The expression "A chain is only as strong as its weakest link" may not apply. A defense that effectively stops an attacker stops that attacker. More precisely, it stops them from traversing some link in the chain. It protects your system only if the defense can't easily be sidestepped. You may have a weak link, like your employees having social media profiles, but that doesn't stop you from deploying strong defenses later in the chain.

An example of a defense that can be easily sidestepped is requiring passwords to be changed regularly. People use a small number of well-understood strategies like appending a 1, and so the third change leads to RememberAlderaan111. In contrast, a defense like IoS requiring that binaries be signed to run is hard to bypass. The attacker can do all the weaponization and exploitation they want, but running a binary requires a signature from the App Store. They may have paths around that; nevertheless, the weak link in the chain, a badly coded binary, doesn't mean the overall chain is only that strong.

Using a kill chain to inform defenses is made more complicated because there are many aspects to defending a system. Defenses that loom large in our minds (patch management, Identity and Access Management) often address single stages of a single chain. To make the learning curve steeper, many commonly cited market segments don't line up well at all. For example, security information and event management (SIEM) is intended to collect and analyze logs. If it does, it becomes helpful across or investigating entire chains of events.

Types of Defenses

When you start thinking about a kill chain, you're often thinking about a system in larger chunks than when you're applying STRIDE. You may be working with parts that others have crafted. In both cases, the defenses are different. They're defensive technologies such as a firewall or a file integrity system. They're defensive operations such as intrusion detection or response. These goals are often met with add-on technology products (or services) rather than by improving the system.

We can conceive of defenses as achieving five major goals: identifying the things we want to protect, protecting them, detecting attacks, responding to attack, and remediating things to an acceptable or improved state. (The goals are borrowed from the NIST Cybersecurity Framework.) There's also a goal of ensuring your defenses are appropriate and well-managed.

For each step of the kill chain, we can think about a variety of responses (the original cyber kill chain paper also adapted a defensive model of deceive, disrupt, deny, destroy, and some other words starting with *D*. It didn't catch on the same way.) However, the essential defenses are protection and detection, especially detection of successful attacks. The success filter is much more helpful when there are many failed attacks. Who cares about the many scanners trying to log in to your Internet-facing VPN, unless they succeed? Deeper inside your systems, I hope the attack is unusual and worth noting.

The goal of this book is to provide deep insight into the threats and a survey of defenses. If you think of them as sides of a coin, then it would be logical to spend roughly equivalent effort on each. However, the relationship is not one to one. They are not sides of a coin, and metaphors are likely to lead you down a garden path.

Defensive Scenarios

There are four types of code we need to secure. First, code we run; second, code we write; third, code we incorporate; and fourth, pipelines that combine them. The code we run includes products we get from elsewhere. Code we run also includes code we write, and we have more flexibility in how we secure that. We may provide that code to others, who may benefit from our security work. The people who created the code we incorporate may or may not have done that, and we may want to evaluate their work as we incorporate their code. Lastly, we can be concerned about the security of systems that build our systems: the pipelines that combine the previous three sets into deployable bundles. These four separate scenarios call for four separate approaches to address each threat, as shown in Table 9.1.

Many traditional security products have tried to bolt security on to code we run, and that approach must overcome many challenges. (This is, in part, why security is often expensive, slow, or ineffective.)

TABLE 9.1 The Four Defensive Scenarios

Scenario	Defenses
Code we run	Operational security (e.g., NIST CSF, ISO 27001)
Code we write	Variously labeled "secure development life cycles" or "AppSec"
Code we incorporate	Supply chain security
Build pipeline	Often labeled "CI/CD pipeline security" but applies even if you don't do CI/CD

For each of these scenarios, we can be concerned about the aspirational security qualities, properties, or defenses that are being built, and we can be concerned about our assurance that it's been built well. Each is important, and they are distinct properties. For example, we might have a firewall that promises to stop all malware. However carefully it's implemented, I am skeptical of the claim and would require strong evidence. In another case, we might have an anti-malware tool, and I might be skeptical of the quality of its parsers.

In both of these cases, I would describe my goal as seeking assurance. Governments frequently use the word in a *mélange* of these senses. Confusingly, the same term is applied to the work by creators in making "an assurance case" and the work by buyers, often delegated to assessors, to check it.

The goal of assurance can be undercut at every point in the development process. During design, not threat modeling or considering "what can go wrong" may lead to development missing crucial threats. Selecting an insecure development environment, not training developers, or ignoring the security qualities of code you include can undercut the best designs. Failing to test can lead to errors being missed. A reputation for litigiousness can lead those who perceive security problems to avoid bringing them to you and a tin ear as you talk to those who do can set off a firestorm of misunderstanding.

Defensive Catalogs

There are a great many catalogs of defensive tools. Most, like the NIST Cybersecurity Framework or the Center for Internet Security's CIS Controls, focus on the operational needs of companies that acquire most of the code they deploy. Some are focused on a particular need, such as the SANS Windows Hardening Guide or Cloud Security Alliance guidance. Yet others are focused on industry, such as healthcare or finance.

An emergent category is requirements for those who are creating (and probably incorporating) code, such as the NIST Secure Software Development Framework. These are sometimes labelled "supply chain security," and that may create confusion for those who are in a supply chain and those who are at the consumptive end of one.

Therefore, I'm not going to attempt to catalog the plethora of defenses that are sold today for personal or business security. (If the vendor selling it to you can't crisply explain what threat they address, impolitely show them the door.) I'm also not going to attempt to catalog the catalogs, and again, the catalog should explain its goals.

Many of them fail to explain what threats they worry about, to their detriment and your cost. (I've given a talk, "Reverse Engineering Compliance," that explains this point in depth [Shostack, 2021].)

Conclusion

Kill chains are a helpful framework to show how attackers bring threats to bear on real systems. Their operational focus brings together the many threats you now understand. Their story-like nature helps make the threats real, and they may help answer the perennial defender's question of "Why would someone do that?" But the threats change slowly, as do the common chains that integrate them.

The chains by which threats to servers, clients, and networks are brought to fruition have changed slowly over the years. The specifics certainly change year to year and the chains decade by decade, but the frameworks will serve you well through your career. They're a core part of what every engineer needs to know.

Epilogue

Like the Sith, the threats in this book are often seen as mysterious or shadowy. Too many engineers have been fooled into thinking that only a fully trained Jedi at the height of their powers can take on these threats. Much you have learned, and more to be learned there is. Overconfidence, must you avoid.

What you've learned in this book are specific threats and ways to counter them. These threats are far more powerful if you ignore them. Some can be addressed with straightforward engineering; others require complex trade-offs with nuance and traps for the careless. As you go forward, consider how each can be brought to bear on your systems. In *Threat Modeling: Designing for Security*, I've defined threat modeling as a family of techniques to help us answer four key questions.

- What are we working on?
- What can go wrong?
- What are we going to do about it?
- Did we do a good job?

As I teach, I've learned that many students struggle to answer the question "what can go wrong?" That is, discovering what threats apply to a system can be the hardest challenge in threat modeling.

It's easy for most people to express a few things that can go wrong, and it's hard for many to specify the technical mechanisms that lead to those outcomes. Some even feel a bit about security like Han Solo feels about the Force.

Han: Hokey religions and ancient weapons are no match for a good
blaster at your side, kid.

Luke: You don't believe in the Force, do you?

Han: Kid, I've flown from one side of this galaxy to the other. I've seen
a lot of strange stuff, but I've never seen anything to make me
believe there's one all-powerful Force controlling everything.
There's no mystical energy field controls my destiny! It's all a lot of
simple tricks and nonsense.

There's some wisdom in Han's skepticism. Some threats *are* simple
tricks. Some claims of threats *are* nonsense. Of course, knocking on
your helmet and shrugging to pantomime that the radio doesn't work
is also a simple trick. We can address threats because of what they do
to us, our products or our customers. And when we do, they lose their
power to control our destiny.

The threats that form the spine of this book, from STRIDE to predictability to parsing, are bound together by kill chains. Knowledge of
the threats enables you to include them as you're designing, creating,
deploying, or operating technical systems. You can now do something
about each.

The heart of engineering is trade-offs. Every engineer must make
trade-offs between properties including cost, quality, and speed. Great
engineers find elegant, clever, or inspiring trade-offs. Frequently, our
trade-offs include things we should have foreseen: power blocks that
are hot to the touch waste electricity, components that can't be recy-
cled destroy the environment, the bridge known as Galloping Gertie
before its collapse was built with a width to length ratio half that of its
contemporaries. Other times, we are surprised. The magic glow of
radioactivity kills the watchmaker? A single packet can take over
a database?

This book, *What Every Engineer Should Learn from Star Wars*, was
designed to bring threats into that trade-off space. From small decisions to large, security is a property of our designs.

The prequels begin with the story of Anakin Skywalker and his corruption and fall. The core trilogy has two intertwined stories of growth. The first is how Darth Vader's yearning for the love of his son leads to his redemption. The second is how Luke, Han, and Leia grow.

Luke, Han, and Leia are thrown together by circumstances outside their control or understanding. Each tries to avoid their hero's journey. Yet through confronting the many challenges and threats that they face, each grows stronger, and they grow stronger together.

You, your products, and even your teams can go through a similar, hopefully less perilous journey. We all have a fear of the unknown, and we have a vague feeling (or even a dread certainty) that our products are less secure than they could have been. But that's the past. The code is literally committed, not just into version control, but sometimes it's burned into silicon and soldered onto boards. We can control only where we go in the future.

When Luke goes to confront Vader at the end of *Return of the Jedi*, he tells Leia, "There's good in him. I've felt it." Even if you don't feel there's good in these threats, confronting them will enable you to find and address them. To deliver security. You can discover them on your own, or you can discover them as a part of how your organization delivers software.

From now, you may choose to continue a lifelong journey into security. If you do, you might choose the light side or the dark to follow, or even decide that you're the chosen one who'll bring balance...

But we're not Jedi, we're engineers.

From the very start and in every part of their delivery, the products and services you engineer can now incorporate security.

It's our only hope.

Glossary

This glossary is primarily intended to supplement NIST's Computer Security Resource Center's Glossary, available at `csrc.nist.gov/glossary/`. Entries that don't have a base in the NIST glossary are marked with a (+). Where my definitions differ, the entry is marked with a (*), and the difference is explained.

ACL A mechanism that implements access control for a system resource by enumerating the identities of the system entities that are permitted to access the resources.

address space layout randomization (ASLR) (+) One of the earlier memory safety techniques, ASLR randomizes memory addresses to make it harder to write exploits. Used imprecisely to refer to memory defenses more generally.

advanced persistent threat (APT) (*) "An adversary with sophisticated levels of expertise and significant resources, allowing it through the use of multiple different attack vectors (e.g., cyber, physical, and deception)…moreover, the advanced persistent threat pursues its objectives repeatedly over an extended period of time, adapting to a defender's efforts to resist it, and with determination to maintain the level of interaction needed to execute its objectives." Generally means government attackers and their agents and cutouts.

asymmetric cryptosystem Any cryptosystem involving more than one key, where at least one key is kept private and one is public or published. For example, RSA or Diffie-Hellman. The published key (or keys) are often vouched for by a public key infrastructure, or PKI, or signed and thus made into a certificate.

authority (+) The ability of a user or other entity to make changes to a system.

business email compromise (BEC) (+) An attack where someone takes over an email account and then uses it to ask for payments to be made to bank accounts they control.

capability (*) Either the noun in its traditional English sense (the power or ability to do something) or an implementation of an authority system, where a capability is a hard-to-guess pointer to an object and an associated permission. For example, 60616 d8b9bbd962b045abc5d8e78c7f3 might be the ability to read /etc/shadow. Only those tools given 6061... can read the file. (NIST does not list this well-established meaning.)

certificate A data structure that contains an entity's identifier(s), the entity's public key (including an indication of the associated set of domain parameters), and possibly other information, along with a signature on that data set that is generated by a trusted party, i.e., a certificate authority, thereby binding the public key to the included identifier(s).

confused deputy (+) A program whose authority is used in unexpected ways by those whose input is fed to it. ("Those whose input is fed" is a broad set, not just those who directly feed data to it.)

Control+Alt+Delete (+) A secure attention sequence used by Microsoft Windows.

credentials (+) The information used to identify and authenticate a principal, such as a username and password combination.

crypto (*) Crypto means cryptography, not cryptocurrency. NIST's sole definition is strangely narrow.

cryptography (*) The discipline that embodies the principles, means, and methods for the transformation of data in order to hide their semantic content, prevent their unauthorized use, or prevent their undetected modification (NIST SP 800-59).

Additionally, Ron Rivest has defined cryptography as the art of securely communicating in the presence of enemies. Implicit in use in this book is that cryptographic systems are fit for purpose: well selected and well implemented.

daemon (+) "A daemon is a type of program on Unix-like operating systems that runs unobtrusively in the background, rather than under the direct control of a user, waiting to be activated by the occurrence of a specific event or condition. Unix-like systems typically run numerous daemons, mainly to accommodate requests for services from other computers on a network, but also to respond to other programs and to hardware activity. Examples of actions or conditions that can trigger daemons into activity are a specific time or date, passage of a specified time interval, a file landing in a particular directory, receipt of an e-mail or a Web request made through a particular communication line. It is not necessary that the perpetrator of the action or condition be aware that a daemon is listening, although programs frequently will perform an action only because they are aware that they will implicitly arouse a daemon." (From `www.linfo.org/daemon.html`.)

document (+) A file intended to be parsed by an interpreter and displayed or used by a person. Others, like HTML, contain code or macros while still being thought of as documents. Some documents, like Python code, blend further toward being executables. I'd like to say that a document interpreter warns you before running code, but see HTML, and so the distinction is less clear than I'd hope.

dogfood (+) To dogfood, or eat one's own dogfood, is to use early versions of your own product to understand its limits. The term was popularized by Microsoft, where the behavior was a norm from the late 1980s through the early 2010s.

EULA (+) End user license agreement. The license that you click through to be allowed to use a product you've purchased. Generally full of incomprehensible legalese, overly long, and not tested for readability or comprehensibility. Eventually, the courts may catch onto the reality that there's a gap between a "meeting of the minds" and today's EULAs.

executable (+)   A program to be run. Most traditionally, it consists of machine code that's run or things with the Unix +x bit, but see *document*.

exploit (+)   (noun) A program that takes advantage of a bug or flaw in a computer system, changing the flow of control to instructions contained in or pointed to by the exploit.

fingerprinting (+)   Fingerprinting entails the collection, categorization, indexing, and retrieval of information that identifies a system or program. For example, operating system fingerprinting relies on ambiguity and implementation choices in the TCP stage, including responses to TTL, window size, max segment size, etc. (Lyon, 2009). Fingerprinting requires the identification and collection of such details, indexed to operating system, and then the collection of details from a system to be identified. Fingerprinting applied to web browsers can often identify a very small population (1,500 or so) of web browsers, based on fonts, plugins, and other characteristics (Eckersley, 2010).

flaw (+)   A design issue that can be used to achieve some goal that's counter to the intent of the designer. Includes failures to meet explicit goals and is also used to describe violations of implicit goals. The term flaw is contrasted with a bug, which is a simple implementation defect (IEEE).

hash algorithm   Hash algorithms map arbitrarily long inputs into a fixed-size output such that it is difficult (computationally infeasible) to find two different hash inputs that produce the same output. Such algorithms are an essential part of the process of producing fixed-size digital signatures that can both authenticate the signer and provide for data integrity checking (detection of input modification after signature).

indicator   A technical artifact or observable that suggests an attack is imminent or is currently underway or that a compromise may have already occurred. (Some definitions are less specific.)

indicator of compromise (IOC) (+)   A subset of indicators that emerge from investigations of compromises rather than imminent attacks.

metadata (+)   Data about other data, for example, creation time of a file, size of a file or message, or source destination of a message.

MITM (*)   Monkey-in-the-middle. Historically man-in-the-middle. "An attack where the adversary positions himself [sic] in between the user and the system so that he [sic] can intercept and alter data traveling between them."

NSA (+)   The National Security Agency of the United States, focused on electronic warfare and intelligence gathering, mostly on the attack side, and with responsibility for helping defend the United States, especially military and intelligence agencies. At one time the largest employer of mathematicians in the world.

one-way function (+)   A one-way function is easy to compute, but it is difficult or impossible to compute its input from its output. Hash algorithms are a subset of all possible one-way functions, for example, the Rabin function of repeatedly squaring some number modulo n is easy to compute and hard to reverse.

one-time pad (+)   A cryptosystem that uses a random stream of key material as long as the message. Used properly, as secure as the key distribution. Reusing the pads means an attacker who xors the ciphertext gets the xor of the plaintext. (That is, let's call ciphertext_1 = message_1 xor pad and ciphertext_2 = message_2 xor pad. If we take ciphertext_1 xor ciphertext_2, we get (message_1 xor pad) xor (message_2 xor pad) and the pad, xor'd with itself, cancels out, and you get target = message_21 xor message_2. Because words like *the* or *headquarters* are more common, you can xor those with target and see if words pop out. When they do, you know one message had *headquarters* and the other had whatever word was revealed.

PBKDF-2 (+) Password-Based Key Derivation Function #2. A one-way function designed with a configurable cost to execute, based on the number of rounds.

permission (*) Authorization to perform some action on a system object. (NIST is less specific.)

persistence (+) Either an attacker's work to retain access to victim systems, or the practice of tracking and checking authentication data, such as a server's SSH public key. A persistence defense is to check that the key is unchanged from use to use. The second sense is used for clarity over the otherwise equivalent "TOFU."

phishing (*) "A digital form of social engineering that uses authentic-looking—but bogus—e-mails to request information from users or direct them to a fake Web site that requests information."

It's common to see *phishing* used to refer to any attack carried in any messaging system. This includes messages with attachments. Those attachments might be documents or executables.

principal (+) The smallest unit to which authority can be granted on a system, such as a user ID.

private key (*) "A cryptographic key that is kept secret and is used with a public-key cryptographic algorithm. A private key is associated with a public key." Many definitions overly restrictively refer to signature schemes, key pairs, or unique entities.

privilege (*) The ability to alter security functions, properties, or rules within a system. NIST's definition, "A special authorization that is granted to particular users to perform security relevant operations," excludes privileges granted to programs.

protocol (+) "A set of rules (i.e., formats and procedures) to implement and control some type of association (e.g., communication) between systems." Many people implicitly prepend "network-" implying that all protocols are network-protocols. A file is a single message with a data structure.

pseudorandom A deterministic process (or data produced by such a process) whose output values are effectively indistinguishable from those of a random process as long as the internal states and internal actions of the process are unknown. For cryptographic purposes, "effectively indistinguishable" means "not within the computational limits established by the intended security strength."

public (key)   The public portion of an asymmetric key.

public key infrastructure   "The architecture, organization, techniques, practices, and procedures that collectively support the implementation and operation of a certificate-based public key cryptographic system. Framework established to issue, maintain, and revoke public key certificates." Look for the one who accepts liability for their claims. *Quis custodiet ipsos custodes?*

random   A value in a set that has an equal probability of being selected from the total population of possibilities and, hence, is unpredictable. A random number is an instance of an unbiased random variable, that is, the output produced by a uniformly distributed random process.

RCE (+)   Remote Code Execution, a common effect of an exploit. "That vuln allows for unauthenticated RCE." *Remote* indicates that the attacker doesn't start with code execution authority on the targeted system.

reference monitor (*)   The traditional term for IT functionality that (1) controls all access, (2) cannot be bypassed, (3) is tamper-resistant, and (4) provides confidence that the other three items are true. Often provided by the operating system kernel, but also by tools such as web servers or databases.

secure attention sequence (+)   A physical action to open a secure channel between a person and a system.

Social Security number (*)   Described in practical terms as a national ID; officiously it is not.

symmetric cryptosystem   A cryptographic algorithm that uses the same secret key for its operation and, if applicable, for reversing the effects of the operation (e.g., an AES key for encryption and decryption).

threat (+)   Amongst NIST's 20 or so definitions are: "Any circumstance or event with the potential to adversely impact organizational operations;" "A possible danger to a computer system, which may result in the interception, alteration, obstruction, or destruction of computational resources, or other disruption to the system."

To those, add "a suggestion that something unpleasant or violent will happen, especially if a particular action or order is not followed."

threat actor   "An individual or a group posing a threat." (Also called *threat agent* or *threat source*.)

TTP   The behavior of an actor. A tactic is the highest-level description of this behavior, while techniques give a more detailed description of behavior in the context of a tactic, and procedures an even lower-level, highly detailed description in the context of a technique.

TOFU (+)   Trust On First Use. See *persistence*.

vulnerability (*)   (1) A weakness in an information system, system security procedures, internal controls, or implementation that could be exploited or triggered by a threat source. (2*) A weakness in software that can be exploited by exploit code. (3*) A weakness in software that, once discovered is clearly a bug that should be fixed. Definitions 2 and 3 are mine, to add specificity. Often shortened to *vuln*.

zero-day (0-day) (+)   A vulnerability for which there is no patch available from the creator when information on the issue is first released. "That was a zero day, but now it's patched." (Pronounced either "zero day" or "Oh day.")

zip bomb (+)   An attack where a compressed file expands more than expected. Don't be fooled by the name; all compression formats have the same problems.

Bibliography

Abrams, Marshall D., Sushil G. Jajodia, and Harold J. Podell. Information security: an integrated collection of essays. IEEE computer society press, 1995

ACM (Association for Computing Machinery), Turing Award Citation, 2013, amturing.acm.org/award_winners/lamport_1205376.cfm

ACM Code 2018 Task Force, ACM Code of Ethics and Professional Conduct, 2018, www.acm.org/code-of-ethics

Adkins, Heather, Betsy Beyer, Paul Blankinship, Piotr Lewandowski, Ana Oprea, and Adam Stubblefield. Building Secure and Reliable Systems: Best Practices for Designing, Implementing, and Maintaining Systems. O'Reilly Media, 2020

Aleph1, "Smashing the stack for fun and profit." Phrack magazine 49 1996-11-08, phrack.org/issues/49/14.html

Amoroso, Edward G. Fundamentals of Computer Security Technology. Prentice-Hall, Inc., 1994

Amazon, aws.amazon.com/macie, last visited November 24, 2017

Amazon, Summary of the AWS Service Event in the Northern Virginia (US-EAST-1) Region, AWS Blog, December 10, 2021, aws.amazon.com/message/12721

Amazon Seller Central, "Restricted Products" sellercentral.amazon.com/gp/help/external/200164330, last visited August 15, 2019

Anderson, Ross, Trojan Source: Invisible Vulnerabilities, Light Blue Touchpaper, November 1, 2021, www.lightbluetouchpaper.org/2021/11/01/trojan-source-invisible-vulnerabilities

Anley, Chris, John Heasman, Felix Lindner, and Gerardo Richarte. The Shellcoder's Handbook: Discovering and Exploiting Security Holes. John Wiley & Sons, 2011

Apple, Inc iOS Security: iOS 12.1 November 2018, www.apple.com/business/site/docs/iOS_Security_Guide.pdf

awhalley, Post-Spectre Threat Model Re-Think, Google Chromium blog, 2018, chromium.googlesource.com/chromium/src/+/master/docs/security/side-channel-threat-model.md

Barr, Jeff, "New Amazon S3 Encryption & Security Features," Amazon Blog, November 6, 2017, aws.amazon.com/blogs/aws/new-amazon-s3-encryption-security-features

Bellovin, Steven M. Defending Against Sequence Number Attacks, RFC 1948, www.rfc-editor.org/rfc/rfc1948

Bishop, Bryan, New York Times reporter refutes Tesla's allegations but 'cannot account' for some discrepancies in data, The Verge, Feb 14, 2013, www.theverge.com/2013/2/14/3990106/new-york-times-reporter-refutes-teslas-allegations-but-cannot-account

Bomey, Nathan, How Chinese military hackers allegedly pulled off the Equifax data breach, stealing data from 145 million Americans, USA Toyda, Feb 10, 2020, www.usatoday.com/story/tech/2020/02/10/2017-equifax-data-breach-chinese-military-hack/4712788002

Bours, Ben, How a Dorm Room Minecraft Scam Brought Down the Internet, www.wired.com/story/mirai-botnet-minecraft-scam-brought-down-the-internet, Dec 13, 2017

Bratus, Sergey, Trey Darley, Michael Locasto, Meredith L. Patterson, Rebecca "bx" Shapiro, and Anna Shubina, "Beyond Planted Bugs in 'Trusting Trust': The Input-Processing Frontier," in IEEE Security & Privacy, vol. 12, no. 1, pp. 83-87, Jan.-Feb. 2014, doi: 10.1109/MSP.2014.1. langsec.org/papers/beyond-bugs-input-frontier.pdf

Burman, Bryan, How to Choose the Right Parameters for Argon2, blog post, June 7, 2019, www.twelve21.io/how-to-choose-the-right-parameters-for-argon2

Burnet, Karla, "Ichthyology: Phishing as a Science" BlackHat Briefings, July 2017, www.blackhat.com/docs/us-17/wednesday/us-17-Burnett-Ichthyology-Phishing-As-A-Science-wp.pdf

Cambridge Dictionary, Cambridge University Press, dictionary.cambridge.org/dictionary/english/threat, last visited December 31, 2019

Cassidy, Kevin, Warning: Your Facebook Privacy Settings Have Been Reset, www.business2community.com/facebook/warning-your-facebook-privacy-settings-have-been-reset-065965 Business2 Community, Jan 7, 2022

CCC, Chaos Computer Clubs breaks iris recognition system of the Samsung Galaxy S8, 2017-05-22, www.ccc.de/en/updates/2017/iriden

CERT (Computer Emergency Response Team), UDP-Based Amplification Attacks, Alert (TA14-017A), January, 2014 (Updated December, 2019), www.cisa.gov/uscert/ncas/alerts/TA14-017A

Checkoway, Stephen, Hovav Shacham, and Eric Rescorla. "Are Text-Only Data Formats Safe? Or, Use This LaTeX Class File to Pwn Your Computer." LEET, 2010

Coldewey, Devin, Oh, Facebook changed its privacy settings again, Techcrunch, August 4, 2021, techcrunch.com/2021/08/04/oh-facebook-changed-its-privacy-settings-again

Crosby, Scott A., Dan S. Wallach And Rudolf H. Riedi, Opportunities and Limits of Remote Timing Attacks, ACM Transactions on Information and System Security, Vol. 12, No. 3, Article 17, Pub. date: January 2009, doi.acm.org/10.1145/1455526.1455530. www.cs.rice.edu/~dwallach/pub/crosby-timing2009.pdf

The CVE Project, CVE-2016-10074, Dec 27, 2016, cve.mitre.org/cgi-bin/cvename.cgi?name=CVE-2016-10074

Davies, Jim, Droids, Minds and Why We Care, in Langley, Travis, and Carrie Goldman, eds. Star wars psychology: dark side of the mind. Sterling New York, 2015

Delaitre, Aurelien M., Bertrand C. Stivalet, Paul E. Black, Vadim Okun, Terry S. Cohen, and Athos Ribeiro. "Sate v report: Ten years of static analysis tool expositions." NIST SP 500-326 (2018), www.nist.gov/publications/sate-v-report-ten-years-static-analysis-tool-expositions

Director of National Intelligence, Cyber Threat Framework, visited October 9, 2022, www.dni.gov/index.php/cyber-threat-framework and A Common Cyber Threat Framework: A Foundation for Communication, March 13, 2017, www.dni.gov/files/ODNI/documents/features/A_Common_Cyber_Threat_Framework_Overview.pdf

Eating your own dogfood, Wikipedia, en.wikipedia.org/w/index.php?title=Eating_your_own_dog_food&oldid=945744836, last visited March 23, 2020

Dorkly, The Death Star Architect Speaks Out, Aug 28, 2015, www.youtube.com/watch?v=agcRwGDKulw

Ducklin, Paul, Serious Security: Rowhammer is back, but now it's called SMASH, Sophos NakedSecurity blog, April 19, 2021 nakedsecurity.sophos.com/2021/04/19/serious-security-rowhammer-is-back-but-now-its-called-smash

Eckersley, Peter, A Primer on Information Theory and Privacy, January 26, 2010, www.eff.org/deeplinks/2010/01/primer-information-theory-and-privacy

Golunski, Dawid, SwiftMailer < 5.4.5-DEV - Remote Code Execution, Exploit-DB, 2016a-12-28, www.exploit-db.com/exploits/40972, legal hackers.com/advisories/SwiftMailer-Exploit-Remote-Code-Exec-CVE-2016-10074-Vuln.html

Emmons, Tom, Largest Ever Recorded Packet Per Second-Based DDoS Attack Mitigated by Akamai, The Akamai blog, June 25, 2020, `blogs.akamai.com/2020/06/largest-ever-recorded-packet-per-secondbased-ddos-attack-mitigated-by-akamai.html`

eSecurityPlanet Staff, "Virus Alert: Bugbear-B Spreading Rapidly Via Email," June 05, 2003, `www.internetnews.com/ent-news/article.php/2217561/Virus+Alert+BugbearB+Spreading+Rapidly+Via+Email.htm`

Faou, Matthieu, Supply-chain attack on cryptocurrency exchange gate.io, ESET We Live Security blog, Nov 6, 2018, `www.welivesecurity.com/2018/11/06/supply-chain-attack-cryptocurrency-exchange-gate-io`

Feldman, Vitaly, "Does learning require memorization? a short tale about a long tail." Proceedings of the 52nd Annual ACM SIGACT Symposium on Theory of Computing. 2020 (arXiv:1906.05271)

Ferran, Lee, Ex-NSA Chief: 'We Kill People Based on Metadata', ABC News, May 12, 2014, `abcnews.go.com/blogs/headlines/2014/05/ex-nsa-chief-we-kill-people-based-on-metadata`

Fisher, Max, "Here's the e-mail trick Petraeus and Broadwell used to communicate," *The Washington Post*, November 12, 2012, `www.washingtonpost.com/news/worldviews/wp/2012/11/12/heres-the-e-mail-trick-petraeus-and-broadwell-used-to-communicate`

Galicia, Albert Puigsech, 7a69Adv#22 - UNIX unzip keep setuid and setgid files, Feb 28, 2005, `marc.info/?l=bugtraq&m=110960796331943&w=2` (Also, CVE-2005-0602)

Fish, Tweets sent Aug 31, 2022, `twitter.com/LazyFishBarrel/status/1565146682819350528?s=20&t=aEBqJhFNm71qrnQeOCOMYA`, `twitter.com/LazyFishBarrel/status/1565146349347037189?s=20&t=aEBqJhFNm71qrnQeOCOMYA`, `twitter.com/LazyFishBarrel/status/1560026636925521924?s=20&t=aEBqJhFNm71qrnQeOCOMYA`

Fleishman, Glenn, Privacy problems on the Web: Even your device's battery life can be used to track you, Macworld, August 28, 2016, `www.macworld.com/article/228548/privacy-problems-on-the-web-even-your-devices-battery-life-can-be-used-to-track-you.html`

Fitzl, Csaba, "Exploiting directory permissions on macOS," March 18, 2020, `theevilbit.github.io/posts/exploiting_directory_permissions_on_macos`

Forshaw, James, "VirtualBox: Windows Process DLL Signature Bypass EoP" bug, filed May 11, 2017, bugs.chromium.org/p/project-zero/issues/detail?id=1257

Fussell, Sidney, The Microphones That May Be Hidden in Your Home, "The Atlantic," Feb 23, 2019, www.theatlantic.com/technology/archive/2019/02/googles-home-security-devices-had-hidden-microphones/583387

GAO, SolarWinds Cyberattack Demands Significant Federal and Private-Sector Response (infographic), April 22, 2021, www.gao.gov/blog/solarwinds-cyberattack-demands-significant-federal-and-private-sector-response-infographic

Gatlan, Sergiu, "Microsoft starts blocking Office macros by default, once again," Bleeping Computer, July 21, 2022, www.bleepingcomputer.com/news/microsoft/microsoft-starts-blocking-office-macros-by-default-once-again

Goodin, Dan, Backdoor built in to widely used tax app seeded last week's NotPetya outbreak, July 5, 2017, Ars Technica, arstechnica.com/information-technology/2017/07/heavily-armed-police-raid-company-that-seeded-last-weeks-notpetya-outbreak

Google, "Google 2-step verification," www.google.com/landing/2step/#tab=how-it-protects, visited Jan 21, 2019

Greenberg, Andy, The Full Story of the Stunning RSA Hack Can Finally Be Told, Wired, May 20, 2021, www.wired.com/story/the-full-story-of-the-stunning-rsa-hack-can-finally-be-told

Gwern, "The Neural Net Tank Urban Legend" www.gwern.net/Tanks, version of 14 Aug 2019

Hafiz, Munawar, Ralph Johnson, Raja Afandi, (2004). The Security Architecture of qmail. In Proceedings PloP, www.researchgate.net/publication/240925283_The_Security_Architecture_of_qmail

Hale, Coda, "A Lesson In Timing Attacks (or, Don't use MessageDigest.isEquals)" Aug 13, 2009, codahale.com/a-lesson-in-timing-attacks

Hamburg, Mike, Paul Kocher, Mark E. Marson, ANALYSIS OF INTEL'S IVY BRIDGE DIGITAL RANDOM NUMBER GENERATOR, Cryptography Research White Paper, March 2012, web.archive.org/web/20141230024150/www.cryptography.com/public/pdf/Intel_TRNG_Report_20120312.pdf

Noah, Yuval, Harari *Sapiens: A Brief History of Humankind*, Harper, 2015

Harris, Bob, "Terminal srm command no longer works" (Forum answer) September 20, 2016, discussions.apple.com/thread/7675060?start=0&t start=0

Herley, Cormac "So long, and no thanks for the externalities: the rational rejection of security advice by users." Proceedings of the 2009 workshop on New security paradigms workshop. 2009

Hoglund, Greg, and Gary McGraw. *Exploiting software: How to break code*. Addison-Wesley Professional, 2004

Hutchins, Eric M., Michael J. Cloppert, Rohan M. Amin, "Intelligence-Driven Computer Network Defense Informed by Analysis of Adversary Campaigns and Intrusion Kill Chains." (2010). Lockheed Martin, www.lockheedmartin.com/content/dam/lockheed-martin/rms/documents/cyber/LM-White-Paper-Intel-Driven-Defense.pdf

Inskeep, Steve, "U.S. Sanctions Cut Off Iranians' Access To Medicine, Iran Says," National Public Radio, August 21, 2019, kuow.org/stories/u-s-sanctions-cut-off-iranians-access-to-medicine-iran-says

IEEE, Avoiding the Top 10 Software Security Design Flaws, IEEE Cyber security blog, November 13, 2015, cybersecurity.ieee.org/blog/2015/11/13/avoiding-the-top-10-security-flaws

Irwin, William. *The Ultimate Star Wars and Philosophy: You Must Unlearn What You Have Learned*. John Wiley & Sons, 2015

Kocher, Paul C., Timing Attacks on Implementations of Diffie-Hellman, RSA, DSS, and Other Systems. In N. Koblitz, editor, Advances in Cryptology - CRYPTO '96, 16th Annual International Cryptology Conference, Santa Barbara, California, USA, August 18–22, 1996, Proceedings, number 1109 in Lecture Notes in Computer Science, pages 104–113. Springer, 1996

Kührer, M., Hupperich, T., Rossow, C., & Holz, T. (n.d.). Hell of a Handshake: Abusing TCP for Reflective Amplification DDoS Attacks

Lakshmanan, Ravie, Warning: PyPI Feature Executes Code Automatically After Python Package Download, The Hacker News, September 2, 2022, thehackernews.com/2022/09/warning-pypi-feature-executes-code.html

Lamport, Leslie, Learning TLA+, last modified 23 December 2021, lamport.azurewebsites.net/tla/learning.html

Lawrence, Eric, "DLL Hijacking Just Won't Die" blog post, 2025, textslashplain.com/2015/12/18/dll-hijacking-just-wont-die

Lawrence, Eric, "Web-to-App Communication: App Protocols" August 29, 2019, textslashplain.com/2019/08/29/web-to-app-communication-app-protocols

Ryan Levick, Sebastian Fernandez, We need a safer systems programming language, Microsoft blog, July 18, 2019, msrc-blog.microsoft.com/2019/07/18/we-need-a-safer-systems-programming-language, listverse.com/2007/12/17/top-10-scientific-mnemonics

Golunski, Dawid, "'PHPMailier Remote Code Execution' Advisory," 25 December 2016, legalhackers.com/advisories/PHPMailer-Exploit-Remote-Code-Exec-CVE-2016-10033-Vuln.html

Golunski, Dawid, "Swift Mailer Exploit Remote Code Exec," 30 December, 2016, legalhackers.com/advisories/SwiftMailer-Exploit-Remote-Code-Exec-CVE-2016-10074-Vuln.html

Golunski, Dawid "Pwnscriptum," undated, legalhackers.com/exploits/CVE-2016-10033/10045/10034/10074/PwnScriptum_RCE_exploit.py (archive/.1 is the headers), last visited Feb 19, 2017

Grassi, Paul A., et al, Digital Identity Guidelines Authentication and Lifecycle Management, NIST Special Publication 800-63B, doi.org/10.6028/NIST.SP.800-63b, March, 2020

Lauinger, Tobias, Abdelberi Chaabane, Sajjad Arshad, William Robertson, Christo Wilson, and Engin Kirda. "Thou shalt not depend on me: Analysing the use of outdated javascript libraries on the web." arXiv preprint arXiv:1811.00918 (2018)

Laurie, Ben and Richard Clayton. "Proof-of-work proves not to work; version 0.2." In Workshop on Economics and Information, Security. 2004. www.cl.cam.ac.uk/~rnc1/proofwork2.pdf

Logitech, "Update: We Will Replace Your Logitech Harmony Links," Logitech Blog, November 9, 2017

Lucas, George, The Hidden Fortress, Criterion Collection, Bonus Material, 2016, accessed at www.youtube.com/watch?v=TEJ6CzG9zVc

Lyon, Andrew W, Kelsey Delayen, Randy Reddekopp, "No Lab Tests" When You Are Born in The Twilight Zone: A Clinical Informatics Case Report, The Journal of Applied Laboratory Medicine, jfaa080, doi.org/10.1093/jalm/jfaa080 as summarized by Paul Eggert in RISKS 32.16, 30 July 2020, catless.ncl.ac.uk/Risks/32/16/#subj12.1

Lysne, Olav, The Huawei and Snowden Questions, Springer, 2018

Maddison, D. R. and K.-S. Schulz, (eds.) The Tree of Life Web Project, tolweb.org/Homo/16418, 2007.

Marchette, David J., *Computer Intrusion Detection and Network Monitoring: A Statistical Viewpoint.* Germany, Springer New York, 2013

Marshall, John, What Are the Odds of Successfully Navigating an Asteroid Field?, Scientific American, August 5, 2015, www.scientificamerican.com/article/what-are-the-odds-of-successfully-navigating-an-asteroid-field

Mastercard, Test Card Numbers, 2020, www.simplify.com/commerce/docs/testing/test-card-numbers

Mazegen, X86 Opcode and Instruction Reference Home, ref.x86asm.net/index.html, and ref.x86asm.net/coder32.html, 2017-02-18

McCarthy, K. Unbreakable smart lock devastated to discover screwdrivers exist • The Register. June 15, 2018, www.theregister.com/2018/06/15/taplock_broken_screwdriver/?page=2

McCulloch, Gretchen, *Because Internet*, Riverhead Books, 2019

McKenna, Chris, 12 Ingenious iOS Screen Time Hacks, October 4, 2019, Protect Young Eyes, protectyoungeyes.com/12-ingenious-screen-time-hacks-how-to-beat-them

Meidinger, Chris "The Phishing Kill Chain," Blog post, Agari Email Security Blog, August 5, 2014, www.agari.com/email-security-blog/phishing-kill-chain

Meghu, Kellman, How NOT To Do Security: Lessons Learned From The Galactic Empire, BSides San Fransicso, 2012

CNBC, Chinese phone maker Huawei punishes employees for iPhone tweet blunder, January 4, 2019, www.cnbc.com/2019/01/04/chinese-phone-maker-huawei-punishes-employees-for-iphone-tweet-blunder.html

Microsoft, 2011 Microsoft, "Ten Immutable Laws Of Security (Version 2.0)," 2011 web.archive.org/web/20170606182438/technet.microsoft.com/en-us/library/hh278941.aspx?f=255&MSPPError=-2147217396

Microsoft, "Auditing Security Events," March 30, 2017, docs.microsoft.com/en-us/dotnet/framework/wcf/feature-details/auditing-security-events

Microsoft, "Audit Policy Recommendations," May 30, 2017, docs.microsoft.com/en-us/windows-server/identity/ad-ds/plan/security-best-practices/audit-policy-recommendations

Microsoft, 2018a Microsoft, 'App Capability declarations,' November 25, 2018, docs.microsoft.com/en-us/windows/uwp/packaging/app-capability-declarations

Microsoft, 2018b [Netuseradd] "NetUserAdd function," 12/04/2018, docs.microsoft.com/en-us/windows/desktop/api/Lmaccess/nf-lmaccess-netuseradd

Microsoft, 2018c Microsoft, 'Open files and folders with a picker' December 18, 2018, docs.microsoft.com/en-us/windows/uwp/files/quickstart-using-file-and-folder-pickers

Microsoft, 2018d Microsoft, "Security Boundaries" May 30, 2018, docs.microsoft.com/en-us/windows/desktop/cossdk/security-boundaries

Microsoft, "What is a User?" May 30, 2018, docs.microsoft.com/en-us/windows/desktop/ad/what-is-a-user

Microsoft, 2020a Microsoft, "Privilege Constants," last visited March 28, 2020, `docs.microsoft.com/en-us/windows/desktop/SecAuthZ/privilege-constants`

Microsoft, 2020b Microsoft, "Privileges," last visited March 28, 2020, docs `.microsoft.com/en-us/windows/win32/secauthz/privileges`

Microsoft, 2021, Order of ACEs in a DACL `docs.microsoft.com/en-us/windows/win32/secauthz/order-of-aces-in-a-dacl`

Microsoft, 2022, WinVerifyTrust Signature Validation Vulnerability, Jan 21, 2022, `msrc.microsoft.com/update-guide/vulnerability/CVE-2013-3900`

Miller, Mark, "Robust Composition: Towards a Unified Approach to Access Control and Concurrency Control" PhD Thesis, Johns Hopkins, 2006

Miller, Bart P. L. Fredriksen, and B. So, "An Empirical Study of the Reliability of UNIX Utilities," Communications of the ACM 33, 12 (December 1990)

Mogul, Richand Shawn Harris, Break the Top 10 Cloud Attack Killchains, Session CSV-T08, RSA Conference, February 2020, `www.rsaconference.com/usa/us-2020/agenda/break-the-top-10-cloud-attack-killchains-session-viewing-point`

Mogull, Rich, Goodbye "Kill Chains," Hello "Attack Sequences," Firemon Blog, 2022, `www.firemon.com/goodbye-kill-chains-hello-attack-sequences`

Momot, F., S. Bratus, Sven M. Hallberg and M. L. Patterson, "The Seven Turrets of Babel: A Taxonomy of LangSec Errors and How to Expunge Them," 2016 IEEE Cybersecurity Development (SecDev), 2016, pp. 45–52, doi: 10.1109/SecDev.2016.019. `ieeexplore.ieee.org/document/7839788`

Morris, Robert and Ken Thompson, "Password Security: A Case History," Communications of the ACM, November 1979 Volume 22, Number 11. `citeseerx.ist.psu.edu/viewdoc/download?doi=10.1.1.128.1635&rep=rep1&type=pdf`

Montalbano, Elizabeth, Supply-Chain Hack Breaches 35 Companies, Including PayPal, Microsoft, Apple. Threatpost, February 10, 2021, `threatpost.com/supply-chain-hack-paypal-microsoft-apple/163814`

Morszczyzna, Mateusz, What's really wrong with node_modules and why this is your fault. Hackernoon, November 27, 2017, `hackernoon.com/whats-really-wrong-with-node-modules-and-why-this-is-your-fault-8ac9fa893823`

Mydans, Seth, "Samoa Sacrifices a Day for Its Future" New York Times, Dec 29, 2011, `www.nytimes.com/2011/12/30/world/asia/samoa-to-skip-friday-and-switch-time-zones.html`

[Onion] CIA Realizes It's Been Using Black Highlighters All These Years, November 30, 2005, www.theonion.com/cia-realizes-its-been-using-black-highlighters-all-thes-1819568147

Nadel, Ben, Canonicalizing A URL By Its Individual Components In Lucee CFML 5.3.6.61, blog, May 22, 2020, www.bennadel.com/blog/3832-canonicalizing-a-url-by-its-individual-components-in-lucee-cfml-5-3-6-61.htm

National Cyber Security Centre, Introduction to logging for security purposes, version 1.0, 8 July 2018, www.ncsc.gov.uk/guidance/introduction-logging-security-purposes

Newcombe, Chris, Tim Rath, Fan Zhang, Bogdan Munteanu, Marc Brooker, Michael Deardeuff Communications of the ACM, April 2015, Vol. 58 No. 4, Pages 66–73 10.1145/2699417, cacm.acm.org/magazines/2015/4/184701-how-amazon-web-services-uses-formal-methods/fulltext

NIST, NIST's Inclusive Language Guidance Aims for Clarity in Standards Publications, April 29, 2021, www.nist.gov/news-events/news/2021/04/nists-inclusive-language-guidance-aims-clarity-standards-publications

NIST, NIST Special Publication 800-90B. Recommendation for the Entropy Sources Used for Random Bit Generation, Meltem Sönmez Turan et al, 2018, nvlpubs.nist.gov/nistpubs/SpecialPublications/NIST.SP.800-90B.pdf

Lyon, Gordon "Fyodor", Nmap Network Scanning, Nmap project, January 1, 2009, nmap.org/book/osdetect-methods.html

Oorschot, Paul C. van "Computer Security and the Internet: Tools and Jewels," Springer, 2020

OWASP, Canonicalization, locale and Unicode, www.owasp.org/index.php/Canonicalization,_locale_and_Unicode, last modified 12 May 2013

Palladino, Valantia, Tech — Logitech to shut down "service and support" for Harmony Link devices in 2018, Ars Technica, November 8, 2017, arstechnica.com/gadgets/2017/11/logitech-to-shut-down-service-and-support-for-harmony-link-devices-in-2018

Parikh, Jugal, Randy Treit, Holly Stewart, Protecting the Protector, Hardening Machine Learning Defenses Against Adversarial Attacks, Blackhat USA, August 9, 2018, www.blackhat.com/us-18/briefings/schedule/#protecting-the-protector-hardening-machine-learning-defenses-against-adversarial-attacks-11669

AntiCompositeNumber (Wikipedia User), Privilege Escalation Diagram, last visited February 17, 2019, `en.wikipedia.org/wiki/File:Privilege_Escalation_Diagram.svg`

Oberhaus, Daniel, The World's Oldest Blockchain Has Been Hiding in the New York Times Since 1995, Vice Motherboard, August 27, 2018, `www.vice.com/en/article/j5nzx4/what-was-the-first-blockchain`

PCI Security Standards Council, Information Supplement, Effective Daily Log Monitoring, May 2016, `listings.pcisecuritystandards.org/documents/Effective-Daily-Log-Monitoring-Guidance.pdf`

Petitcolas, Fabien, Kerckhoffs' principles from « La cryptographie militaire », webpage, `www.petitcolas.net/kerckhoffs/index.html` last visited August 27, 2022

Pieczul, Olgierd, Simon Foley, and Mary Ellen Zurko. 2017. Developer-centered security and the symmetry of ignorance. In Proceedings of the 2017 New Security Paradigms Workshop (NSPW 2017). Association for Computing Machinery, New York, NY, USA, 46–56. DOI:`doi.org/10.1145/3171533.3171539`

Pocock, Chris, The Revolutionary but Thorny U.S. Predator-Reaper Program, AINOnline, June 13, 2015, `www.ainonline.com/aviation-news/defense/2015-06-13/revolutionary-thorny-us-predator-reaper-program`

Poulsen, Kevin "'Nimda' worm hits net," Security Focus, September 18, 2001, `www.securityfocus.com/news/253`

Ptacek, Thomas H., and Timothy N. Newsham. Insertion, evasion, and denial of service: Eluding network intrusion detection. Secure Networks inc Calgary Alberta, 1998. `users.ece.cmu.edu/~adrian/731-sp04/readings/Ptacek-Newsham-ids98.pdf`

Reeder, Rob, Expandable Grids: A user interface visualization technique and a policy semantics to support fast, accurate security and privacy policy authoring. PhD thesis, Carnegie Mellon University Computer Science Department. CMU tech report number CMU-CS-08-143. July, 2008

Reick, Philip, Answer to Parse Phone Number into component parts, Stack Overflow, October 22, 2008, `stackoverflow.com/questions/227473/parse-phone-number-into-component-parts`

Roberts, Paul, MIT: Discarded hard drives yield private info, IDG News Service, 2003, `www.computerworld.com/article/2580013/mit-discarded-hard-drives-yield-private-info.html`

Roth, Emma, Intel's 12th Gen CPU can't handle the Bar exam, The Verge, July 13, 2022, `www.theverge.com/2022/7/13/23209784/intel-law-students-12th-gen-processor-bar-exam-examplify-examsoft`

Saldana, Grace China's Newest Bio-Weapon Unleashed, FreedomWire, July 30, 2020, `freedomwire.com/china-bioweapon-seeds`

Sanger, David E., Obama Order Sped Up Wave of Cyberattacks Against Iran, *New York Times,* June 1, 2012, `www.nytimes.com/2012/06/01/world/middleeast/obama-ordered-wave-of-cyberattacks-against-iran.html`

Shachtman, Noah Most U.S. Drones Openly Broadcast Secret Video Feeds, Wired, October 29, 2012, `www.wired.com/2012/10/hack-proof-drone`

Schmitt, Emanuel and Jan-Niklas Voigt-Antons. 2020. Predicting Tap Locations on Touch Screens in the Field Using Accelerometer and Gyroscope Sensor Readings. In HCI for Cybersecurity, Privacy and Trust: Second International Conference, HCI-CPT 2020, Held as Part of the 22nd HCI International Conference, HCII 2020, Copenhagen, Denmark, July 19–24, 2020, Proceedings. Springer-Verlag, Berlin, Heidelberg, 637–651. `doi.org/10.1007/978-3-030-50309-3_43`

Seebach, Peter, OOXML: What's the big deal?, IBM Developerworks, 19 Feb 2008, `web.archive.org/web/20091003044227/www.ibm.com/developerworks/library/x-ooxmlstandard.html`

Sharma, Ax, Dev corrupts NPM libs 'colors' and 'faker' breaking thousands of apps, Bleeping Computer, January 9, 2022, `www.bleepingcomputer.com/news/security/dev-corrupts-npm-libs-colors-and-faker-breaking-thousands-of-apps`

Schneier, Brice "Attack trees." Dr. Dobb's journal 24, no. 12 (1999): 21-29

Hanna Seariac, What happens if I don't put my phone on airplane mode?. Deseret News, September 22, 2022, `www.deseret.com/u-s-world/2022/9/22/23365792/phone-airplane-mode-why`

Shostack, Adam, Buffer Overflows and history a request, `www.emergentchaos.com/archives/2008/10/buffer-overflows-and-history-a-request.html`, October, 2008

Shostack, Adam, Lessons Learning Workstream, `shostack.org/resources/lessons`, 2022

Shostack, Adam, Reverse Engineering Compliance, Blackhat Asia 2021, `www.youtube.com/watch?v=j7nDXgLahhU&list=PLCVhBqLDKoONr9yrBmUKf6gb-FifkeEGL&index=10`

Shostack, Adam, *Threat Modeling: Designing for Security* (Wiley, 2014)

Siguza, "Psychic Paper," `siguza.github.io/psychicpaper`, May 1, 2020

Sinan, Mehmet Inci, Berk Gulmezoglu, Gorka Irazoqui, Thomas Eisenbarth, and Berk Sunar, "Seriously, get off my cloud! Cross-VM RSA Key Recovery in a Public Cloud" Preprint, 15 Sep 2015, `eprint.iacr.org/2015/898`

[Smug] Comfortably Smug, The Radicalization of Luke Skywalker: A Jedi's Path to Jihad by Comfortably Smug, December 11, 2015, `decider .com/2015/12/11/the-radicalization-of-luke-skywalker-a-jedis-path-to-jihad`

Snyk, Zip Slip Vulnerability, 2018, `snyk.io/research/zip-slip-vulnerability`

Soltani, Ashkan, Edward W. Felten, Matt Blaze, Steven M. Bellovin, Bruce Schneier, Joseph Lorenzo Hall, Morgan Marquis-Boire, Nicholas Weaver, Stephen Checkoway, Dan S. Wallach, Adam Shostack, Rebecca Wright, Carrie E. Gates, Scott Bradner, Susan Landau, Ben Adida, Nadia Heninger, Philip Zimmermann, and Sharon Goldberg. Amicus Brief in Carpenter vs United States, August 15, 2017, `knightcolumbia.org/content/ supreme-court-brief-technologists-warn-against-warrantless-access-cell-phone-location-data`

Stern, Alan, and David Grinspoon. Chasing New Horizons: inside the epic first mission to Pluto. Picador, 2018

Sunstein, Cass R., *The World According to Star Wars*, Dey Street Books, 2016

Sussman, Noah, "Falsehoods programmers believe about time" blog post, Sunday, Jun 17th, 2012 and `infiniteundo.com/post/25326999628/ falsehoods-programmers-believe-about-time` "More falsehoods programmers believe about time; "wisdom of the crowd" edition," Wed Jun 20th `falsehoodsabouttime.com`

Thompson, Ken, 1984. Reflections on trusting trust. Commun. ACM 27, 8 (Aug 1984), 761–763. DOI: `doi.org/10.1145/358198.358210`

Tims, Anna "Postcode loophole enables fraudsters to hijack eBay parcels," *The Guardian*, September 22, 2019, `www.theguardian.com/money/ 2019/sep/22/fraudsters-hijack-ebay-parcels-postcode-scam`

Tofel, Kevin, Your iPhone 6 has a barometric sensor and this weather app wants to use it, ZDNet, June 15, 2015, `www.zdnet.com/article/ dark-sky-weather-app-iphone-6-plus-barometer`

Udell, Jon, Access control, monoculture, and accountability Infoworld, September 17, 2004, `www.infoworld.com/article/2664548/ access-control-monoculture-and-accountability.html`

Unicode Consortium, Confusables. Version 3.9, `util.unicode.org/ UnicodeJsps/confusables.jsp?a=Yoda&r=None`, last visited Feb 14, 2022

Ullrich, Steffen, "Breaking DKIM - on Purpose and by Chance," October 2017, `noxxi.de/research/breaking-dkim-on-purpose-and-by-chance.html`

Washington State Department of Agriculture, Public asked to turn in suspicious seeds mailed from other countries, press release July 29, 2020, `agr.wa.gov/about-wsda/news-and-media-relations/news-releases?article=31411`

Weinbaum, Cortney, Steven Berner, Bruce McClintock, SIGINT for Anyone, The Growing Availability of Signals Intelligence in the Public Domain, RAND, 2017, `www.rand.org/pubs/perspectives/PE273.html`

Whitwam, Ryan, Scientists Rename Genes So Excel Won't Reformat Them as Dates, ExtremeTech, August 7, 2020, `www.extremetech.com/extreme/313567-scientists-rename-genes-so-excel-wont-reformat-them-as-dates`

Wildenhain, Tom, On the Turing Completeness of MS PowerPoint, April 9, 2020, `www.andrew.cmu.edu/user/twildenh/PowerPointTM/Paper.pdf`

Winkler, Ira, Tracy Celaya Brown, You Can Stop Stupid, Wiley, 2020

Young, Adam, and Moti Yung. "Cryptovirology: Extortion-based security threats and countermeasures." In Proceedings 1996 IEEE Symposium on Security and Privacy, pp. 129–140. IEEE, 1996. `citeseerx.ist.psu.edu/viewdoc/download?doi=10.1.1.44.9122&rep=rep1&type=pdf`

Zalewski, Michal. *The tangled Web: A guide to securing modern web applications.* No Starch Press, 2011

Story Index

Throughout this book, I've used Star Wars as a sort of memory palace—a way for you to put your new knowledge into fun cubbyholes. If you've forgotten the technical details but remember the storyline it was tied to, well, you could just reread the book, but failing that…this index might be your only hope.

The sources are listed in Star Wars Universe chronological order, not order of release in our galaxy. Within each, a short scene description or a quotation is followed by a reference to the chapter and most immediate heading to encourage you to re-read for the reference. (The table of contents lists sections; this story index contains lower-level headings.)

Episode I: The Phantom Menace

- "Fear leads to hate. Hate leads to anger. Anger leads…" (Conclusion of Chapter 7, "Predictability and Randomness")
- Anakin destroys a droid control ship (Abundance and quotas in Chapter 5, "Denial of Service and Availability")

Episode III: Revenge of the Sith

- "You were my friend!" (URLs in Chapter 4, "Information Disclosure and Confidentiality")

Obi-Wan (Television Series)

- Obi-Wan meets a child Leia, breaking my claims in Chapter 1, "Spoofing and Authenticity." Perhaps "You served my father" should now be read as an authenticator?

Rogue One

- Archives at Scarif (Physical storage in Chapter 4, "Information Disclosure and Confidentiality")
- Building a Death Star (Opening of Chapter 7, "Predictability and Randomness")

Star Wars: A New Hope

- Princess Leia's ship being pursued (Opening words of "Introduction;" opening words of Chapter 4, "Information Disclosure and Confidentiality")
- R2-D2 displays the hologram (Opening words of Chapter 1, "Spoofing and Authenticity")
- "These aren't the droids you're looking for" (Opening words of Chapter 6, "Expansion of Authority and Isolation")
- Destruction of Alderaan (The threat: Repudiation in Chapter 3, "Repudiation and Proof")
- Luke and Han dress as Stormtrooper TK-421 (Human identifiers in Chapter 1, "Spoofing and Authenticity")
- Han shoots the comms console (Ephemeral or persistent in Chapter 5, "Denial of Service and Availability")
- R2-D2 shuts down the garbage compactor (Compute in Chapter 5, "Denial of Service and Availability")

- Obi-Wan shuts down the tractor beam (Opening words of Chapter 2, "Tampering and Integrity" and Ephemeral or persistent in Chapter 5, "Denial of Service and Availability")
- "If you strike me down now, I shall become more powerful than you can imagine." This would have been in Chapter 6, "Expansion of Authority and Isolation," but it's a hard line to make work.
- Millenium Falcon escapes the Death Star (Opening words of Chapter 2, "Tampering and Integrity", and of Chapter 6, "Expansion of Authority and Isolation")
- A tracking device is placed on the Millenium Falcon (Conclusion of Chapter 6, "Expansion of Authority and Isolation")
- Rebels analyze the Death Star Plans
  - The Rebel systems are exposed to ransomware (Tampering with Storage in Chapter 2, "Tampering and Integrity")
  - Discussion of the Death Star plans and transparency (Assume Transparency in Chapter 7, "Predictability and Randomness")
  - Finding and taking advantage of a weakness in the Death Star (Opening words of Chapter 9, "Kill Chains")

The Empire Strikes Back

- Luke is told "Your weapons, you will not need them" as he enters the dark side tree (Least Privilege and Separation of Chapter 6, "Expansion of Authority and Isolation")
- Raising an X-Wing Fighter out of a swamp (Memory safety, Chapter 8, "Parsing and Corruption")
- Han flies through the asteroid field, saying "never tell me the odds" (Cryptographic threats in Chapter 7, "Predictability and Randomness")

Return of the Jedi

Index